WORKING WITH CHILDREN AND YOUTH WITH COMPLEX NEEDS

20 SKILLS TO BUILD RESILIENCE

Working with Children and Youth with Complex Needs provides a detailed description of techniques and rich stories of how social workers, psychologists, counselors, and child and youth care workers can help young people become more resilient. With ample case studies and fascinating explanations of research, Dr. Ungar shows why we need to work just as hard changing the environments that surround children as we do changing children themselves. Building on lessons learned from clinical, community, and residential settings, Dr. Ungar discusses 20 skills that can enhance the effectiveness of frontline mental health services. Along with descriptions of the skills necessary to talk with clients about the factors that put their mental health at risk, *Working with Children and Youth with Complex Needs* also presents systemic practices clinicians can use in their everyday work. Engaging with children's extended family, addressing issues of community violence, racism, and homophobia, and helping parents and teachers understand children's maladaptive coping strategies as sometimes necessary are among the many practical strategies that are discussed which clinicians can use to enhance and sustain the therapeutic value of their work.

Michael Ungar, PhD, is a family therapist and professor of social work at Dalhousie University in Halifax, Canada. He is also the founder and co-director of the Resilience Research Centre, which coordinates large multisite research studies in over a dozen countries. Among his many contributions to his community have been his roles as co-chair of the Nova Scotia Mental Health and Addictions Strategy Advisory Committee, executive board member of the American Family Therapy Academy, and scientific director of the Children and Youth in Challenging Contexts Network.

WORKING WITH CHILDREN AND YOUTH WITH COMPLEX NEEDS

20 SKILLS TO BUILD RESILIENCE

Michael Ungar

 Routledge
Taylor & Francis Group

NEW YORK AND LONDON

First published 2015
by Routledge
711 Third Avenue, New York, NY 10017

and by Routledge
27 Church Road, Hove, East Sussex BN3 2FA

Routledge is an imprint of the Taylor & Francis Group, an informa business

© 2015 Michael Ungar

Library of Congress Cataloging in Publication Data
Ungar, Michael.
  Working with children and youth with complex needs : 20 skills to build resilience / Michael Ungar.
    pages cm
  1. Resilience (Personality trait) in children. 2. Resilience (Personality trait) in adolescence. 3. Social work with children. 4. Social work with youth. 5. Child psychotherapy. 6. Adolescent psychotherapy. I. Title.
  BF723.R46U54 2014
  618.92'8914—dc23   2014015693

ISBN: 978-1-138-80072-4 (hbk)
ISBN: 978-1-138-80073-1 (pbk)
ISBN: 978-1-315-75530-4 (ebk)

Typeset in Stone Sans and Stone Serif
by Keystroke, Station Road, Codsall, Wolverhampton

Disclaimer: The Children and Their Families

In order to protect the privacy of all the individuals with whom I have had the privilege to work, the stories I share in these pages are based on the lived experiences of actual young people and their families but details have been changed significantly. The lives of multiple individuals have been combined and identifying information fictionalized to preserve people's confidentiality.

CONTENTS

CONTENTS

CHAPTER 1

A SOCIAL ECOLOGICAL APPROACH TO CLINICAL WORK

Monday Morning, 9:20 A.M. (Part 1)

Michelle arrived twenty minutes late for her weekly appointment at the mental health and addictions treatment center where I worked. For months I'd been seeing this 17-year-old, impulsive, white, adolescent, whose purple hair and pierced bottom lip made her look far tougher than she really was. Though Michelle eventually eased herself into her seat, a Styrofoam cup of coffee clasped in both hands, I knew these scheduled counseling sessions had done little except make Michelle much smarter about the consequences of her heroin use. It was remarkable, and a stroke of luck, that Michelle's group home staff hadn't kicked her out even though she continued to abuse drugs. Every time her 20-year-old boyfriend relapsed, she did too. Michelle insisted that he was the only person who really cared about her. He may also have been the only person she could rely on to be there when she turned 18 years old. When that happened, she would be forced to leave permanent foster care.

"I've had another fight with staff," Michelle told me. She had been late for curfew and high when she did return. The group home staff had threatened to revoke phone privileges and Michelle had slammed her door so hard the handle broke. I'd spoken with the staff many times before. They knew Michelle was at risk of ending up homeless or dead immediately after her 18th birthday. But what more could they do to help? She refused to engage in any work to create a smooth transition into adult independent living. In truth, they were just as stuck as everyone else who were trying to work with Michelle to convince her to transform her life into something better.

"What are you going to do after you age out of foster care?" I asked, realizing that any talk of drugs and drinking were going to go nowhere that day.

"I've got my boyfriend and his grandmother. He'll be out of jail before my next birthday and I can live with them. I would let the group home staff set me up in my own apartment, but my transition worker said my boyfriend couldn't live with me." Michelle rolled her eyes and stared into her coffee cup. "F—- them. They've got no right to tell me who I can live with once I'm 18," she said, then slumped down in her chair.

While most people saw Michelle as an angry young woman with serious problems, I came to know her as a lonely child with unmet psychological and material needs, living in a world that had badly neglected her for years. After a horrible start in a home where she witnessed frequent domestic violence, Michelle's mother eventually threw Michelle out when she was 14 years old because of Michelle's increasing drug use, violence in the home, and sexualized behavior toward her mother's boyfriends. None of these behaviors surprised her caseworkers.

To make matters worse, Michelle had had an awful relationship with the police for the last three years. They'd been investigating her experience of sexual abuse by an online pedophile who had made contact with her and a dozen of her classmates through Facebook. Michelle's case still hadn't reached trial and might never. Not surprising, Michelle had refused trauma counseling. "I've been through worse," is all she'd say about the incident.

I believed her. When she was 16 years old and had suffered through four foster placements in two years, Michelle asked to return to her mother's home. She was told that if she did her younger sister would have to be removed and placed in care. Her mother did what Michelle expected and refused to take her back or advocate for her right to come home.

Unsure what I could do to help that Monday morning, I paused a long time before saying to Michelle, "Maybe you can tell me what else we should be talking about today."

Michelle raised her eyes and for a moment I thought I could see the wet shine of tears. "I just want them to listen to me. Can you do that for me? Get them to stop talking at me and just listen to what I want?"

I nodded and reassured Michelle that I would try, though secretly I wasn't sure I had the power to get anyone to do anything that Michelle wanted them to do. Mustering my courage, and with a deep breath that seemed to bring with it the faintest promise of hope, I looked straight at Michelle and asked her, "So, what exactly would you tell everyone if you could get them to listen?"

Changing Social Ecologies: Three Problems

Meeting Michelle, I was entranced by her persistence, as well as the efforts of her professional caregivers to provide her with as much security as they could within the limits of their agency's resources and mandates. Later in this chapter, I'll revisit the work I did with Michelle to show the skills I used to help her. My work with Michelle is just one of many examples in this book of a *social ecological approach* to treatment designed for use by counselors, therapists, and other mental health care providers from diverse professional backgrounds.

I use the phrase "social ecological" to make clear that I mean an intervention that addresses all aspects of an individual's interactions with her environment: social and educational services, extended family, school, community, and economic and political structures. The phrase, however, refers to more than just interactions with the people in each setting. It is also about the built environment, though one can't forget that the shape of that environment reflects people's values (for example, the location of child welfare offices, the positioning of wheelchair ramps, the physical layout of subsidizing housing units). Earlier models of ecological clinical practice (Belsky, 1980; Germain & Gitterman, 1980; Kemp, Whittaker & Tracy, 1997) have certainly shaped my thinking, but a social ecological approach relies on a somewhat different and more up-to-date understanding of ecology (where our description of ecological relationships has dramatically changed over the last thirty years, becoming less causal and hierarchical, and with greater emphasis on the equal contribution made by all elements of an ecosystem from the smallest microbe to the largest multicellular organism), epigenetics (with its less fatalistic emphasis on how environments trigger gene expression), resilience, postmodernism, and integrated models of service delivery.

After all, whatever services Michelle was being offered reflected a set of beliefs about what young people like her need and the social and political systems that decide who gets which services delivered in what ways. Policies, practices, and funding are always provided in a manner that reminds us what society as a whole says is important. This social ecological perspective will become much clearer, and much more concrete, as I describe the work Michelle and I did together that helped her cope individually while also dramatically changing her access to the resources that she needed to stay safe and heal.

While a systems-based, ecological approach to clinical work is not new, there has been very little research that shows it is effective. This book is meant to change that. Other notable efforts to describe an ecological practice that builds on our understanding of resilience include Resilient Therapy, a community-oriented model of therapy popular in the United Kingdom (Hart, Blincow & Thomas, 2007). It is one model that acknowledges the need to pay attention to social justice factors and is intended to take "resilience and turn it into set of actions and working practices, mechanisms designed to generate better outcomes than would be expected" (p. 15). Likewise, the model of community psychology promoted by Isaac Prilleltensky (2012) also focuses on aspects of inequality and the broader social determinants of health that shape well-being. These models and others have influenced the social ecological practices, principles, and skills that are described in the following chapters. This approach also builds on a decade of research with children and youth exposed to extremely adverse living conditions, family stressors, and individual challenges. I used the results of my own research in 20 countries, and that of my many colleagues, to develop a social ecological model of intervention. This model gives clinicians a toolbox to help the people with whom they work (typically referred to as clients or patients) develop the protective factors associated with well-being in contexts of adversity. That research has shown that for children exposed to higher levels of stress (the focus of my work), their resilience has much *less* to do with individual factors than it does with the way the child's environment provides the child with the resources necessary for well-being. No surprise, then, that when I thought about what my research could mean to my clinical work with children I was forced to think ecologically rather than about individuals separate from the complex environments that make it more or less likely they thrive under stress.

The problem with implementing a social ecological practice, however, is threefold. First, there is a *problem of competence*. Most clinicians are not community developers or professional advocates. Nor do they spend their day helping young people fight systemic oppression (racism, homophobia, bullying, etc.), find stable housing, make schools safe, or effect change to the many other environmental factors that create and sustain well-being (these are often called the social determinants of health). No matter what their discipline, very few clinicians have the training or skills necessary to be effective case managers and community workers.

Second, there is a *problem of resources*. Programs that have tried to turn clinicians into ecologically-minded therapists have usually required specialized programing, lots of staff resources, and extra money. While other approaches that are resource-heavy have been proven effective (for example, Multisystemic Therapy [Swenson et al., 2000] and The Penn Resiliency Program [Gillham et al., 2007]), it can seem that an ecological practice is something done by someone other than the clinician mandated to see clients in direct practice. Intensive in-home support programs, group work in schools, inter-agency treatment teams for complex cases, clinical reflecting teams, and many other important ecological interventions may be effective, but they don't meet the immediate needs of the majority of counselors who work in settings that emphasize direct clinical practice with an individual or the individual's closest family members. For these clinicians, an ecological practice may seem unwieldy and lacking specific clinical techniques that can be used when resources are scarce and clients' problems and social ecologies extremely complicated. While I cannot make this work simpler than it is, in the pages that follow I have provided descriptions of skills that can be used by mental health care providers who want to broaden their focus from individual therapy to helping individuals change the worlds that disadvantage them.

However, there is a *problem of evidence* when working ecologically. This is the third big challenge to implementation. It is difficult for family therapists, residential workers, child welfare workers, school guidance counselors, public health nurses, community psychologists, child and youth care workers, hospital social workers, and dozens of other professionals to justify the time they devote to an ecological practice when there is so little evidence that working to change a child's broader social ecology is time well spent and cost-effective. In the absence of evidence that ecological models work, most clinicians ignore what they intuitively know: that time devoted to addressing the social determinants of well-being, exploring a child's marginalization, and including in treatment the child's natural supports are more helpful than another session alone with an individual, or a child and her caregiver.

Too often, we assume individuals who are exposed to problems beyond their control can make meaningful changes in behavior while still living in social environments that remain toxic. Will an anxious child stop being anxious as long as there is still gun violence in his housing project, or bullies who call him stupid at school? Can we reasonably expect a child to stop running away from a home where domestic violence flares every Saturday night? Can an adolescent with a physical disability thrive if his local recreation center is inaccessible because of a flight of stairs? If that same child is in foster care, will his foster parents receive enough financial support to adequately meet their child's needs? Research with the most vulnerable children shows very clearly that they heal best when we shape their environments (Jaffee et al., 2007; Prilleltensky, 2012). In the following chapters I'll describe practice principles and skills that make a social ecological approach effective.

Self-assessment

Before you read further, look at the quick self-assessment tool which is on page 17 at the end of the chapter. You can also find an online copy of the tool on my website, www.michaelungar.com. You may be pleasantly surprised to see how many ecological practice principles and skills are already a part of your work with young people or get clues to which areas of practice need to be part of your growing edge. The numbered descriptions from 0 to 3 (half points are fine too) offer a way to assess fidelity (adherence) to what I'll show later are best practices. If you consistently rate your work with clients a 3 then it is very much in keeping with the principles of a social ecological approach to counseling.

You may want to score yourself now, before you read the following chapters, then again after you've had a chance to integrate more social ecological principles and skills into your practice. Without having read the descriptions of each principle and skill, however, some of the items in the self-assessment may seem vague. Feel free to skip over any questions you don't fully understand and come back to them later after reading the more detailed explanation.

If you have the ability to video record or audio record sessions with a client, you'll be able to see the extent to which your practice reflects these principles now and how your work changes over time. Keep in mind that a single session may not show all of the aspects of the model that I will discuss in the following chapters. Over several sessions, however, all these elements of good practice should be observable.

The Need for an Expanded Set of Clinical Skills

Anyone trained in techniques to enhance mindfulness (Miller, Rathus & Linehan, 2007), who does cognitive behavioral therapy (Feldman, 2007), or treats addictions (Leschied et al., 2004) can pick up a manual and read step-by-step instructions for what one does to help clients change and the research that proves it works. How, though, do we ensure that treatment pays attention to the root causes of marginalization that our clients experience rather than turning real world issues like racism into an individual's personal challenge (for example, providing anger management training to a child who attacks people when they make racist comments)? How do we ensure that the changes a child makes during counseling are sustainable when the supports and services the child needs are either unavailable or inaccessible at home (for example, a child who is incarcerated may have access to a caring worker but be placed on a 12-month wait-list for services after discharge)? Without good answers to these kinds of questions, the strengths of an individual like Michelle will remain hidden or misunderstood as maladaptive coping strategies, when they are very sensible solutions in dangerous, emotionally toxic social ecologies.

While my clinical work with Michelle takes place in what looks like a fairly traditional office-based setting, an ecological practice is useful in many different settings where mental health care providers work. It's an excellent approach for family therapists to expand the scope of their practice, residential workers to develop case plans that will continue after a client leaves treatment (I worked for many years in children's group homes, young offender facilities, and mental health treatment centers), in-home support workers who need to think about both psychological and social stressors, teen health center nurses who must provide care to young people without angering parents, and social workers, psychologists, psychotherapists, and psychiatrists who are tired of diagnosing problems that have more to do with their patients' social ecologies than psychopathology. An ecological practice can be (and has been) adapted to these settings.

Conversations that take place, like the one I described earlier with Michelle, are just as likely to occur on a residential unit, driving to a doctor's appointment, or in a secure treatment setting. They can occur over a kitchen table in a child's home or at a child's school with the child's teacher looking on. I've even done this work in coffee shops and under trees in a park when my office was too formal or too scary for a child who wasn't ready for that level of one-on-one intense clinical work. Regardless of the setting, the techniques I used to work with Michelle are effective because they focus attention on the child's social ecology and changes that others close to the child need to make rather than putting all the responsibility for change on the child herself.

Before tipping my hand and discussing in detail the techniques I used when working with Michelle, it's crucial that we agree that like most young people, Michelle showed plenty of potential to do well on her own. I would even describe her as having "hidden resilience" (Ungar, 2004). She wanted people in her life. She could control her drug abuse, at least for a time. She was thinking about her future, even if that included living independently with a boyfriend who was almost certain to continue to abuse drugs and steal.

Change the opportunities available to Michelle and she might make different choices. That's the magic of understanding resilience as more than an individual's ability to cope with adversity. Resilience is just as much about the way a child's social ecology opens new opportunities to overcome problems, or helps a child avoid exposure to risk in the first place.

Clearly, we have an internal capacity to thrive but that capacity to overcome adversity must be nurtured and supported (Seccombe, 2002). Counselors can play an important role here; for example, Nancy Scheper-Hughes (2008) argues that a focus on post-traumatic stress and the disorder that follows over-emphasizes our fragility. Though we mustn't ignore the marginalization and exploitation that many children like Michelle experience, our assumptions of vulnerability and frailty overlook what individuals are capable of achieving when the people and institutions in their lives (their social ecologies) provide them with opportunities to excel (Cyrulnik, 2011).

An Unconventional Approach to Practice

As a guidebook for clinical practice with children, youth, and their families, this one is going to take an unconventional position and show that helping young people change is as much about changing the people and institutions with which they interact as it is about changing individuals themselves. The more complex the challenges an individual like Michelle faces, the more important it is to change the environment *first* before we try to change individual thoughts, feelings, or behaviors. The principles and skills associated with this social ecological model of practice align well with many of the core competencies required of social workers, marriage and family therapists, child and youth care workers, psychologists, guidance counselors, and other allied mental health professionals. As I'll show in Chapter 3, we, as professionals, have long recognized the need to think and work ecologically, integrating our work with the principles reflected in our codes of ethics and the core competencies that translate them into practice. What we have lacked, however, is detailed practice-informed and research-based interventions that can help us to work more effectively with people in ways that are sensitive to the complexity of the problems they face. We have had no shortage of great advice, but very little evidence to support us when we advocate for clients, promote contextual sensitivity, reflect on our power and privilege as therapists, or focus our work on changing social ecologies rather than changing people. As Madsen and Gillespie (2014) explain with regard to their work with families involved with child protection services, "Helping people to take a larger view of their lives can be a profoundly empowering to them. We want to acknowledge that we live in a socio-cultural context in which historically some people have come to matter less than others." If we are going to meet our obligations as professionals, however, we need a substantial model of ecological practice that we can be confident is effective.

Any clinician who has worked in community settings with people who are extremely marginalized, exposed to high levels of violence, or suffering from severe disabilities or mental health challenges already knows that changing the environment jumpstarts individual processes of growth. Most of the evidence-based practices, those that are used to treat problems as different as post-traumatic stress, conduct disorder, and learning challenges, focus most on helping individuals develop the cognitive skills and adaptive behaviors believed to contribute to well-being (see, for example, Feldman, 2007; Manassis, 2012). There is an odd ideological fervor to some of these interventions since we know that *change is unsustainable without access to an environment that supports the client's process of growth*. However, it is timely that several of the best-known cognitive psychologists have recognized that without social change individual change is impossible in contexts where there are significant social, economic, and political challenges (Bandura, 1998; Cicchetti, 2010).

As clinicians we understand this, but in the absence of models of ecological practice that have an evidence base to prove they are effective, we tend to focus solely on what we can easily control during the time we spend with our clients: that's clients themselves. Unfortunately, this leads to an evaluation paradox. Some interventions are far more amenable to measurement of outcomes than others because what they are trying to change is relatively simple and narrowly defined (like expressions of anger, rates of substance use, or experiences of anxiety). How do we prove that for children like Michelle with very complex needs living in very complex environments a combination of individual, family, and community interventions offers the most effective treatment? The answer is that we must begin with what we have learned from practice, what we call "practice-based evidence" (Lebow, 2006).

Practice-based Evidence and Social Ecological Interventions

Many clinicians leave their offices to attend case conferences at children's schools, invite parents into family sessions, advocate for clients to access better financial aid, testify on behalf of clients in court when children are being removed by Child Welfare authorities, and work as staff members of treatment teams in community and institutional settings like group homes for young people with persistent mental illnesses. These are examples of what I mean by social ecological interventions. While anecdotally we know that these efforts to shape a client's experience of the world have a positive impact on a client's psychological and social adjustment, there is very little scientific proof that this systems-oriented clinical work can be as or more effective than individually-oriented practice. Herein lies a serious challenge. Clinicians are forced to squeeze these ecological interventions into their clinical practice and hope nobody will notice enough to complain.

In this regard, working to adapt systems to meet people's needs can be somewhat political. As counselors, we may have to question our job descriptions, confront the reluctance of our colleagues to see their roles more broadly, force our institution to share human and financial resources, and sell funders on the idea that clinicians who are compensated for changing a client's social ecology will be more effective at helping clients themselves change.

Here is an example: A child who is failing at school because of a complex array of problems that include a learning disorder, social exclusion, and parental neglect is going to require someone to provide good individual support along with interventions that address broader ecological barriers to successful coping. In practice, the counselor who uses an ecological approach is unlikely to ask this child "What do *you* need to do to succeed at school?" and then focus on changing the child's study habits or self-esteem. The counselor will instead say to the child, "What does *your school* need to do to help you succeed? What do *your parents* need to do? And what can *I*, as your counselor, do that will help you come to school more often?" This second set of questions obligates the therapist to work ecologically, changing systems while still supporting a child's adaptation under stress. In my practice, that has meant advocating for a child to change schools (when his school exposes him to violence and exclusion), organizing meetings of multiple service providers, and finding funding to cover the child's added costs of transportation. As if that's not enough, it also meant convincing my supervisor that if I helped address these contextual risks, the child would be much more likely to work with me on his behavioral problems and accept help from a teacher's aide. My supervisor, in turn, had to deal with a bureaucracy that had rules about which interventions I could bill for. Meetings with school principals and time spent on the phone finding transportation dollars were not typically seen as clinical interventions. The good news is that where these efforts are made, my experience and that of my colleagues tells me we become more effective clinicians. We help the most vulnerable of children engage successfully with their service providers. Other community-oriented practitioners who are focused on enhancing resilience, like Hart, Blincow and Thomas (2007), have termed this pattern of intervention "resilient moves."

An Intentional Model of Practice

As the last example shows, an ecological practice focuses attention as much on the social determinants of well-being (like safety in one's family and community, a sustainable attachment to caregivers, and access to education) as it does individual psychological factors related to biology and personality. It works because it reflects what we have learned from the following areas of research and practice:

1. Adaptation of systems theory that reminds us to include families and communities in treatment (Imber-Black, 1988; Lourie, Stroul & Friedman, 1998; Madsen, 1999, 2009; Prilleltensky, 2012).
2. Appreciation for the analyses of power and co-construction of meaning that are a part of post-structuralist (Dickerson & Zimmerman, 1996) and feminist models of therapy (Dominelli & McLeod, 1989; Weedon, 1997).
3. Bronfenbrenner's (1979, 2005) theory of the social ecology of human development that provides a multisystemic lens with which to think about individual growth and development in different contexts.
4. Research on resilience with marginalized populations of children which has shown that many protective factors predict which children will do well despite adversity (Bonanno, Westphal & Mancini, 2011; Cyrulnik, 2011; Masten, Monn & Supkoff, 2011; Ungar, 2011, 2012; Werner & Smith, 2001).
5. The study of natural ecologies where relationships between elements are now understood to be less linear, causal, or hierarchical than we thought previously (Naess, 1989; Wackernagel & Rees, 1996).

While we know that a child's social ecology influences developmental outcomes, we remain uncertain how to adapt research findings and theoretical models to the clinical interventions and systemic changes that are necessary to help children and their families succeed. Tragically, what doesn't get recognized as good practice doesn't get funded by service providers. The evidence, however, is clear: changes to children's social ecologies can have a greater impact on psychological and behavioral outcomes than focused interventions on children themselves, especially for children who face more severe challenges (Prilleltensky, 2012).

Resilience as Navigation and Negotiation

To repeat a well-known observation of Kurt Lewin, the grandfather of social psychology, "There is nothing so practical as a good theory" (1951, p. 169). Research on resilience, especially that of more ecologically-minded researchers, is producing a detailed description of how children, youth, and families overcome adversity (Bottrell, 2009; Harvey, 2007; Hobfoll, 2011; Ungar, 2005, 2008). That research, often with people who live lives as stressful as Michelle's, is proving that resilience is *not* an individual's capacity to overcome adversity. The metaphor of people being like metal springs that bounce back after being squished is nothing more than a polite way of blaming people who don't succeed (who don't bounce back) for their being unable to change conditions beyond their control. To see resilience as a quality of the individual reflects an ideology of rugged individualism that has convinced us that because one individual "beats the odds" every other individual in similar circumstances should be able to do the same. This detestable idea is challenged by research with people who live in challenging contexts around the world, in both high-income nations like the United States, Canada, and the UK, and those from low- and middle-income countries like Cambodia and Brazil (Bell, 2011; Panter-Brick & Eggerman, 2012; Ungar, 2007; Weine et al., 2012). For many, success is beyond people's reach until someone (a therapist, teacher, family member, friend, politician, or significant other) makes mental health resources available and accessible.

To illustrate, Kimberly DuMont and her colleagues (DuMont, Ehrhard-Dietzel & Kirkland, 2012) showed that among a group of mothers who have characteristics that put them at risk of child abuse or neglect (for example, living in vulnerable communities with high rates of poverty, infant mortality, and teen pregnancy), many protective factors distinguished parents who harmed their children from those who did not. Almost all of these factors are not individual qualities that the mothers themselves control. Social supports that provide stressed parents with respite care, educational opportunities, employment, and family income, combined with appropriate expectations of children's developmental progress (reinforced by the mother's cultural beliefs) and empathy for children's feelings, create a rich collection of protective factors.

Furthermore, there were marked differences between ethnoracial groups in DuMont et al.'s study. Hispanic mothers were more likely than African American and non-Hispanic mothers to avoid abusive behaviors. Accordingly, very little of the overall difference between the parents could be accounted for by individual qualities of the parents themselves, but instead seemed to reflect broader social processes like access to social support and culturally related experiences that helped mothers be better parents. Preventing child abuse, it seems, is best done by changing a mother's social ecology rather than changing the mother herself.

Such findings help us to see that while we have remarkable capacity *individually* to cope well with stressors, and many of us do just that, the greater the stress load, the less likely it is that individuals will be resilient. Stevan Hobfoll (2011), based on years of research in Israel with both Jews and Arabs, wryly observes, "We must be careful not to romanticize this striving, as our research already shows that the initial optimism about how many people are resilient in the face of major stress . . . is greatly exaggerated in circumstances where stressors are more massive or chronic" (p. 128).

It appears that people who cope well and overcome adversity succeed at two processes: navigation and negotiation (Ungar, 2005). Resilient individuals (families or communities) are those who are able to *navigate* their way to the resources they require. These navigations, however, can only succeed if the resources people need are *available* and *accessible*. Practically speaking, an individual must exercise enough personal agency (motivation and personal power) to seek the resources she needs while her social ecology must have the capacity to put those resources where individuals can make use of them. For example, a health care system can be flush with mental health professionals (in other words, they are available) but these human resources are not accessible to the most marginalized without such things as subsidized service fees, cultural sensitivity by clinicians, public transportation, and out of hours service.

So far, so good. However, making resources available and accessible is only going to impact wellbeing if what is provided is *meaningful* to individuals who need the service. As my work with Michelle showed, it is important that clients know they can *negotiate* for what is important to them and successfully make their goals the focus for therapy. Bringing all these ideas together, resilience can be defined as follows:

In the context of exposure to significant adversity, resilience is both the capacity of individuals to *navigate* their way to the psychological, social, cultural, and physical resources that sustain their well-being and their capacity individually and collectively to *negotiate* for these resources to be provided and experienced in culturally meaningful ways.

(Ungar, 2008, p. 225)

An ecological practice makes it possible for young people and their families to navigate and negotiate for resources that are meaningful to them.

Of course, that doesn't mean we should completely neglect individual factors either. A growing number of studies of resilience are pointing to genetic factors (and their environmental triggers), neurological processes (and the neuroplasticity that results from a facilitative environment) and personality types as all contributing to a child's well-being under stress (Folkman, 2011; Luthar, 2006). For example, if we look at resilience to traumatic events, we know that characteristics like the ability to show some restraint and self-regulation of emotions, a touch of extroversion to solicit support from others after exposure to traumatic events, the capacity to be calm in new situations, cheerfulness, enthusiasm, and the capacity to take pleasure in life, are all personality traits that distinguish those who cope well from those who are likely to suffer from Post-Traumatic Stress Disorder (PTSD; Miller & Harrington, 2011). However, it is a good environment that puts the resources people need to do well in front of them. Personal potential in a toxic social environment may never be realized.

Three Ways to Intervene

There are many ways that Michelle's team of professional supports could have helped her realize such potential for growth and avoid the debilitating effects of trauma. Here are three aspects of what should be part of every mental health practitioner's job description:

- *Direct Clinical Practice:* Direct practice with individuals and families is still the most common form of mental health intervention. It is typically focused on changing thoughts, feelings, and behaviors (Ivey & Ivey, 2007). The emphasis is on the relationship between the counselor and the client that has been shown to be the one aspect of clinical work that contributes to change more than any other (Duncan, Miller & Sparks, 2004; Orlinsky, Rønnestad & Willutzki, 2004).
- *Case Management:* When patients with mental and physical disabilities were deinstitutionalized and hospitals closed, clinical staff were forced to develop new ways of helping people develop the life skills necessary to live independently. Case management grew as an approach to helping individuals develop the networks of support and the life skills they need to survive. It extended the mandate of therapists to include the brokering of access to resources like housing and support groups. In the process, it turned clinicians into advocates for the rights of vulnerable populations (Heinonen & Spearman, 2006).
- *Community Work:* Sometimes, counselors must shift their focus from individual and family interventions to work with groups experiencing a common challenge, or the wider community. For example, in contexts where there has been a natural disaster or political violence, therapists may become community developers, intervening to address collective experiences

of trauma and the broader social determinants of health like racism and inequality (Almeida, Vecchio & Parker, 2008; Hart, Blincow & Thomas, 2007; Gewirtz, Forgatch & Wieling, 2008; Pancer et al., 2012). As a model for intervention, an ecological approach to practice does not require mental health professionals to stop working with individuals and families. It does, however, emphasize a continuum of service that places importance on collaboration between mental health counselors (those who help individuals change) and community developers (those who help communities meet people's needs).

All three approaches help children, youth, and families find new ways to cope under stress. They help young people succeed at two important tasks: (1) *navigate* to the personal and social resources they need to experience well-being and (2) *negotiate* for resources to be provided in ways that are meaningful to children and youth from diverse contexts and cultures.

Monday Morning, 9:20 A.M. (Part 2)

Helping Michelle navigate and negotiate was not easy. As her counselor, I thought Michelle would do well to talk about her experience of sexual abuse and her response to traumatic events, to reconnect with school, put in place a harm reduction strategy to decrease her drug abuse and control the influence of the boyfriend, and accept help from her transition worker. Michelle, meanwhile, had learned that authority figures could not be trusted even if she knew she needed their help. For her, the future was a foggy uncertainty and she was unlikely to let go of the one person, her boyfriend, whom she believed was there for her, no strings attached.

Compounding Michelle's problems was the fact that even if Michelle told her workers, "I need my own apartment," they were compelled by outdated policies to place barriers in front of her that prevented her from achieving the housing, safety, attachments, and support she required to manage her drug use. Housing First initiatives teach us that people change when they feel physically secure (Tsemberis et al., 2003). Psychological interventions are more effective the less the client is exposed to factors that threaten well-being, which means mental health is sometimes more dependent on the quality of the client's environment than the quality of the client's cognitions. With this in mind, I had to ask myself:

- Could Michelle exercise some say over who she lives with in her independent housing unit? Could her workers respect her choice of sexual partner and support her as the relationship runs its course?
- Could Michelle insist that her group home workers be the ones who help her transition out of care rather than being forced to start a new relationship with another social worker?
- Could Michelle's contact with her family be supported without it resulting in the removal of her younger sister from the home?
- Could Michelle's need to bring her court case to a conclusion be respected and the process expedited?
- Could Michelle's need to use drugs to maintain a peer group be understood? Could she be taught the harm reduction techniques she needed to reduce the consequences of her risky behaviors without jeopardizing the few relationships she had?

Thinking ecologically means engaging in a relational therapeutic approach to counseling that intentionally combines the best of what we know about clinical practice, case management, and the community work that helps us advocate for clients like Michelle.

My Clinical Practice with Michelle

"So, what exactly would you tell everyone if you could get them to listen?" I asked Michelle. She thought about my question for a moment, then told me she didn't want to be alone and she was actually happy to remain connected to people who had been her workers for the past several years. She was anxious about turning 18 years old and being on her own. If she couldn't get an apartment and share it with her boyfriend, she would rather move in with him and his mother. Unfortunately that would distance her even further from her support staff, something that neither Michelle nor her workers wanted to see happen.

On one level our conversation was about how I could advocate with the child welfare agency mandated to care for Michelle; on another, we were talking about insecure emotional attachments, abandonment, and the way drugs helped Michelle self-soothe. We decided that Michelle was not a bad kid, but a good kid in a bad situation that could be changed.

We began with a plan for secure housing. While I could do little more than make phone calls and attend case conferences, I did manage to coach Michelle how to better advocate for herself. We contacted an organization for children in care, and through their support explored Michelle's rights. Eventually, Michelle negotiated a compromise with social services: they would set her up in a small independent living unit and her boyfriend could visit as often as he liked as long as he maintained a separate domicile and he refrained from bringing drugs into the home. If the couple were going to use drugs, it was expected that they would do so at the boyfriend's residence.

With that settled, it was my turn to suggest some treatment goals that I was pretty confident reflected Michelle's other priorities. First, I asked Michelle to consider talking about her relationship with her mother and what it meant to her. Second, I invited her to talk about the sexual abuse and her frustration with the lack of progress prosecuting her abuser.

Drug abuse was not our focus for some time, mostly because Michelle wanted nothing to do with that conversation beyond occasional advice regarding harm reduction strategies. We eventually talked about these strategies at length, but only after Michelle was confident I'd heard her thoughts on her mother, her time in care, and the online predator who had tricked her into meeting him.

We worked together for nine months before Michelle decided she was ready to be on her own. There were setbacks, of course. Her boyfriend physically assaulted her while on probation and she forgave him despite needing a visit to the emergency department for stitches. Two months later she was temporarily discharged from her group home after she was caught using drugs in her room. That incident almost destroyed the longer-term plan for independent living. Within seven days, though, Michelle was allowed back into the group home as long as she promised to see me more often. Everyone, including Michelle, was relieved.

There were also sessions with Michelle and her mother, who agreed to come to see me on the condition that the focus was on helping Michelle transition to independent living safely and not the problems she'd experienced parenting her daughter. There was even one session with Michelle and her boyfriend before he abused her. Having met him and watched them together, it was much easier to understand what he meant to Michelle and why she went back to him. He was a reckless, impulsive young man who when high could be dangerous, but straight and sober he made Michelle feel like a princess (at least that's how Michelle described her experience).

Finally, we brought into our sessions a member of Michelle's support staff at the shelter and used that time together to talk about both the group home's commitment to Michelle and their worries about her future. Though the work may sound confusing, it actually flowed easily, talking about how Michelle could navigate to the resources she needed to sustain well-being while negotiating for those resources to be provided in ways that made sense to her.

Common Factors that Predict Good Outcomes

The processes that protected Michelle psychologically and physically are remarkably similar to those of other children and families living in challenging contexts around the world. Street children in Colombia, migrant youth in China, and Inuit students in Canada's Arctic show common coping strategies like relying on adult mentors, distancing themselves from toxic home environments, making the most out of personality traits that are culturally appropriate and valued by others, or resisting the cultural stereotypes that threaten self-worth (Ungar, 2011).

For populations with complex needs who face significant levels of adversity, there are seven common protective factors that appear repeatedly in my research (Table 1.1). Though all seven have been shown to contribute in ways large and small to the successful coping of children who are stressed or marginalized, they are particularly helpful when a child's environment is full of risk and her life has been a complex series of decisions with few opportunities to make good choices.

Table 1.1 Seven factors associated with resilience (Ungar et al., 2007)

Resource Category	Explanation
1. Relationships	Relationships with significant others, peers, mentors, and family members within one's home and community.
2. Identity	A personal and collective sense of who one is that fuels feelings of satisfaction and/or pride; sense of purpose to one's life; self-appraisal of strengths and weaknesses; aspirations; beliefs and values; spiritual and religious identification.
3. Power and control	Experiences of being able to care for oneself and others; personal and political efficacy; the ability to effect change in one's social and physical environment in order to access resources; political power.
4. Social justice	Experiences related to finding a meaningful role in one's community; social equality; the right to participate; opportunities to make a contribution.
5. Access to material resources	Availability of financial and educational resources; medical services; employment opportunities; access to food, clothing, and shelter.

Table 1.1 continued

Resource Category	Explanation
6. Cohesion	Balancing one's personal interests with a sense of responsibility to the greater good; feeling as if one is a part of something larger than oneself socially and spiritually; one's life has meaning.
7. Cultural adherence	Adherence to everyday culture-based practices; assertion of one's values and beliefs that have been transmitted between members of different generations or between members of one generation; participation in family and community cultural practices.

Making Practice Socially Just

In my experience, most graduates of social work, psychology, nursing, medicine, and child and youth care programs are introduced to the reasons why each of these seven factors are important. Many also receive instruction in the politics of disadvantage and marginalization, and understand *conceptually* the need to put principles of social justice into practice. The problem is that in our actual clinical work these principles are, as Isaac Prilleltensky observes, "conspicuously absent" (2012, p. 2). Read the literature on child welfare practice, for example, and one is hard pressed to find a verbatim transcript of a meeting between a parent and a social worker or psychologist that occurs during a crisis that reflects in any practical way principles of social justice (for an exception, see Hart, Blincow & Thomas, 2007; Ungar, 2011). While the problem is stubborn and entrenched in an earlier view of the therapist as detached, the likelihood of "countertransference" minimized by the impersonal separation of the one counseling and the one being counseled, there are many who see instead potential for better practice when issues of social justice are front and center. Angie Hart and her colleagues have promoted teaching health care professionals to develop an "inequalities imagination" (Hart, Hall & Henwood, 2003, p. 481) that positions within therapy a thorough understanding of social justice issues at the heart of practice. It is a practical strategy. After all, inequality and social exclusion leak into clinical processes, overwhelming people's capacity to cope and placing real world limits on their opportunities to change.

What, then, does a practice that attends to issues of racism, sexism, homophobia, and other forms of exclusion look like, especially when these issues are not the reasons why clients come to counseling? How do we resolve being solution-focused, strengths-based, and client-centered while at the same time introducing a social justice perspective to those with whom we're working? When is it acceptable to lead, and when should we follow? As Prilleltensky (2012), in his discussion of well-being, suggests, "What I am arguing for is that it is equally valid to assess the wellness of the organization or community independently from the experience of a person in such a system. In other words, I would like to argue that to complement persons' assessments of their own experience in a setting, it is useful to identify characteristics of the setting that are empowering, liberating, and health-giving" (p. 3). Clinically, that means asking clients to consider how their families, schools, service providers, and communities are either making them mentally ill or creating the conditions to overcome mental health challenges like eating disorders, anxiety, and addictions.

A Focus on Delinquency

While a social ecological model of practice can be used with problems as diverse as elder abuse of a senior who is isolated from her extended family or a delinquent youth, I've chosen in this book to focus on the clients I am most familiar with, children and youth who exhibit serious antisocial behavior and their families. It is much easier to illustrate the principles and skills of an ecological practice by discussing all the phases of intervention in relation to just one type of problem.

Serious antisocial behavior includes a range of behaviors that result in referral to mental health services (i.e., conduct disorder, depression), youth justice services (i.e., criminal behavior, violence), child welfare agencies (i.e., running away from home, involvement in the sex trade), school counselors (i.e., truancy), public health professionals (i.e., high-risk sexual behaviors), and addictions services (i.e., substance use). While the problems young people experience are often interrelated, there is little rationale for why a youth is referred to one system or the other when he presents with a complex array of concurrent disorders and comorbidities (Henggeller & Sheidow, 2012). A shortage of services tends to result in more intrusive and restrictive treatments for delinquent youth than might be necessary. Mental health services for children and youth are particularly problematic because of the level of unmet need among young people (Kirby & Keon, 2006; U.S. Dept. of Health and Human Services, 1999) and because conduct disorder is associated with adult criminality, marital problems, combative employee–employer relations, unemployment, and poor physical health later in life. Conduct disorder also predicts educational underachievement, substance use and dependency, anxiety, depression, and suicide (Jané-Llopis & Anderson, 2005). While it is never too late to intervene, early intervention has been shown to always be the better option.

The problem with individually-oriented treatment for this population is that it can overlook the complexity of the multiple systems that become involved with young people with serious antisocial behavior. The youth most in trouble with the law are often found to be in the greatest need of mental health services and responsive foster care providers (Conger & Armstrong, 2002; Loeber et al., 1998; Murphy, 2002). Similarly, homeless youths and children in care require intensive case management and mental health supports (Cauce et al. 1998; Litrownik et al. 1999). Juvenile justice programs require stronger connections with public schools to achieve effective re-integration when discharging youth to their communities (Hellriegel & Yates, 1999). Child welfare clients are often shown to be in need of mental health care and have higher rates of service utilization (Arcelus, Bellberby & Vostanis, 1999; Haapasalo, 2000; Kroll et al., 2002; Webb & Harden, 2003) as well as needing access to a myriad of other support services such as special schools and responsive court systems (Dohrn, 2002; Sagatun-Edwards & Saylor, 2000; Saathoff & Stoffel, 1999; Wilson & Melton, 2002).

Given these intersecting systems and the complex needs of young people with serious antisocial behavior, there is a growing case to be made for an ecological conceptualization of why young people misbehave and how to intervene. Several comprehensive reviews (for example, Liberman, 2007; Loeber, Burke & Pardini, 2009) have summarized findings across studies that identify a relatively consistent array of individual, family, peer, school, and neighborhood risk factors for antisocial behavior. Within each, there are patterns that repeat. Parenting practices such as how children are disciplined and supervised, especially after school, have been shown to put youth at risk of delinquency (Pettit et al., 2001). Other caregiver factors like drug use and mental health are also related to the development of antisocial behavior (Cohen, Hien & Batchelder, 2008), with aspects of individual functioning such as cognition and biological processes like autonomic arousal triggered by factors found in a youth's environment. Outside of a youth's household, factors such as a lack of prosocial activities, low academic functioning, and deviant peer involvement also influence the development of antisocial behavior (Dishion, 2000; Mikami & Hinshaw, 2006; Shin, Daly & Vera, 2007). A good intervention with this population needs to think about all these ecological factors even if the referral is meant to provide the individual with personal therapy for behavioral problems.

Summary

An ecologically trained clinician asks clients to consider substitute coping strategies that are meaningful and that bring with them long-term success (resilience). Training in the skills necessary to influence both individual psychological factors and the social determinants of well-being gives mental health care providers a toolbox of skills they can use intentionally to broaden therapeutic interventions beyond those focused on individuals or immediate family members.

As this introductory chapter has shown, many clinicians are already case managers, advocates, and system changers. Those aspects of their work, however, go largely unnoticed. While positive thinking and "grit" might predict better psychological outcomes for the general population, we can help more children with complex needs faster when we change their environments first. In the chapters that follow, we'll explore ways to help children, youth, and families with complex needs living in challenging contexts navigate and negotiate effectively.

EXERCISE 1.1

A Social Ecological Approach to Counseling: Self-Assessment Tool

Name: _____   Date: _____

Section A: Total Score _____

Section B: Total Score _____

Thinking about your practice, how would you rate yourself on each of the following principles and skills? How much is each evident in your work?

You can use this self-assessment to think about your work in general, or you may want to consider what you did with a particular client during one contact or session. If you prefer, it may be easier to think about the entire course of intervention you and your client have engaged in together. After all, no single session is likely to show all these principles and practices in action, though a good ecological approach to counseling will show many being applied over time.

You can also include comments in the spaces provided if they are needed to help explain your answers.

SECTION A:

There are principles of practice that, when reflected in our work as clinicians, help to ensure that the focus of intervention is not just on individuals, but also on changing the social ecologies that either cause problems or help to make people more resilient.

20 Principles of Practice

1. **The counselor discusses strategies with the client to make use of the resources that are available and accessible.**

I discuss what I know, and what the client knows, regarding how to access different individual, social and physical resources. Together, we identify any challenges to accessing resources and make plans to overcome these challenges. There are clear strategies developed to help the client access resources.

This statement describes my work:

Not at all	A little	Quite a bit	A lot	Does not apply to the type of work I do
0	1	2	3	n/a

Comments . . .

2. The counselor explores with the client the client's definition of problems and possible solutions.

I explore with the client what she/he/they identify as the reason counseling is needed, and how problems and possible solutions affect the client and other people close to the client.

This statement describes my work:

Not at all	A little	Quite a bit	A lot	Does not apply to the type of work I do
0	1	2	3	n/a

Comments . . .

3. The counselor discusses what the client hears about his or her problems and solutions.

I explore a range of messages (positive and negative) that the client hears about her/his/their problems and the solutions that have been tried (past and present).

This statement describes my work:

Not at all	A little	Quite a bit	A lot	Does not apply to the type of work I do
0	1	2	3	n/a

Comments . . .

4. The counselor explores with the client which resources are the most meaningful.

I discuss with the client which individual, social, and physical resources are the most meaningful, reflecting on the client's culture and context to determine the resources that are likely the best fit to help the client.

This statement describes my work:

Not at all	A little	Quite a bit	A lot	Does not apply to the type of work I do
0	1	2	3	n/a

Comments . . .

5. The counselor integrates different phases of the intervention.

The focus of my work with the client changes as I get to know the client better and trust builds (engagement). Our collaborative assessment provides new information about individual and contextual risks and strengths, the informal supports and formal services that are available to the client, and possible solutions to the problems the client experiences. There is evidence during the intervention that new information is used to refocus the work (change the contract), update expectations for change and how we work together, and plan for the client to succeed after the clinical work ends (transition out of counseling). Each part of the work informs the other as we move along.

This statement describes my work:

Not at all	A little	Quite a bit	A lot	Does not apply to the type of work I do
0	1	2	3	n/a

Comments . . .

6. The counselor shows awareness of use of self.

I pay attention to my own beliefs regarding what the client needs to do. I am careful not to assume I know the solution to the client's problem.

This statement describes my work:

Not at all	A little	Quite a bit	A lot	Does not apply to the type of work I do
0	1	2	3	n/a

Comments . . .

7. The counselor shows the intentional application of theory to practice.

My work shows the intentional use of social ecological principles. The questions that I ask and activities that are done are intended to help the client navigate to the resources she/he/they need and negotiate for the services and supports she/he/they feel are most meaningful. While other approaches to counseling may be evident, the client experiences a coherent flow to the work.

This statement describes my work:

Not at all	A little	Quite a bit	A lot	Does not apply to the type of work I do
0	1	2	3	n/a

Comments . . .

8. The counselor shows awareness of diversity.

I show sensitivity to the unconventional (atypical) solutions that the client uses to solve problems. Context and culture are discussed when solutions are expored.

This statement describes my work:

Not at all	A little	Quite a bit	A lot	Does not apply to the type of work I do
0	1	2	3	n/a

Comments . . .

9. The counselor assesses the client's strengths, identifying coping strategies that the client has used in the past, along with the social and physical resources that were required for these strategies to succeed.

I explore examples of the client's coping strategies from the past and present, discussing both what the client did as well as what services the client accessed, who in her/his/their personal network and community helped, and the capacity of the client's environment to help make change possible.

This statement describes my work:

Not at all	A little	Quite a bit	A lot	Does not apply to the type of work I do
0	1	2	3	n/a

Comments . . .

10. **The counselor creates a clear contract, either written or verbal, with well-described goals for the period of intervention. The counselor negotiates goals for the intervention with the client.**

I work with the client to negotiate an understanding of the problems and how that understanding impacts the client's life. I set priorities and timelines with the client, and agree on how we will follow-up to ensure a plan is implemented.

This statement describes my work:

Not at all	A little	Quite a bit	A lot	Does not apply to the type of work I do
0	1	2	3	n/a

Comments . . .

11. **The counselor focuses a portion every session on reviewing or renewing the contract for service.**

I review near the beginning of each session the contract, and during each session, I acknowledge new issues that the client mentions, reminding the client of the contract she/he/they have agreed to for counseling. When necessary, I ask the client if she/he/they would like to re-contract.

This statement describes my work:

Not at all	A little	Quite a bit	A lot	Does not apply to the type of work I do
0	1	2	3	n/a

Comments . . .

12. The counselor is willing to challenge the client's problematic patterns of coping and motivate change. The counselor negotiates with the client the coping skills that will be worked on during the session.

I skillfully discuss with the client which coping skills are effective and the long-term consequences of not making changes. New skills are discussed and those that are most meaningful practiced during the session.

This statement describes my work:

Not at all	A little	Quite a bit	A lot	Does not apply to the type of work I do
0	1	2	3	n/a

Comments . . .

13. The counselor is effective at showing genuine concern. The counselor sustains a positive relationship with the client.

I display optimal levels of warmth, concern, and genuineness, encouraging the client to engage in discussions she/he/they are ready to have.

This statement describes my work:

Not at all	A little	Quite a bit	A lot	Does not apply to the type of work I do
0	1	2	3	n/a

Comments . . .

14. Threats to the client's safety and the safety of others are addressed and strategies put in place to protect everyone from risks.

I engage the client in discussions about her/his/their safety and the safety of others close to the client. When safety is threatened, plans to address safety concerns are developed and implemented.

This statement describes my work:

Not at all	A little	Quite a bit	A lot	Does not apply to the type of work I do
0	1	2	3	n/a

Comments . . .

15. The counselor acknowledges that changing social structures is as important as changing individuals. The counselor explores solutions that are multisystemic and complex.

I explore the many different factors contributing to the client's problems and contract to work on multiple solutions that address both individual and contextual challenges.

This statement describes my work:

Not at all	A little	Quite a bit	A lot	Does not apply to the type of work I do
0	1	2	3	n/a

Comments . . .

16. The counselor explores the client's internal and external barriers to growth.

I help the client identify a range of both internal and external barriers that prevent them from achieving her/his/their goals. I explore examples of how these barriers have had an impact, positive and negative, on the client's life.

This statement describes my work:

Not at all	A little	Quite a bit	A lot	Does not apply to the type of work I do
0	1	2	3	n/a

Comments . . .

17. The counselor anticipates and prepares for the client's transition back into relationships with informal supports or other formal service providers after the intervention ends.

I do whatever I can to include during the intervention (either in person, or through periodic contact outside of scheduled meetings) individuals and services that can support the client during and after the intervention.

This statement describes my work:

Not at all	A little	Quite a bit	A lot	Does not apply to the type of work I do
0	1	2	3	n/a

Comments . . .

18. The counselor advocates with, or on behalf of, the client, or shows the client how to advocate independently.

I spend time discussing strategies to advocate with, or on behalf of, the client, or show the client how to advocate for herself/himself/themselves.

This statement describes my work:

Not at all	A little	Quite a bit	A lot	Does not apply to the type of work I do
0	1	2	3	n/a

Comments . . .

19. The counselor does not convince the client to comply with rules and regulations.

I briefly point out the consequences of problem behaviors but spend most of my time with the client exploring why the client's current behavior is experienced by the client as adaptive. I appreciate that resistance to rules and regulations may be a coping strategy the client finds useful when other strategies seem less effective.

This statement describes my work:

Not at all	A little	Quite a bit	A lot	Does not apply to the type of work I do
0	1	2	3	n/a

Comments . . .

20. The counselor redirects questions about unconscious determinants of behavior to social ecological factors.

I acknowledge any questions or concerns about intrapsychic determinants of behavior (like personality traits, unconscious motivations, and early childhood trauma) but redirect the client to focus on identifying the social ecological factors that are necessary to solve problems.

This statement describes my work:

Not at all	A little	Quite a bit	A lot	Does not apply to the type of work I do
0	1	2	3	n/a

Comments . . .

SECTION B:

Putting these principles described in Section A into practice takes special skills. Here are 20 skills observed in video recordings of counselors whose work shows evidence of a social ecological model of intervention.

Navigation Skills

	This statement describes my work:				Does not apply to the type of work I do
	Not at all	A little	Quite a bit	A lot	
1. Make resources available. I help the client identify the internal and external resources that are available.	0	1	2	3	n/a
2. Make resources accessible. I discuss how the client can access the resources that are available.	0	1	2	3	n/a

	This statement describes my work:				Does not apply to the type of work I do
	Not at all	**A little**	**Quite a bit**	**A lot**	
3. Explore barriers to change. I discuss the barriers to change the client experiences, and which resources are most likely needed to address which barriers.	0	1	2	3	n/a
4. Build bridges to new services and supports. I discuss with the client the services and supports that I am familiar with and my role as a bridge builder to help make new resources available and accessible.	0	1	2	3	n/a
5. Ask what is meaningful. I explore with the client which resources are the most meaningful given the client's context and culture.	0	1	2	3	n/a
6. Keep solutions as complex as the problems they solve. I explore solutions that are as complex (multisystemic) as the problems they address.	0	1	2	3	n/a
7. Find allies. I explore possible allies who can help the client access resources and put new ways of coping into practice.	0	1	2	3	n/a
8. Ask whether coping strategies are adaptive or maladaptive. I help the client explore whether the solutions she/he/they are using to cope in challenging contexts are adaptive or maladaptive, and the consequences to the choices the client makes.	0	1	2	3	n/a
9. Explore the client's level of motivation. I discuss with the client her/his/their level of motivation to implement new preferred solutions.	0	1	2	3	n/a

	This statement describes my work:				Does not apply to the type of work I do
	Not at all	A little	Quite a bit	A lot	
10. Advocate. I advocate with, or on behalf of, the client, or show the client how to advocate independently, to make resources more available and accessible.	0	1	2	3	n/a

Negotiation Skills

	This statement describes my work:				Does not apply to the type of work I do
	Not at all	A little	Quite a bit	A lot	
1. Thoughts and Feelings I explore with the client thoughts and feelings about the problem that brought the client to counseling.	0	1	2	3	n/a
2. Context The client and I explore the context in which the client's problems occur, and the conditions that sustain them.	0	1	2	3	n/a
3. Responsibility The client and I discuss who has responsibility to change patterns of coping that are causing problems for the client, and/or for others in the client's life.	0	1	2	3	n/a
4. Voice I help the client's voice be heard when she/he/they name the people and resources necessary to solve problems in challenging contexts.	0	1	2	3	n/a

	This statement describes my work:				Does not apply to the type of work I do
	Not at all	**A little**	**Quite a bit**	**A lot**	
5. New Name When appropriate, I offer different names for a problem, and explore what these new descriptions mean for how the client and I will work together.	0	1	2	3	n/a
6. Fit I invite the client to choose one (or more) new description(s) of the problem that fit with how she/he/they see the world.	0	1	2	3	n/a
7. Resources The client and I work together to find the internal and external resources the client needs to put new solutions into practice.	0	1	2	3	n/a
8. Possibilities I help the client see that she/he/they have more possibilities for change, and a larger number of coping strategies than she/he/they believed possible.	0	1	2	3	n/a
9. Performance I help the client identify ways to perform for others her/his/their new coping strategies.	0	1	2	3	n/a
10. Perception I help the client to convince others that she/he/they have changed, or are doing better than expected.	0	1	2	3	n/a

CHAPTER 2

WHY A SOCIAL ECOLOGICAL PRACTICE WORKS

The most difficult times clinically are those when we feel lost, overwhelmed by another's problems, or naively believe we have the solutions to fix someone's life but fail miserably. Without an organizing set of rules (a theory of change) we risk floundering, following people's problem-saturated stories without any hope of helping them find solutions that are meaningful for them. Counseling with a theory of change in mind provides us with a roadmap that helps us know where to start, how to proceed, and when to encourage a transition to something new. It makes our clinical practice intentional. The roadmap we use needn't be overly prescriptive, spelling out the specifics of every word we say. The best theories inform a practice that is flexible, allowing us to apply theory to practice in ways that are sensitive to people's contexts and cultures.

This chapter, then, is mostly about the theory behind why a social ecological practice works rather than the specific skills that make it work. It also provides a concise introduction to some of the most important things we know about patterns of resilience and the processes that make resilience possible. For those who want to read immediately about the skills necessary to put theory into practice, you should proceed to Chapter 4. You can always come back to this chapter and the next one later.

My purpose here, then, is to show that a good model of clinical practice should help counselors make their work contextually and culturally responsive. Whatever your model of practice, it should facilitate resilience, creating the conditions for the young people with whom we work to experience positive psychological and social development even when burdened by physical and psychological disorder or the marginalization that results from living in socially disadvantaged families and neighborhoods. To do this, the counselor focuses on the two processes of navigation and negotiation. These are the engines of change used by mental health care providers who think ecologically. But what specific kinds of navigations and negotiations are likely to produce the greatest amount of change? Answering this question is the focus of this chapter.

An Example of Theory in Action: Colin

Since grade three, Colin has lived in a community where he has been exposed to violence almost daily. Children there quickly learn to survive by being aggressive and delinquent. Colin, however, is a mild-mannered, well-cared-for, white, working-class child who stands out at school as one of the brighter students. He comes to school every day with a lunch bag nicely packed by his mother who works full-time as a professional driver. Unlike his peers, Colin's problems aren't neglect. They are the bullies who torment him because he is so well looked after.

At age 16, Colin was referred to a colleague of mine, Jennifer, a child and youth care worker who is part of a team of service providers who offer families in crisis support in their homes at times convenient for them. Jennifer asked me to help her develop a better plan for the clinical work she was doing with Colin. As hard as she had tried to help Colin, she just couldn't make the bullies go away. Colin was at risk of dropping out of school because of the constant torment. At first, we were both doubtful that anything else could be done for Colin that hadn't already been tried. Our hesitancy to predict success was only reinforced when Jennifer met with both Colin and his mother, Becky, in their home early one weekday evening. Becky was very clear what she thought Colin's problem was: "He needs more self-esteem. Damn it, teach him how to stand up for himself!"

Colin wasn't convinced that was his problem. He insisted he had tried to stand up for himself and had done everything in his power to get away from the bullies. In grade school he'd avoided the bullies by walking to school rather than taking the bus. He'd purposefully found activities to do at lunchtime so he wouldn't have to be on the playground. He'd even made a few friends, though they too mostly cowered when the bullies noticed them. When Colin's lunch was stolen or he was pushed down and slapped, he told his teacher and his principal. The bullies were suspended, which only made them laugh at Colin more. "We just got three days at home playing Nintendo," they told him and spit in his face. By the time Colin reached Junior High, the bullies had begun to vandalize his home, throwing eggs at his windows, or putting dog excrement in his mailbox. Colin's mother called the police and they spoke to the boys' parents, but still nothing changed. By this point, Becky was driving her son to school every day so he wouldn't have to be alone on the street.

"If only he'd fight back," Becky said.

Colin did eventually pick a fight with one of the bullies. "I told him, 'Okay, let's go outside and do this'," Colin told Jennifer. A teacher overhead him instigating the fight and suspended Colin. It was at that point that Colin's mother had requested help and agreed to let Jennifer into her home. She hoped one more attempt at counseling might help her son.

"It's so frustrating," Jennifer told me when we met for consultation. "It's not fair what's happening to Colin. But nobody is changing it."

I agreed, and wondered if she was going to do what the mother had asked and provide Colin with therapy to increase his self-esteem. She thought about it, but it didn't feel right, she said, to be putting all the responsibility for change on Colin's shoulders. The question remained, though, what else could she do except try to change Colin's self-concept and behavior?

It's a common problem that individual and family therapists encounter, no matter what their theoretical orientation. At one time or another, we all ask ourselves, "How can I influence the social factors that surround my client?" "Do I focus just on the individual, or can I do something to change my client's environment?" Whether we work in office-based clinical settings, residential settings like group homes and hospitals, or community clinics that are less formal, we still encounter the same problem. How does one have a practice that is both individually focused and socially conscious? How do we not only help individuals beat the odds stacked against them, but also change those odds so that clients are more likely to thrive? Just as importantly, will a more ecological practice work?

"Do you think Colin's problem is a lack of self-esteem?" I asked Jennifer.

"His mother thinks so," she replied slowly, "but I think the problem is the bullies."

I thought about this for a moment. It struck me that Colin had shown a remarkable amount of self-esteem. Colin had persisted and gone to school each day. He'd told his teachers about the bullying even though it had made the bullies retaliate against him and his family. It struck me that the problem was that Colin's mother didn't see her son as coping well in an impossible situation and that what Colin needed first was recognition for the self-esteem he'd already shown. Once we convinced Becky how competent her son really was, I wondered if we couldn't continue to work with Colin to identify solutions that made sense to him. Neither Jennifer nor I had experience living in the community where Colin was growing up, nor did either of us really know what it was like to be bullied for such a long period of time by boys who brought guns to school. We decided we'd have to trust Colin to help us find solutions that made sense to him in his world and had at least half a chance of succeeding if put into practice.

A case plan using the principles of navigation and negotiation was developed:

- Jennifer would work with Colin to review everything he'd already done to stand up to the bullies. She would ask him whether he felt he had shown self-esteem each time. Her approach would challenge 'thin' descriptions of Colin (those that lack appreciation of Colin's socio-historical context) as failing or lacking self-esteem by engaging him in a conversation that would support a view of Colin as resilient in a terribly adverse context. Colin's perception of himself would be made a little louder and given more power when his problems were being discussed.
- Colin's mother would be invited to participate in these conversations. Jennifer would help Colin convince Becky that he had actually been showing a lot of personal power in how he had protected himself. In this way, the intervention would be systemic, changing how Becky interacted with her son and her definition of his problem and its solution.
- If Colin still felt he needed help to improve his self-esteem, Jennifer would work with him to challenge faulty cognitions and change behaviors that were disempowering. Her application of techniques borrowed from Cognitive Behavioral Therapy. Those treatments could be used to develop Colin's ability to resist feeling depressed or mimicking the violence he experienced.
- Meanwhile, if Colin agreed, Jennifer would host an after-school meeting for a few of Colin's friends. She would ask them what they thought about Colin's situation, whether he had shown courage dealing with the bullies, and most importantly, what they thought he could do to keep himself safe. By making Colin's peers the experts, and listening to them describe what they were up against, Jennifer hoped to challenge Mom's perception of Colin as failing to tackle his problem and to explore the contextual challenges to Colin standing up for himself more (Would it be safe? Would others support him?).
- Though there had been many case conferences in the past, Jennifer wanted to meet with Colin's school and see if anything more could be done to keep him safe. She wanted to be Colin's case manager and advocate for Colin and coach him on how to advocate more effectively for himself.
- Finally, Jennifer needed to talk to her manager at the agency where she worked and get her support. She needed to know that the extra hours she'd be accumulating organizing case conferences and meetings alone with Colin's mother (to help her understand the process Jennifer was using) would be seen as hours fulfilling Colin's contract for service which was explicit with regard to addressing his "psychological problems and family dynamics." She worried that sessions alone with Becky might not fit her funder's idea of what individual and family work looks like.

This is, though, what an ecologically-oriented clinical intervention looks like: clinical work and case management combined into a seamless intervention that facilitates navigations and negotiations by individuals and families who have few resources and complex needs. The approach does not require elaborate collaboration between counselors (a large group of therapists working together behind a one-way mirror is a luxury, but not a necessity), client therapy groups, or any other techniques that are often impractical outside of well-resourced clinical training centers. Any time Jennifer spends on activities that are beyond the traditional role of clinician doing individual or family therapy is justified as time spent changing the social and physical ecologies that surround Colin. Her supervisor may have balked a little at the time Jennifer was spending changing Colin's social ecology rather than working directly with Colin, but she couldn't argue with the results. Both Colin and Becky were pleased with the service they were getting and fully engaged. Furthermore, those extra hours working ecologically reduced the duration and intensity of the individual work Jennifer had to do with Colin.

A Social Ecological Approach to Clinical and Community Interventions

Colin's case plan is a good demonstration of how a social ecological practice can be combined with other approaches to counseling. Jennifer may eventually use Cognitive Behavioral Therapy to address Colin's self-concept, or borrow aspects of Narrative Therapy to change Colin's mother's perception of her son's problem. Changing individual or family therapy into an effective multi-systemic therapy in contexts of adversity means helping people make changes where changes are needed most: their social ecologies. Colin didn't need to work on his self-esteem as much as he needed to get recognition for the coping strategies he had already used in a very challenging context. As was shown in Chapter 1, psychological resilience cannot be nurtured in higher risk situations until the risks a child faces are dampened.

The work with Colin adheres to six rules that make change processes effective for people who live in contexts where there are few supports and high levels of stress. The same rules, however, may not be all that effective for clinical work with people who experience less severe problems or problems that are relatively uncomplicated (for example, a child from a well-resourced, safe home is arguing with his mother about how much homework he should do after school).

Rule #1: Early is Better, but it's Never Too Late

When designing interventions, it is always preferable to provide help early, before problems become more complex and patterns of coping that cause problems grow to be deeply entrenched. Early intervention changes life trajectories. For example, at the level of biological developmental processes, we know how important it is to provide a better beginning for children. Neuroplasticity, the brain's capacity to recover from exposure to prolonged traumatic events and neglect, can be developed through positive and supportive experiences that prevent further deprivation (Luthar & Brown, 2007). In other words, environments that provide optimal conditions for human development, like soil rich in nutrients, are an investment in early prevention that makes resources more easily available and accessible to disadvantaged children. It is an "upstream" cost-effective alternative to counseling and other forms of "downstream" intervention after problems have become serious, which is especially effective when there is "constelled disadvantage" (Hart, Blincow & Thomas,

2007, p. 14), the challenge posed by a myriad of factors that come together to produce complex problems. In these difficult contexts, children survive because of changes to both external factors such as the child's social and economic status or exposure to violence, and internal factors like the subtle changes in behavior and cognition that result from a positive attachment to a caregiver.

The factors that have the potential to turn a child from vulnerable to resilient are temporal. Specifically, time influences resilience in two ways. First, developmentally, we know that people will cope with adversity with varying degrees of success at different points in their psychosocial development, depending on the number of stressors in their environment (the burden) and their capacity (the resources) to cope. Second, different historical periods demand of us different coping strategies. For example, in a period of economic boom, leaving school and moving out on one's own early may protect the self-esteem of a child with a severe learning disability if he is able to quickly find work and support himself. During a prolonged recession, however, he may have to remain in school longer and living at home if there are no opportunities for employment.

We are much more familiar with what Laub and Sampson (2003) term "cumulative continuity" (p. 51) of problem behaviors like delinquency over time: "Delinquency incrementally mortgages the future by generating negative consequences for the life chances of stigmatized and institutionalized youth" (p. 51). Delinquency, therefore, has a temporal dimension too. It weakens social bonds and leads to the necessity of adult crime. Fortunately, there are other factors that are likely to make a delinquent youth resilient as an adult, interrupting negative life trajectories. First, just becoming an adult changes a young person's level of delinquency as many status offences, crimes that only a young person can commit like under-age drinking, stop being criminal acts. Later, marriage, time in the military, and full-time employment, all predict better attachments and opportunities to change patterns of adult criminal behavior. These experiences are dependent on how well the youth's social ecology responds to the needs of the young person.

However, there is no easy way to predict with certainty that any single protective factor will permanently change problem behaviors. Each intervention is, however, "grist for the mill," adding a little more to the potential strengths an individual has to resist falling into problematic patterns of coping. There is a great deal of variability in responses, with some compensatory patterns of coping producing a steeling effect: the child compensates for exposure to traumatic events like abuse by developing coping skills that allow her to maintain a sense of equilibrium and continue to do well. Later, the adult who experienced abuse as a child is shielded from the mental health problems that are related to adversity because of the coping skills she learned earlier in her life (Feder et al., 2010; Friborg et al., 2006).

The only drawback to compensatory coping strategies is that they sometimes backfire. When researchers studied whether American soldiers returning from tours of duty in Iraq and Afghanistan were more or less likely to experience PTSD, they discovered that soldiers who had been abused as children and who as children used avoidance and withdrawal strategies to cope made great soldiers during their tours of duty. The same soldiers were the ones most likely to experience PTSD when they returned home (Bonanno & Mancini, 2012; Cacioppo, Reis & Zautra, 2011). Soldiers without a history of abuse and soldiers with histories of abuse who had used other strategies like externalizing behaviors (i.e., angry outbursts, running away, truancy) tended to report lower levels of PTSD in large part because they were better at talking about their experiences after discharge. The example is interesting as it reminds us that a coping strategy that may be very adaptive for a child when younger, allowing an abused child to continue to perform adequately outside of his home, can later become an unsustainable maladaptive strategy to cope with trauma. In the case of the soldiers with abuse experiences and histories of avoidant coping, they were less able to access informal social supports (for example, the camaraderie of other veterans) which can be crucial to coping with the trauma related to being a combatant during war.

Rule #2: 70-20-10

From clinical practice and a review of studies of resilience, we know that approximately 70% of children will cope well with the challenges they face in adverse family, school, and community contexts *if* they are provided with the psychological and social supports they need (see, for example, Bonanno, 2013; Sroufe et al., 2005). For most children who face significant adversity, that means sustained structural supports like safer streets, good schools, attachments to peers involved in prosocial activities, a financially stable home, and freedom from violence or harsh discipline at home and at school. It also means good government policies informed by research that set as a priority the provision of services that match the needs of communities. Despite a popular belief to the contrary, children's level of motivation to achieve positive developmental milestones like high school graduation or to resist substance abuse is actually less important than the resources children are provided by their caregivers, educators, and policy makers (Ungar, 2011). When well-monitored, well-cared for and provided quality education and other supports, most children succeed even if they have low levels of motivation to excel. In contrast, motivated children in social ecologies that deprive them of caring adults, good schools, and opportunities for recreational "highs" (like sports, music, and adventure) are not as likely to succeed in as great numbers as less motivated but better resourced children.

To illustrate, an initiative called Pathways to Education (www.pathwaystoeducation.ca) is a community-based program that has been shown to be effective increasing high school completion rates among students from disadvantaged communities where rates of graduation can be as low as 25%. Staff work with adults in the community to identify one public housing project or neighborhood school where the majority of children are exposed to factors associated with early school leaving such as poverty, parents who left school early, community violence, or high rates of teenage pregnancy. Because the sample is purposeful, every child in the catchment area is offered extra help beginning in grade nine. The intervention includes one-on-one support and advocacy, group mentoring with caring adults, academic tutoring that children are expected to attend after school with trained educators, and financial support (money is put into a trust account each year the child attends high school) which, by the time the child graduates, is enough to pay for the first few years of college, university or a vocational program. By changing the environment around the child and making it more supportive, high school completion rates more than doubled and rates of absenteeism dropped as much as 52% in the first year. Students who participated showed rates of engagement in post-secondary education higher than the national average, and were much more likely to complete their degrees than post-secondary students. These positive outcomes can be attributed to the changes in the availability and accessibility of the supports children needed to succeed at school. Individual motivation to change was not the primary focus of Pathways to Education.

Sadly, longitudinal studies also show that approximately 30% of children who experience significant adversity require more than just good homes, schools, or community centers to overcome the trauma resulting from abuse, marginalization, relocation, individual mental disorders, or the disordered behavior of their caregivers (Moffitt et al., 2001; Werner & Smith, 1992). In those cases, approximately two thirds of the children who do not respond to structural changes in their families, schools, or communities (or 20% of the total at-risk child population) respond well to tertiary level mental health interventions that help change complex, harmful reactions to past victimization and current psychological problems. This number is arrived at by estimating the typical level of effectiveness reported for most therapeutic interventions (about two thirds of clients of mental health services show improved functioning after counseling) (Lebow, 2006). Together, the combination of structural supports, effective clinical interventions and case management can ensure that at least 90% (70% plus 20%) of young people in adverse contexts enter adulthood relatively well-functioning.

What happens to the remaining 10% of children who experience significant levels of adversity? Despite the advantages of safe supportive environments and therapeutic help, many are still likely to move into their adult years with troubling patterns of problem behavior (Moffitt et al., 2001). The good news, though, is that many of these individuals do, in time, heal the wounds inflicted on them by adverse early childhood experiences (Laub & Sampson, 2003). Their success will be partly the result of their growing capacity to think more clearly about their actions and anticipate the consequences. Their pattern of growth will also be related to the opportunities they have for employment, intimate relationships, and a sense of belonging and purpose in their communities.

The 70-20-10 rule highlights a pattern in the research and evidence from the clinical practice literature that suggests that not all individuals who face significant challenges need individual or family therapy, though many do, especially when structural changes to the individual's environment are not enough to change their problem behavior. Unfortunately, even with extra clinical help, we can expect that 10% of all individuals with complex needs will not show much short-term improvement in their behavior. For these individuals interventions are, to quote Earla Vickers, one of my clinical mentors, "money in the bank" that can pay dividends much later in life.

Rule #3: Protective Processes Work

We misspeak when we describe someone as "resilient," as if there is one final state they can achieve, like a cake that is fully baked and ready to be taken from the oven. We are also mistaken when we say a child shows resilience, as research clearly shows that the capacity to recover from stress is not a static quality of the child, but the result of processes that make growth possible (Masten & Obradović, 2006). Factors associated with resilience are the fuel that makes protective processes effective. For example, a good relationship with one's parent and the capacity of that parent to monitor her child are both factors that facilitate the process of healthy child–parent interactions that make the child more likely to be resilient.

To illustrate, Reid is a 12-year-old child with above average intelligence and a talent for sports, but living in subsidized housing with his mother who has been diagnosed with Borderline Personality Disorder. Over the years she has struggled to attach to her son but her abusive behavior has never been severe enough to warrant Reid's removal. Much of Reid's success is attributable to a supportive school, though the school can only do so much to keep Reid safe. It was his school Principal who noticed that Reid was reluctant to go home and helped the boy get involved in a number of school activities. She also called child protection services to ensure that Reid was being properly monitored by authorities. Arguably, if Reid hadn't been engaged in the protective processes that resulted from healthy interactions at school and with service providers, it is likely that he would have fallen into patterns of behavior such as delinquency or depression.

With regard to clinical and community interventions, this focus on process is particularly important. It is far easier to change the environment around an individual in ways that open opportunities for new resources than it is to fortify an individual to make him strong enough to cope in an environment that fails to adequately provide him with what he needs to do well.

Rule #4: Cumulative Resilience

The more protective processes individuals engage in that enhance their capacity to cope, the more likely they are to show good developmental outcomes. Studies of strengths show the same pattern. Across a population, prosocial behaviors like school attendance and attachments to peers are related to a long list of internal and external factors (Benson, 2003; Donnon & Hammond, 2007). In general, the more these factors are available to the individual, the better the individual weathers stressful life events.

The relationship between the number of protective factors, protective processes and positive outcomes is curvilinear. This is important for counselors to understand when developing case plans. One positive health-enhancing factor in a child's life, like a non-delinquent peer group, is good. That peer group and an opportunity to get extra help at school is even better, doubling the chances the young person will do well. Add to this list a parent who communicates with his child's teachers, a violence-free home, a community that values education, the transmission of cultural traditions to the child, access to recreational facilities, and the young person is likely to be engaged in multiple processes that ensure long term developmental benefits. Research shows that these factors combine in ways that make them more than just the sum of their individual influence. Their influence grows exponentially, one increasing the positive impact of all the others.

For counselors this means we need to think about case plans as a complex and interrelated set of possible solutions to problems that occur at different systemic levels (individual, family, school, community). The more positive processes we help clients engage in, the more impact each process will have. Changing behavior, then, is a matter of providing access to enough protective processes to help people cope effectively in threatening environments.

Rule #5: Differential Impact

One of the most distinguishing aspects of the study of resilience is that it always pays attention to the amount of risk a child is exposed to. Change the amount of risk and the long-term impact a protective process will have changes too. In other words, protective processes exert different amounts of influence on developmental outcomes depending on the amount of adversity individuals experience (Ungar, 2013).

Factors that are protective when there is exposure to a great deal of stress may have no benefit at lower levels of stress, or could even cause an individual harm. For example, adoption is usually seen as an advantage for an abandoned child but is experienced by a child with a secure attachment to an adult as a terrible and life-disrupting traumatic event. The rule of differential impact explains this pattern. Furthermore, the amount of benefit a protective process brings to a child also varies by how richly resourced the child's world is. Comparing two orphans, we know that for orphans who suffered severe early neglect before they were adopted, a secure attachment to an adoptive family will result in a disproportionately greater amount of positive influence on the neglected child when compared to an adopted child who did not suffer early neglect (Beckett et al., 2006). In other words, adoption benefits the most badly treated children the most.

The same pattern is observed in other interactions that take place in a child's wider social ecology. For example, a good relationship with one's teachers at school and the feeling of belonging that follows is very important to youth from homes and communities where there are few emotional supports, but does very little to increase a young person's engagement at school if he is already well anchored at home and has plenty of extra-curricular activities. Here again is the same pattern of differential impact (Shernoff & Schmidt, 2008). School engagement is much more important to children from disadvantaged backgrounds who do not have after-school supports than children who have lots of opportunities to show their talents and form positive relationships with caring adults outside of school (Ungar & Liebenberg, 2013).

Likewise, acculturation may be a good thing for children and adults from the dominant culture but resisting acculturation can protect the mental health of first and second generation immigrants when it prevents them from becoming alienated from their culture of origin (Berry et al., 2006; Simich et al., 2009). Acculturation can actually cause harm to populations coping with the stress of migration and integration into a community where they experience racial or ethnic prejudice.

For counselors, understanding the differential impact of protective processes helps fine-tune goals for intervention. Depending on the individual client's exposure to adversity and the complexity of the client's needs, different processes may be more or less helpful. This is a very important distinction and one that is often overlooked by both clinicians and policy makers. This differential impact is the result of both children's perceptions of the resources available to them, both real and imagined, and the opportunity structures that make it possible for them to use resources. It also reflects their differential susceptibility to risk factors related to gene expression (Belsky, Bakermans-Kranenburg & van Ijzendoorn, 2007; Belsky & Pluess, 2009a, 2009b). In other words, individual factors related to both cognitions and genetics influence whether a protective process exerts a large or small influence on a client. For counselors, this may explain why an effective intervention with one individual fails to help another.

This is the kind of complexity that an ecological practice addresses far better than clinical models that rely on explanations of human development that assume homogeneity in the way individuals from different contexts and cultures will respond to stress. When we ignore differences, we overlook how we can match interventions to individuals. For example, Fergusson and Horwood (2003) make the distinction between protective processes (those that are beneficial to those exposed to risk factors but of no benefit to those not exposed) and compensatory processes (the process associated with resilience benefits both those exposed and not exposed to adversity). They report results from a 21-year study, the Christchurch Health and Development Study, with an unselected birth cohort of 1265 children born in 1977 in Christchurch, New Zealand. Those results show that what is and is not a source of resilience depends on the context in which interactions between people and resources take place: "When externalizing and internalizing in adolescence are considered, it is apparent that each sex has what appear to be gender-specific strengths and vulnerabilities, with femaleness providing resilience to externalizing but vulnerability to internalizing. . . The results show that what may confer resilience to one outcome, may increase vulnerability to another" (p. 147). As the example suggests, even gender will decide which types of protective processes work best for which person. This is not surprising given that a child's gender exposes them to many forms of risk and dramatically changes their access to health resources.

We need, therefore, to put most of our energy into looking for the protective processes that are effective for those who are the most marginalized. This makes a social ecological model of intervention different from Positive Psychology, which has tended to focus on population-wide factors that reflect the values of the dominant culture (see, for example, Peterson et al., 2008). We could imagine, for example, a situation where dominant culture youth fail miserably when assessed for skills that minority culture youth use to thrive. To illustrate, language acquisition skills in a country like the United States are far better developed among immigrants than Americans of Anglo-European descent or those who have fully acculturated, yet we do not measure the *absence* of multilingualism as a *deficit* among American school children. We don't typically talk about children as vulnerable and lacking potential to flourish because they *only* speak English. In a country comprised mostly of English speakers, the majority of children need only one language to survive. Of course, it's not the same for cultural minorities and immigrants for whom multilingualism is a protective factor with profound influence on their life course. Generalized assessments of the protective factors that are the building blocks of Positive Psychology do not, however, focus on capacities that are most relevant to minorities. Instead, there is a bias toward aspects of behavior valued by cultural elites.

The same argument can be made with regard to the ability to resist racism, or "code switch," when transitioning between one cultural group and another. Children behave in ways that either celebrate their differentness through clothing, language, and other behaviors, or find ways of being chameleon-like conformists and fitting in. These skills are important to sustaining a positive identity and sense of coherence when one is a cultural outsider. They are typically developed, however, only by cultural minorities (we could say that cultural minorities show strengths in this area). Therefore, as these examples show, there is a need for counselors to understand how a protective factor can have a negligible effect on a population but skew developmental outcomes (and exert a differential amount of influence) on a particularly disadvantaged group of children. As one can imagine, this important observation can dramatically change what occurs in counseling and the goals that are set.

Finally, the rule of differential impact also explains why the provision of human services is so important to disadvantaged children and families, but has little impact on developmental outcomes among those who face little or no adversity (Sanders et al., 2013). Browne's (2003) work illustrates this difference. In an effort to provide lower socio-economic status (SES) children and those involved with child welfare services with access to extra-curricular activities, funds were provided to help children participate in activities after school. The program realized back the investment through decreased demand for medical services and mental health counseling. Investments in services do not, as a rule, exert a significant impact on children who face fewer risks and don't need them (Masten, 2006; Ungar, 2012).

Rule #6: Hidden Resilience (Maladaptive Coping)

Sometimes young people cope in ways that others perceive as harmful but that clients themselves argue are protective. Children adapt to their environments in ways that make sense to them given the psychological and social resources that are available. When these patterns of coping are thought by others to be unacceptable, but clients see their coping as effective, we can describe their coping as maladaptive and their resilience as hidden (Ungar, 2004).

The theory of maladaptive coping (or pathological adaptation) suggests that in contexts with few options, certain behaviors may protect the child from threats to their psychological well-being even though these behaviors bring with them problems like disapproval from caregivers, school suspensions or forced treatment (Ng-Mak et al., 2010). Problem behaviors in poorly resourced environments can simply be an individual's best "choice" (though there really is very little choice!) to make do with what little she has.

Interventions to change maladaptive coping strategies can, therefore, offer substitutes that bring with them equally effective means to achieve the same psychological benefits that dangerous, deviant, delinquent, and disordered behavior already provide. The child who is looking for a sense of belonging and security but lacks a stable home may turn to delinquent peers because he has no other way to protect himself and feel affirmed. The young woman who becomes sexually active may find through her sexual activity a way to develop a positive identity when other paths to self-esteem appear blocked. Neither strategy (joining a delinquent peer group or early sexual activity) are socially acceptable, but research shows that maladaptive coping is most likely to occur when contexts are poorly matched to the personalities and strengths of individuals (Cruz-Santiago & Ramirez-Garcia, 2011; Ebersöhn, 2007). For example, in ethnographic accounts of youth in gangs young people talk about their criminal experience as an opportunity to be entrepreneurial, to feel safe, or to feel the self-esteem that comes with belonging to a powerful group of peers (Pinnock, 1997; Totten, 2000). Likewise, marginalized young women who become sexually active early may account for their experience as a rite of passage that makes them feel adult-like in much the same way that other children experience their driver's license and high school graduation as their rites of passage (Allen et al., 2007; Taylor, Gilligan & Sullivan, 1995).

When counseling to change children's behavior, it is important to consider whether the children and their caregivers can successfully navigate and negotiate for the resources they need to thrive. When satisfying substitutes to troubling behavior are available and accessible, change is likely to occur. After all, people navigate toward problem behaviors because those behaviors become the most meaningful. For example, a family where the parents (especially the mother) haven't completed high school may create a context in which education is undervalued and children are given permission to disengage from school early. Change the resources available to the child by providing the child with an educational mentor, financial assistance for post-secondary education, and tutors to ensure academic success, and many children will choose to stay in school and graduate. In other words, the meaning of school can be changed through a comprehensive approach that involves both individually-focused interventions with the child to assess learning challenges and motivate a child to learn along with structural changes that make it easier for children to learn. It's this second prong of the intervention, the adaptation of the environment, which is as or more important as individual therapy in contexts where education is undervalued and underfunded. In those instances, individual children and their families need to be engaged in the construction of a new definition of education as a pathway to success that is available to them while lawmakers must be coaxed to understand that investing in schools is a better investment than prisons.

The argument goes even further when we consider behaviors that may be socially undesirable but which are functional for a minority. An interesting example is the tendency of youth who perform poorly at school to leave before graduation. The strategy may appear to disadvantage them except that by their own account leaving a situation where they feel their self-esteem is threatened, and where opportunities for a good job in the future are perceived as few and far between even if they have a high school leaving certificate, may be a protective strategy relevant in a particular socio-historical context (Dei et al., 1997).

Collectively, as a community of mental health professionals, we have largely overlooked differences among ethnic and racial minorities. As Pratyusha Tummala-Narra (2007) wrote recently as an introduction to a case study of a bi-racial 30-year-old American woman plagued by anxiety, "While there is empirical evidence for the effectiveness of several psychotherapeutic approaches for certain psychological problems, such as phobias and depression, empirical evidence that any of these is effective with ethnic minority populations is sorely lacking" (p. 209). The therapy that unfolded grew well beyond a cognitive treatment, exploring the woman's experience of racism, sexual abuse, and the systemic prejudice she encountered when interacting with the police. It was in that context that therapy was effective because it was done in a way that was sensitive to the client's understanding of the world and the barriers she experienced daily.

While mental health care providers are trained to help individuals, we can also practice in ways that influence an individual and family's meaning system and, on occasion, the perception of policy makers of the appropriate solutions to wickedly stubborn problems like school drop-out or non-disclosure of sexual abuse. The chapters that follow emphasize direct clinical practice, but always with attention to the need to understand the context in which our interventions take place and our multiple roles as clinicians, case managers, residential workers, and advocates for socially just services.

Chapter Summary

Whether working in an office-based service, a residential setting, or a community program, counselors need to be able to help people navigate to the resources and services they need and negotiate for resources to be provided in ways clients find meaningful. A theory of change for a social ecological clinical practice directs our attention to how young people adapt to their environments in ways that make their navigations and negotiations effective. The more effective children are as navigators and negotiators, the more resilient they will be in challenging contexts. In this chapter, I've provided six rules to explain why a social ecological practice works, linking aspects of contextualized, culturally sensitive therapy with children and families to what we already know about resilience.

As has been shown, a social ecological practice encourages us to look at young people as making the best use possible of their strengths (what they already do well). When children face multiple challenges, however, counselors must appreciate that coping strategies may not result in socially acceptable patterns of navigation and negotiation (maladaptive coping and hidden resilience). When counselors understand young people's coping patterns as adaptive, they are in a better position to help them find substitutes for problem behaviors that bring solutions every bit as good as (and likely better than) the ones they found on their own when resources were scarce.

CHAPTER 3

PRINCIPLES AND SKILLS FOR A SOCIAL ECOLOGICAL PRACTICE

Interventions are not random events but intentionally sequenced patterns of conversation and activities that succeed at helping people find new ways of coping with adversity. That adversity can be as varied as toxic interpersonal relationships at home that expose a child to violence and neglect, a physical disability that prevents a child from social inclusion with her peers (and the resulting threats to the child's self-esteem that follow), or a school's refusal to put in place an effective case plan for a child with ADHD who needs a highly structured learning environment in order to perform well.

To be effective, a social ecological approach to intervention can either follow a well-prescribed pattern of techniques, or, if employed more flexibly, show the creative use of many different skills. In my experience, new therapists tend to rely on more scripted interventions (I know I did) until they gain the experience and confidence to dress up treatment with their own personal style. In this chapter I'll explain the five phases of intervention that an ecologically-oriented therapist uses and the different principles necessary to guide the work with clients from start to finish (though, as we'll see, counseling never really ends, it simply transitions).

Three Important Aspects of a Social Ecological Practice

A social ecological practice is distinguished by a number of practice principles that I'll discuss later in this chapter, and 20 skills illustrated in Chapters 4 and 5. Every one of these principles and skills help people navigate and negotiate more effectively. After reviewing videos of counselors using a social ecological model of clinical practice in different settings and reflecting on what makes their practice so effective, my colleagues and I found three unique and essential aspects of practice:

1. *Navigation*: Intervention helps clients identify the internal and external resources that are available to them and then evaluates the accessibility of those resources. When counselors are effective at helping clients navigate, clients find new coping strategies and exploit the resources that become available. It's these new ways of coping that make clients living in complex and challenging social ecologies more resilient the next time there is a crisis. The single mother coping with a substance abuse problem who is identified to child welfare services because she was seen verbally abusing her adolescent children (who themselves are in trouble with the law) needs both individual counseling and social support if she is going to heal and parent effectively. Whether she gets the resources she needs is another question,

one that depends much more on social policy, a community's commitment to providing social services, and the social discourse that either blames her for her problems or portrays her as a person made vulnerable because of circumstances beyond her control.

2. *Negotiation*: Intervention helps clients influence which resources they receive, by whom, how, when, and where. A discussion of the relative power of those who control resources and those who need them is almost always a part of counseling sessions that reflect the principles of a practice that is sensitive to people's social and physical ecologies. Social discourses that reinforce power for some or make the client entirely responsible for her problems are looked at critically. In the case of a single mother under investigation by child welfare authorities, helping her to negotiate better would mean having her voice heard when it comes time to develop an intervention plan for her and her children. Does she need her children removed or an in-home support worker a few days a week? Are the children really better off taken away from their mother, or will the disruption of attachments cause more harm than good? Will the voices of the children also be heard as services are negotiated? Negotiation means the counselor advocates with, and on behalf of, the client, or shows the client how to advocate for herself. New solutions are discussed that are meaningful to the client, reflecting the client's culture and context. Strategies to resource solutions are also discussed. The client is asked to consider how she can influence access to the resources that are available and who she needs help from to put new solutions to problems into practice. If a mother being investigated by child welfare authorities insists she can handle her children without professional help, then how can her social support network be mobilized to help her and her children remain together? To negotiate means to avoid predetermination of what clients need nor assume the counselor knows best what successful adaptation is going to look like for individual clients.

3. *Five overlapping phases of intervention (engagement, assessment, contracting, work, transition)*: Each of the five phases of intervention (which I'll discuss in detail in a moment) occur simultaneously when working ecologically. This is necessary as a social ecological practice emphasizes non-linear systemic thinking in which clients and counselors are constantly negotiating goals, refining contracts, updating assessments, and changing the focus of the work to match the client's needs. In the case of a single mother with children, a therapeutic contract might first address the woman's need for addictions counseling, then reassess her capacity to parent in a stressful environment, re-contracting to create the conditions necessary for a stable home for her children despite exposure to poverty or community violence. A decentered practice (one focused on the client's environment rather than the client herself) promotes the inclusion of the clients' natural supports and other service providers in counseling when possible. It also tackles persistent risk factors like inadequate financial support to the family, stigma, and social exclusion, all issues of social justice affecting the family's ability to survive on their own. By focusing on the many people who can help the family cope long-term, and changing the family's environment, an effective counselor will be able to smooth a client's transition from dependence on formal service providers to the nurturing relationships with natural supports that make change sustainable.

Five Phases of Intervention

Based on careful observation of clinicians at work and review of case files, therapeutic interventions can be broken down into five overlapping phases. Together, they keep the client and counselor engaged in a fluid process of navigation and negotiation that ensures people do not become dependent on the efforts of professionals to fix their problems. Instead, clients are encouraged to build and sustain a weave of relationships that have the potential to be an ongoing source of support even after counseling ends. The five phases of intervention are:

1. *Engage:* Counselors facilitate connections with the people with whom they work, building trust and inspiring confidence that the therapist-client relationship will succeed at creating new ways of coping that are as, or more, desirable than the client's current coping strategies. The client will sense that the counselor is both curious about the client's lived experience and humble enough to listen attentively and appreciate what can be learned from the client's stories of survival.
2. *Assess:* Counselors help clients reflect on patterns of belief and behavior, as well as experiences of marginalization and challenge, that have caused them problems in the past and present. Just as importantly, counselors help clients reflect on solutions they've tried and latent capacities that are waiting to be mobilized.
3. *Contract:* Counselors help people decide what they want to change, how they want to go about changing, and when.
4. *Work:* Counselors walk people through a process that makes change possible. These changes can take place at the level of beliefs and behavior or be more process-oriented, creating new patterns of interaction and meaning systems. The work phase changes young people's ability to navigate and negotiate, improving access to internal resources (for example, a sense of attachment to a caregiver), external resources (for example, a safe residential placement), or both at the same time.
5. *Transition:* Counselors help young people perform new strategies for coping with problems, or help their clients navigate to places where children's problems are no longer a negative force in their lives. Whether a child has changed or a child's social ecology has been modified to better meet a child's needs, the result is a child who is able to succeed and is recognized by others as doing well. As people and people's social ecologies are transformed, they transition from needing their counselor to help them to relying on others who are more readily available and with whom a relationship is sustainable.

Unlike some approaches to counseling that describe the five phases as occurring sequentially with only brief periods of overlap (i.e., first we engage, then we assess, and so on) ecologically-oriented therapists describe the five phases as occurring simultaneously (See Figures 3.1 and 3.2). The final phase, usually called termination, looks much more like a phase of transition than a hard stop. Helping children and their families navigate and negotiate is always more successful when there is:

- Ongoing engagement of the child and an ever-widening network of supporters.
- A never-ending assessment that adds detail as problems and solutions are better understood.
- Periods of contracting and re-contracting as new goals emerge.
- Innovative work that tailors itself to peoples' complex, atypical, culturally-distinct patterns of coping.

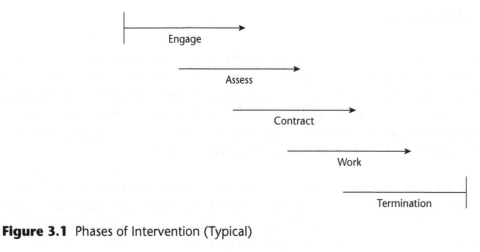

Figure 3.1 Phases of Intervention (Typical)

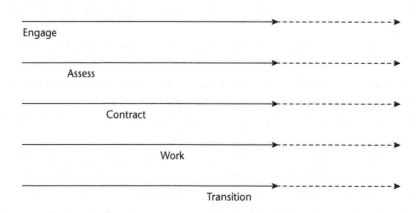

Figure 3.2 Phases of Intervention (Social Ecological)

- Help for clients to transition smoothly out of counseling and back into relationships with the natural supports that already exist or to build bridges to new ones.

For example, a good therapeutic process ensures that transitions are anticipated and the people and services that will support a child after counseling ends are engaged in the therapeutic process up front, included in the assessment and contracting phases, are integral to the work that is done, and encouraged to continue to involve themselves with the client well into the future. Who comes to counseling, and the role each takes, is part of an overall clinical strategy to help people create their own communities of care after the counselor–client relationship ends.

Case Study: Sally

It can be difficult to work this holistically, making each phase of the intervention part of a cohesive, coherent, and well-coordinated therapeutic process. My work with Sally, a 14-year-old white girl who had recently moved to a new suburban middle-class community, is a good illustration. During the first few months at her new school, Sally attempted suicide twice in the school bathroom. Both attempts were more attention seeking than serious efforts to end her life. Nevertheless, Sally's school psychologist, guidance counselor, and a specialized psychosocial support worker who acted as her case manager were all very concerned about Sally's behavior. After the second suicide attempt, Sally was taken out of regular classroom programming, something that further isolated her.

A referral to a regional children's hospital resulted in no firm treatment plan as Sally's behavior was not serious enough to justify psychiatric treatment or medication. Sally's parents reported the same pattern of self-harming behaviors at her old school over the previous three years. Little by way of effective treatment was offered. If Sally made gestures to harm herself, she was sent home. Home, however, provided few supports. Sally's mother worked long hours and her father struggled with alcoholism. Most days, it was Sally who prepared dinner for the family, unless her and her father got into one of their many fights. When that happened, Sally left to spend time at her 16-year-old boyfriend's home. His mother let Sally stay there overnight, sharing her son's bed, as long as Sally returned home the next day.

When I got the referral at the individual and family counseling agency where I worked part-time, the focus was narrowly on Sally and her mental health problems. While I began by engaging Sally in treatment, it quickly became apparent that the people who I needed to engage were those who Sally needed for support: her parents, her school psychologist, her guidance counselor, her case worker at child welfare, Sally's boyfriend, and his mother. Sally's parents were my first priority though it wasn't easy to find a time Sally's mother could meet, nor was it easy to get her father to join us. We eventually managed a meeting late on a Friday afternoon four weeks after I began seeing Sally at my office after school.

The school staff were easier to reach and made themselves available when they could. In total, I met with every one of them at least once, either at my office or at the school. Mostly, they spent their time with me telling me how much they were concerned about Sally and the changes she needed to make if she were to be allowed to come back to regular classroom programming. When I shifted the conversation from an individual, psychopathology focus and asked them what they could offer Sally to make it easier for her to feel connected at school, the conversation changed. It focused on specialized programming to help Sally reintegrate into a regular grade 8 classroom and more support during recess and lunch to find extra-curricular activities that Sally could be included in.

Engagement with all these formal and informal supports contributed to a plan for what happened after counseling ended. While we explored the factors that triggered Sally's self-harming behavior, much of what we paid attention to were the changes that were needed at home and at school to remove those triggers. Slowly, we identified ways that others could give Sally the feeling that she was emotionally connected. Our contract specified goals for individual change and changes to Sally's environment. Each person who joined us for a session helped add to the detailed assessment which described a number of different coping strategies Sally had used, others had used around her (for example, her father's drinking) and those that she hoped to use in the future, whether realistic (for example, making one close friend) or not (for example, becoming a fashion model so people would notice her). Contracts were revised as we moved from the ways Sally would be expected to change, to what others were doing that exacerbated Sally's efforts to feel safe at home and among her peers at school. Even Sally's boyfriend and his mother were invited to attend a session. Though an unusual situation for a girl of Sally's age, her relationship with her boyfriend and his family was an atypical but accessible resource for Sally through which she was managing to maintain a sense of self-worth and get attention. It was noteworthy that she had never done anything to harm herself while at their home.

Our work together settled into a comfortable routine of talking about Sally's thoughts and feelings and engagement with an ever-expanding network of people who we asked for support. Each person added to the assessment and became a part of the contract. Each helped us further the work we were doing by improving Sally's access to resources she argued were meaningful to her. For example, when her parents insisted Sally break off her relationship with her boyfriend ("He's too old for you and we don't like it when you stay overnight there") our time together was spent figuring out ways to reassure Sally's parents that Sally was finding something she needed through the relationship. A safety plan was put in place to ensure the young couple practiced safe sex (though Sally insisted they were not sexually active).

When working with a young person like Sally, it can be difficult to know where one should focus attention. How can the different phases of treatment intertwine without becoming a confusing mess? There are always so many factors to consider. The following list of practice principles and essential skills are meant to be like a well-stocked pantry. In the hands of a good chef, ingredients can be used in different combinations as needed to create a delicious meal. Not all great meals need a well-defined recipe, though most of us follow recipe books when we attempt to cook up something new. Counselors, like chefs, need the tools of their trade easily accessible. They also need to be well-versed with regard to what each ingredient contributes to the final product.

20 Essential Principles for a Social Ecological Practice

While the three aspects of practice (navigation, negotiation, and overlapping phases of intervention) are critical to making counseling ecologically-oriented, there are 20 principles that help to ensure interventions remain focused as much on people's social ecologies as their individual strengths and challenges. (A sheet that can be photocopied at the end of this chapter provides a brief list of all 20 principles.) While not all 20 principles are unique to ecological models of practice, they all help to ensure an effective intervention. As you read through the following list of principles, consider when during the five phases of intervention you could use them and which combinations are likely to work best for which client.

Navigation and Negotiation Principles

Principle #1: The counselor explores with the client the client's definition of problems and possible solutions. Counseling starts with asking the client for her/his/their understanding of the problem that motivated her/him/them to seek help. The focus of the intervention is on understanding what the client has experienced as a problem and what types of solutions are most likely to fit with the way the client sees the world.

Principle #2: The counselor discusses strategies with the client to make use of the resources that are available and accessible. The focus of intervention is on what both the client and counselor know about accessing resources when resources are available. Counseling explores aspects of individual and collective strengths, helping clients become aware of talents and capacities she/he/they may have overlooked that could help expand her/his/their choice of coping strategies. Past experiences are discussed in order to reflect on how individuals and environments interact and the solutions that the clients, and others, have used to solve problems.

Principle #3: The counselor discusses what the client hears about her problems and solutions. Time is spent exploring the range of messages, both positive and negative, that the client hears about her problems and the solutions that she is most comfortable pursuing. There is usually a great deal of time spent deconstructing who has the power to decide which solutions are best and who benefits most when a client chooses one coping strategy over another.

Principle #4: The counselor explores with the client which resources have been the most meaningful over time. Observation of an ecologically trained counselor at work typically shows a period of reflection on patterns of coping the client has used over time and why these coping strategies were preferred (and if they were effective).

Principle #5: Threats to the client's safety and the safety of others are addressed and strategies put in place to protect everyone from risks. Threats to the client's safety are discussed and strategies put in place to protect the client, the client's family and community from risk of harm. A social ecological approach to issues of safety avoids over-reaction to the risks posed to clients and others when one is unfamiliar with the context in which the client lives.

Principle #6: The counselor acknowledges that changing social structures is as important as changing individuals. The counselor explores solutions that are multisystemic and complex. Many organizations, including the International Union of Psychologists, the American Family Therapy Academy and national associations of social workers encourage their members to think about their work as having political overtones. Clinical therapy can be used to promote social justice when it addresses biopsychosocial barriers to well-being. Efforts to coordinate informal supports and formal service providers create communities of concern that can take collective action to address the social injustices clients experience.

Principle #7: The counselor explores the client's internal and external barriers to growth. The counselor helps the client identify a range of internal and external barriers that prevent her/him/them from achieving desired goals. The impact of these barriers on the client's life are discussed in order to see if they are worth challenging. Counseling helps make clients aware of the systemic barriers to change that she/he/they experience, including her/his/their experience of marginalization in communities that look at the client as an outsider or different.

Principle #8: The counselor redirects questions about unconscious determinants of behavior to social ecological factors. There is little need to focus on the unconscious determinants of problem behavior when working ecologically. While psychotherapy has its place for some clients who are motivated to reflect on why they behave as they do, a social ecological approach is more concerned with whether a particular behavior, thought, or feeling is experienced by the client as helpful. Psychotherapy may work for people in challenging contexts if there is enough money and time to complete treatment, but reflection on unconscious motivations for behavior seldom helps us understand the role a failed environment plays in shaping coping strategies. To try to change the unconscious roots of behavior is too long a process and likely to cause clients and therapists to overlook more malleable factors like a client's exposure to abuse, rejection by others, and the functional but maladaptive ways clients have coped with the very real problems that occur in complex social ecologies.

Five Phases of Intervention Principles

Principle #9: The counselor integrates different phases of the intervention. Each of the five phases of intervention has an impact on the other. As a client's interactions with her/his/their social ecology changes, there is a need to revisit who the counselor should engage with, details of the assessment, the specifics of the contract, and the implications of what is learned to the work phase and transitions that will occur later.

Principle #10: The counselor assesses the client's strengths, identifying coping strategies the client has used in the past along with the social and physical resources that were required for these strategies to succeed. The ecologically-oriented counselor focuses less on a client's psychosocial developmental milestones (for example, "When did you first enter school?", "When did you begin to have more independence from your parents?", "At what age did you find your first full-time job?") or family history during the assessment phase and more on the development of protective processes that the client has used in challenging contexts. A genogram, for example, when done ecologically, is only superficially about people's birth dates and relationships. It is much more interesting to plot on the genogram the history of problems ("Who drank heavily or used drugs in your family of origin?", "Who else self-harmed, or attempted suicide?") and their solutions ("Who didn't drink?", "How are you different from others in your family who avoid their responsibilities?"). A straightforward period of history taking can often feel like something that the clinician needs but bores the client who has come to counseling to get on with the work.

Principle #11: The counselor creates a clear contract, either written or verbal, with well-described goals for the period of intervention. The counselor negotiates goals for the intervention with the client. It may be obvious, but counseling often goes awry because it is unclear what the goals for treatment are. One week, Sally, who I introduced earlier, is in my office complaining about being in a special class that separates her from her peers, the next she is angry with her parents because of the chores they make her do when her father is drinking. Just because we approach counseling with a multisystemic perspective doesn't mean that our goals shouldn't remain focused and interventions targeted to one or two problems were it is possible to influence outcomes.

Principle #12: The counselor focuses part of every session on reviewing or renewing the contract for service. Near the beginning of each session the contract is discussed and changes made if required. New information from the ongoing assessment, or changes to the plan for transition (for example, who are you going to go live with after discharge from secure treatment?) are reflected in the contract for service. In turn, the contract guides who is included in counseling (engagement) and the specific work that needs to be done.

Principle #13: The counselor anticipates and prepares for the client's transition back into relationships with informal supports or other formal service providers after the intervention ends. Sally was my client for less than a year. For her to succeed longer term, the important people in her life needed to participate in counseling too. After all, they were the ones who provided Sally with a sustaining web of supports that could repeat the interventions begun during formal counseling. An ecologically-oriented practice, like other therapies, acknowledges that people do best when they transition from the clinician's office to their family's couch, their school principal's kindly gaze, a mentor who sees their potential for change, and the dozens of other possible informal and formal community supports available to them.

The Counselor's Use of Self Principles

Principle #14: The counselor shows awareness of use of self. Good ecologically-oriented counselors are transparent with regard to their cultural bias, professional beliefs, intentions, and actions. The client is never made to feel like counseling is more about the counselor's vision of successful adaptation and less about what the client feels comfortable doing. The illusion of expertise is deconstructed, meaning that the counselor avoids becoming a source for answers. Instead, the counselor makes it clear to the client that the counselor's role is to help find solutions that are contextually and culturally relevant to the client.

Principle #15: The counselor is effective at showing genuine concern. The counselor sustains a positive relationship with the client. Not only do counselors use empathic listening skills during the intervention to convey to the client how important she/he/they are, counselors also pay attention to other issues like client safety, client confidentiality (except when the law mandates clinicians disclose a client's intention to harm herself or others), options for service with other service providers, and what the intervention will be like for the client, explained in a way that the client understands. Whenever possible, the counselor is transparent as to what he or she knows about the client from third-party sources. Finally, effort is made to create continuity over time in the counselor–client relationship. Whenever possible, counselors remain with their clients through the entire process of change, and make themselves easily accessible after counseling ends and clients need to reconnect temporarily.

Principle #16: The counselor shows the intentional application of theory to practice. Interventions reflect a coherent theoretical perspective with regard to how and why clients change behaviors, thoughts, and feelings (see Chapter 2). When done well, the counselor's work is experienced as intentional and helpful opening doors to new opportunities for clients. The questions asked and tasks accomplished are coherent parts of an overall approach to intervention that can be easily described. The client experiences confidence that she/he/they and the counselor are working together to find the resources that will give the client a reasonable chance of success when coping with "wicked" problems.

Principle #17: The counselor shows awareness of diversity. While counselors cannot possibly be expected to fully understand everyone else's culture or context, they are expected to show sensitivity to the unconventional (atypical) solutions that people use to solve problems in ways that make sense to them. A good counselor looks for contextually and culturally relevant resources that can help people address the problems they want to change. Counseling explores how clients are both the same and different from others in their families and communities.

Principle #18: The counselor is willing to challenge the client's problematic patterns of coping and motivate change. Once a trusting relationship is formed, a portion of any clinical session can be used to discuss the real world consequences to decisions that the client makes. The counselor needn't refrain from pointing out problems that arise when clients act in troubling ways. This is done, however, after a relationship is established and in a way that shows curiosity for how the client views her own behavior and why the solutions she uses are meaningful to her. What appears to be a problem to the counselor (Sally's self-harming behavior at school), may be experienced by the client as a perfect adaptation when there are few other choices to achieve her goals. When a client resists an intervention, the ecologically-trained counselor views that behavior as a clue that it's time to re-contract for goals that are more meaningful to the client. Resistance is not necessarily proof the client wants to end treatment. Alternative patterns of coping that offer powerful substitutes for problem behaviors should be sought that will motivate the client to distance herself from troubling patterns of coping she's used in the past. Clinical sessions can provide an opportunity to rehearse and then evaluate new ways of coping to see if they help or hinder the client's capacity to cope.

Principle #19: The counselor advocates with, or on behalf of, the client, or shows the client how to advocate independently. Time is devoted to strategizing how the counselor and client, together and apart, can advocate for resources to be made available and accessible. Sally and I worked together to help her find effective ways to show people how frustrated she was. We also explored ways Sally and I could advocate for changes at her school and at home to decrease Sally's social exclusion and experience of neglect.

Principle #20: The counselor does not convince the client to comply with rules and regulations. If we understand client behavior as adaptive in challenging contexts, then the counselor should not become an agent for institutional or state control. In other words, it can't be our role to convince people to behave in ways that we and others say is acceptable. The more we work with people who face significant challenges because of mental illness, poverty, or other types of social exclusion, the less we can hold to the naïve belief that our preferred solutions for them are always in their best interest. People are, in general, motivated by the need for social status and acceptance. While we may point out the consequences of anti-social behavior to a delinquent adolescent, or explain why resistance to mandatory drug treatment or voluntary compliance with a course of medication will result in less freedom (for example, more surveillance, more rules, more restrictions on behavior), the imposition of rules will not help counselors to understand why clients experience their problem behaviors as adaptive. Simply put, we can't help people change if we don't first appreciate how they are already coping in tough situations. Of course, behavior that is threatening to harm the client or others cannot be condoned. In those rare instances, it is better if someone other than the counselor is the one who enforces rules of conduct, though in every counselor's career there is likely to be times when he or she has to pick up the phone and notify authorities that a client, or someone close to the client, is in imminent danger. This must always be the choice of last resort. It is very difficult to save the clinical relationship afterwards. After all, who is going to trust us when we say, "I want to understand how you cope and the decisions you've made to survive" and then impose a set of behaviors we judge to be meaningful or protective.

While the above lists of practice principles may look daunting, remember, most clinicians already approach aspects of their counseling ecologically. Unfortunately, these elements of best practice have been largely ignored when we evaluate outcomes. With a few exceptions, like work by Duncan, Miller and Sparks (2004) on client satisfaction and Isaac Prilleltensky's approach to community psychology (Prilleltensky, 2012), we have largely overlooked these processes of clinical work that are complementary to individual psychotherapy. Accomplishing all 20 of these essential, but not unique aspects of a social ecological practice will make our work effective, contribute to the building of resilience among clients, and should help clients sustain changes made during clinical interventions, regardless of whether those took place in a residential, community, or office setting.

The Counselor's 20 Skills

A counselor who is able to integrate into her clinical practice the principles and elements just described, creating a seamless five-phase intervention, is going to succeed at providing an intervention that pays attention to the client's complex needs in challenging contexts. Putting these elements into practice, however, requires a number of skills. Many of these will be familiar to clinicians from other training, though their application here makes for an intentional model of ecological practice that will be far more effective than random attempts to think about resources, meaning, context, and culture. In this chapter, I'll simply list the 20 skills. (A sheet that can be photocopied at the end of this chapter provides a brief list of all 20 skills.) In later chapters, they'll be discussed in more detail and what they look like in clinical, residential, and community treatment settings. I will also provide examples of questions that counselors ask to make their practice more ecological.

Keep in mind as you review the list of skills that they were developed through observation of senior therapists conducting ecologically-oriented interventions with clients who presented with complex needs in resource-poor environments.

10 Navigation Skills

1. Make resources available
The counselor helps the client identify the internal and external resources that are available.

2. Make resources accessible
The counselor discusses how the client can access the resources that are available.

3. Explore barriers to change
The counselor discusses the barriers to change the client experiences, and which resources are most likely needed to address which barriers.

4. Build bridges to new services and supports
The counselor discusses with the client the services and supports that the counselor is familiar with and her or his role as a bridge builder to help make new resources available and accessible.

5. Ask what is meaningful
The counselor explores with the client which resources are the most meaningful given the client's context and culture.

6. Keep solutions as complex as the problems they solve
The counselor explores solutions that are as complex (multisystemic) as the problems they address.

7. Find allies
The counselor explores possible allies who can help the client access resources and put new ways of coping into practice.

8. Ask whether coping strategies are adaptive or maladaptive
The counselor helps the client explore whether the solutions she/he/they are using to cope in challenging contexts are adaptive or maladaptive, and the consequences to the choices the client is making.

9. Explore the client's level of motivation
The counselor discusses with the client her/his/their level of motivation to implement new preferred solutions.

10. Advocate
The counselor advocates with, or on behalf of, the client, or shows the client how to advocate independently to make resources more available and accessible.

10 Negotiation Skills

1. Thoughts and feelings
The counselor explores with the client thoughts and feelings about the problem that brought the client to counseling.

2. Context
The counselor and the client explore the context in which problems occur, and the conditions that sustain them.

3. Responsibility
The counselor and client discuss who has responsibility to change patterns of coping that are causing problems for the client, and/or for others in the client's life.

4. Voice
The counselor helps the client's voice be heard when she/he/they name the people and resources necessary to make life better.

5. New names
When appropriate, the counselor may offer different names for a problem, and explore what these new descriptions mean for how the counselor and the client will work together.

6. Fit
The client chooses one (or more) new descriptions of the problem that fit with how she/he/they see the world.

7. Resources
The client and counselor work together to find the internal and external resources the client needs to put new solutions into practice.

8. Possibilities
The client experiences possibilities for change that are more numerous than expected.

9. Performance
The counselor and the client identify times when the client is performing new ways of coping and discuss who will notice the changes.

10. Perception
The counselor helps the client find ways to convince others that she/he/they have changed, or are doing better than expected.

A Word about Professional Competencies and Ethical Practice

Though beyond the scope of this book to survey professional requirements across all disciplines, it is worth noting that a social ecological practice aligns well with many of the most important professional competencies and standards for ethical practice that are common to mental health care disciplines working in diverse settings. Consistently, core competencies include requirements that professionals think and act ecologically. For example, we are supposed to do the following:

- *Be conscious of professional boundaries and roles*: A social ecological practice tends to see the therapist as contextually embedded, a part of the client's community (or not), and seeks to understand how this potential familiarity with context helps or hinders the clinical work.
- *Advocate for clients*: A social ecological practice is explicit with regard to advocacy. The therapist either mentors the client in how to advocate for himself or advocates on behalf of the client.
- *Perform our duties ethically and within the bounds of our expertise*: An ecological-oriented practice is sensitive to context and the power imbalances inherent in client–therapist relationships. It is an explicitly ethical practice that avoids the unintended harm done to clients when contextual risks are ignored during counseling or case plans reflect the bias of the therapist.
- *Engage diversity and difference*: While a social ecological practice has some standardized tools and common procedures for intervention, the focus on diversity and difference is explicit in the work. Even when clients and therapists look the same, or share the same culture, class, sexual orientation, ability, or history, the uniqueness of each person's lived experience should become an active ingredient in what takes place during therapy.
- *Be life-long learners, with the humility to ask others, including clients, for advice*: A social ecological practice assumes that clients' contexts are so complex and varied that the therapist is always needing to learn what will work for different people in different situations. Responding to the needs of clients requires the humility and curiosity to engage clients in the search for solutions that fit well for them, positioning them as key informants on their lives. It also means that effective clinicians seek out supervision from peers and mentors to help them reflect on their practice and explore the complexity of their clients' lives.
- *Advance human rights and social and economic justice*: When changing clients' social and physical ecologies through mental health interventions, there is an overt effort to address clients' experiences of marginalization. Human rights are discussed during counseling through conversations about exclusion/inclusion, race, ethnicity, ability, gender, sexual orientation, and class. People's problems are seen as a consequence of more than individual problems; they are related to the social determinants of health. Problems are not the responsibility of individuals alone to solve. Part of an effective ecological practice is to engage in policy debates and promote changes that will benefit future clients.
- *Use models of practice that are evidence-based and practice-informed*: A social ecological practice reflects decades of work by systems-trained clinicians and builds on analysis of cases and the extensive research on protective factors. It manualizes what clinicians have been doing all along when they looked beyond their client to the client's context for mental health resources.
- *Make changes sustainable*: Counselors who work ecologically engage with others who can change clients' contexts in ways that make it easier for clients to sustain the changes they have made. There is a great deal of focus on extra-therapeutic activities that bring supports into therapy. Therapists advocate with their clients' natural supports for additional help. Together, these and other interventions are among the many strategies that ensure changes made during counseling continue.
- *Demonstrate expertise during all five phases of intervention (engage, assess, contract, work, transition) with individuals, their families, and communities*: While not all mental health professionals define their clientele as individuals, families, and communities, in practice many find themselves engaged at multiple ecological levels when change is needed. An effective

counselor ensures that all five phases of intervention overlap, and that individuals are not left alone to take responsibility for problems that have social and historical dimensions (for example, unemployment, sexual violence, stigma).

- *Use judiciously ecological practice principles and skills*: There may be times when individualized treatment is required, or where the therapist must represent the best interests of her community and participate in interventions that go against the client's will. Mandatory reporting, court-ordered assessments, treatment for those who are institutionalized, are all aspects of clinical practice that make counselors focus much more on the client than is typical of a social ecological practice. In such cases, the counselor is an agent of the state who acts to keep the client and the client's family and community safe. Responsibility for change is shared, or weighted toward the client.
- *Participate in research and program evaluation*: Without documenting the success of a social ecological model, it will be difficult to convince funders to allocate dollars to activities that are not exclusively centered on the individual client. Helping the parent of a child (who is the designated client) navigate state support services, or working with a school board to make it easier for a child with an anxiety disorder to attend a regular classroom, are activities that need to be recorded and measured if they are to be recognized as best practices. That which is measured and shown to be helpful has a greater possibility of being funded.

Competencies like these can be grouped into subdomains of conceptual (there is understanding of the theoretical roots of the approach, the risks associated with counseling, and the reasons behind the interventions), perceptual (the counselor recognizes that the client is embedded in a wider context and takes into consideration the client's health status, needs for specialized services, and hypothesizes what other services are needed and why), executive (the therapist applies the techniques necessary to work effectively), evaluative (the therapist reflects on practice and monitors outcomes), and professional (the therapist meets professional standards and demonstrates self-reflection while working) skills. A social ecological practice needs counselors to do all these things if their work is going to fit well with the standards set for competent and ethical practice. As you read more about the principles and skills that are the foundation stones of an ecological intervention, you should be able to identify your own professional core competencies in the material.

Chapter Summary

Building on observations of counselors themselves, the 20 principles and 20 skills for a social ecological practice discussed in this chapter provide the tools necessary for a model of intentional practice that helps individuals and families with complex needs get the resources they need to change problem behaviors. When done well, the changes clients and their social ecologies make are sustained through increases in people's capacity to navigate and negotiate for the resources that are most meaningful to them. In practice this means changing a client's capacity to navigate and negotiate (and the responsiveness of the client's social and physical ecology to make accessible the resources the client needs) rather than putting all our efforts into changing individuals. While some aspects of navigation and negotiation rely on the client to show personal motivation and changes in behavior, a social ecological approach to counseling emphasizes multisystemic change that is always complex. Individual change is never enough unless environments change too.

Moving back and forth from theory to practice, this chapter has provided an overview of the five overlapping phases of intervention that make a social ecological practice so responsive to the needs of clients. I then described three broad principles that underlie this approach to practice and 20 essential but not necessarily unique principles of the work an ecologically-trained counselor does. Next, I provided an abridged description of 20 intertwined skills evident when my colleagues and I reviewed videos of counselors working ecologically. I concluded with a brief discussion of how an ecological approach to practice reflects the core competencies and standards of ethical practice required of many professionals.

In the chapters that follow we'll explore in greater detail the skills that make a social ecological practice effective.

20 Principles for a Social Ecological Practice

Navigation and Negotiation Principles

Principle #1	The counselor explores with the client the client's definition of problems and possible solutions.
Principle #2	The counselor discusses strategies with the client to make use of the resources that are available and accessible.
Principle #3	The counselor discusses what the client hears about her problems and solutions.
Principle #4	The counselor explores with the client which resources have been the most meaningful over time.
Principle #5	Threats to the client's safety and the safety of others are addressed and strategies put in place to protect everyone from risks.
Principle #6	The counselor acknowledges that changing social structures is as important as changing individuals. The counselor explores solutions that are multisystemic and complex.
Principle #7	The counselor explores the client's internal and external barriers to growth.
Principle #8	The counselor redirects questions about unconscious determinants of behavior to social ecological factors.

Five Phases of Intervention Principles

Principle #9	The counselor integrates different phases of the intervention.
Principle #10	The counselor assesses the client's strengths, identifying coping strategies the client has used in the past along with the social and physical resources that were required for these strategies to succeed.
Principle #11	The counselor creates a clear contract, either written or verbal, with well-described goals for the period of intervention. The counselor negotiates goals for the intervention with the client.
Principle #12	The counselor focuses a portion of every session on reviewing or renewing the contract for service.
Principle #13	The counselor anticipates and prepares for the client's transition back into relationships with informal supports or other formal service providers after the intervention ends.

The Counselor's Use of Self Principles

Principle #14	The counselor shows awareness of use of self.
Principle #15	The counselor is effective at showing genuine concern. The counselor sustains a positive relationship with the client.
Principle #16	The counselor shows the intentional application of theory to practice.
Principle #17	The counselor shows awareness of diversity.
Principle #18	The counselor is willing to challenge the client's problematic patterns of coping and motivate change.
Principle #19	The counselor advocates with, or on behalf of, the client, or shows the client how to advocate independently.
Principle #20	The counselor does not convince the client to comply with rules and regulations.

20 Skills for a Social Ecological Practice

Navigation Skills

Navigation Skill #1   **Make resources available**
The counselor helps the client identify the internal and external resources that are available.

Navigation Skill #2   **Make resources accessible**
The counselor discusses how the client can access the resources that are available.

Navigation Skill #3   **Explore barriers to change**
The counselor discusses the barriers to change the client experiences, and which resources are most likely needed to address which barriers.

Navigation Skill #4   **Build bridges to new services and supports**
The counselor discusses with the client the services and supports that the counselor is familiar with and her or his role as a bridge builder to help make new resources available and accessible.

Navigation Skill #5   **Ask what is meaningful**
The counselor explores with the client which resources are the most meaningful given the client's context and culture.

Navigation Skill #6   **Keep solutions as complex as the problems they solve**
The counselor explores solutions that are as complex (multisystemic) as the problems they address.

Navigation Skill #7   **Find allies**
The counselor explores possible allies who can help the client access resources and put new ways of coping into practice.

Navigation Skill #8   **Ask whether coping strategies are adaptive or maladaptive**
The counselor helps the client explore whether the solutions she/he/they are using to cope in challenging contexts are adaptive or maladaptive, and the consequences to the choices the client is making.

Navigation Skill #9   **Explore the client's level of motivation**
The counselor discusses with the client her/his/their level of motivation to implement new preferred solutions.

Navigation Skill #10   **Advocate**
The counselor advocates with, or on behalf of, the client, or shows the client how to advocate independently to make resources more available and accessible.

Negotiation Skills

Negotiation Skill #1	**Thoughts and feelings** The counselor explores with the client thoughts and feelings about the problem that brought the client to counseling.
Negotiation Skill #2	**Context** The counselor and the client explore the context in which problems occur, and the conditions that sustain them.
Negotiation Skill #3	**Responsibility** The counselor and client discuss who has responsibility to change patterns of coping that are causing problems for the client, and/or for others in the client's life.
Negotiation Skill #4	**Voice** The counselor helps the client's voice be heard when she/he/they name the people and resources necessary to make life better.
Negotiation Skill #5	**New names** When appropriate, the counselor may offer different names for a problem, and explore what these new descriptions mean for how the counselor and the client will work together.
Negotiation Skill #6	**Fit** The client chooses one (or more) new descriptions of the problem that fit with how she/he/they see the world.
Negotiation Skill #7	**Resources** The client and counselor work together to find the internal and external resources the client needs to put new solutions into practice.
Negotiation Skill #8	**Possibilities** The client experiences possibilities for change that are more numerous than expected.
Negotiation Skill #9	**Performance** The counselor and the client identify times when the client is performing new ways of coping and discuss who will notice the changes
Negotiation Skill #10	**Perception** The counselor helps the client find ways to convince others that she/he/they have changed, or are doing better than expected.

CHAPTER 4

THE FIRST SET OF SKILLS: HELP CLIENTS NAVIGATE

As the previous chapters have shown, an ecological approach to counseling grew from clinical practice and research with young people and their families living on the margins of our communities. Building on the lessons learned, we know we can nurture and sustain the well-being of children, youth, and their caregivers in adverse social and physical environments when the resources they need are made available and accessible. It isn't just their individual capacities that determine their success, but also, as I'll show in this chapter, the capacity of children's environments to facilitate individual processes of navigation.

Navigating well is easier when one has the motivation, personality, and talents to take advantage of opportunities. But it is more likely to occur if one's social ecology provides those opportunities through good social policy, a supportive family, and community networks. It's also easier to navigate if, when problems become overwhelming, clinical interventions are sensitive to the context in which an individual or family lives. Even an unmotivated foster child who is forced from his family and placed in residential care will survive reasonably well if his caregivers are attentive, his schooling adequate, his community safe, his culture respected, there are opportunities for age-appropriate recreation and socialization, and he is given a realistic promise that he will be able to realize his goals in life. In other words, an optimal environment increases the odds that a child does well over time (Harvey, 2007). The remarkable thing about this interaction between environments and individuals is that, as Ann Masten (2001) has pointed out, in the course of experiencing the "ordinary magic" of their lives, many vulnerable individuals find the resources they need to experience resilience.

The family is an especially wonderful source for that magic when they are available and willing to help. As Froma Walsh (2011), the first scholar and author to describe the factors that contribute to the resilience of families, explained, when it comes to a traumatic event that threatens a family, each family member can influence how the family as a system responds. To the extent that the family maintains positive everyday functioning like emotional sharing, meaning-making, self-organizing to get instrumental tasks accomplished, and the pursuit of collective goals, the family will sustain its collective resilience and the resilience of its individual members.

Counseling is only necessary when there is not enough magic, or the magic is dark, pulling a child into delinquency, early school drop out, and risky sexual activity. In those cases, maladaptive coping strategies can be the only way a child can find the resources he needs to survive in dangerous social ecologies.

Parents, too, can become trapped in unhealthy patterns when resources are few or inaccessible. The visionary work of Bill Madsen and his colleagues (Root & Madsen, 2013), invites families who are involved with child protection services (CPS) to create a Collaborative Helping map that identifies both the stressors and supports that make family violence more likely to occur. In practice, that means Madsen has the workers he trains consider four clusters of questions to help clients name the risks their children face and identify what they need to help them navigate to resources that will support them. Parents are asked:

1. What are your hopes for your children? What kind of family would you prefer to be? (Vision);
2. What gets in the way of your Vision for your family? What are we worried about? (Challenge);
3. Who and what support you in obtaining your Vision for your family? What is working well? (Support);
4. What needs to happen? How can we draw on supports to address obstacles to ensure Safety, Permanency, and Well-Being? (Plan).

While Madsen works mostly with families involved with CPS, his work reminds us to think ecologically rather than psychologically even in very challenging contexts where children's lives are at risk.

To co-create answers to his questions about vision, challenges, supports, and plan, Madsen asks clients (most of whom are very reluctant to engage with their social workers) not only to consider what they did and its impact on their child, but much more importantly, to separate themselves from their problems. Instead of individual psychopathology, the focus is on how stressors in a person's life contribute to abusive behavior, the barriers families experience to change, and the supports parents need to be the kind of parent they really want to be. While the abusive behavior is still the caregiver's responsibility to change, Madsen's clients are encouraged to talk about their lives in context. Poverty, histories of family violence, a lack of family supports, alcoholism and substance abuse, homelessness, racism, sexism, and other problems are all factors that make it more likely abuse occurs. These factors stress caregivers, burdening them with the frustrating problem of being an ideal parent with very few supports. Borrowing the narrative idea that people are not their problems, Madsen focuses his attention on the problem behavior and unites with the client to resist its pull into abuse behavior (see White, 2007). For example, the parent with a drinking problem is asked to consider how alcohol tricks the parent into becoming so drunk that she can't deal with her child in a nonviolent way. The father who sexually molested his child is invited to both take responsibility for his behavior and see what he did as a reflection of a set of beliefs about his privilege as a man and the power over others that comes with it.

The context in which people navigate to find the solutions to their problems is never absent from the work being done, which means the solution is to help caregivers be more effective in their battle with the factors that make it likely they will abuse. Madsen's approach invites parents to collaboratively create a vision for what they want their children to remember of their childhoods and then help find the supports to tackle the barriers to making those visions possible. If an ecological practice can be useful in these contexts, imagine what helping people navigate can mean to families with far fewer challenges.

Case Study: Francois

I learned a great about the interaction between individual strengths, barriers to inclusion, and informal and formal supports and services through my work with Francois, a 14-year-old boy whose success shows what it takes to be resilient. Francois was referred to a study I co-led on children who are doing well despite serious challenges (Ungar et al., 2012). Born into a working-class family, Francois suffers from Albinism which greatly affects his sight and, as a consequence, the pace at which he is able to learn. In many less-resourced communities, and with a less supportive family, Francois' multiple challenges may have meant a lifetime of social isolation and little chance for adapted education or future economic independence. Despite his disability, however, and because he is fortunate to live where he does, he is able to attend a regular school program. Accommodations have been made to ensure he receives the extra support of a teacher's aide and computer-assisted technology both at school and at home. These government-subsidized supports have not only prevented Francois from being at risk academically, they have also prevented him from becoming socially excluded or developing the mental health problems that accompany stigma. Mind you, his outgoing personality helps too. Even though his sight is limited, he still manages to get into frequent mischief in his community. Spend a day with Francois and you'll see a boy who enjoys getting himself into trouble, behavior that is mostly tolerated by his parents. It's as if Francois' naughtiness helps him fit in with his peers despite his disability.

Beyond school, Francois has at least one good friend with whom he plays video games. He spends time cooking for his family or engages in unstructured play like bouncing on his friend's trampoline. When out in his community, Francois hides his disability when he can, wearing sunglasses to make himself look like a rap star though his white hair and pale skin are clues to something else. When observed in his community, Francois passes for "normal" in most contexts, though a group of bullies used to pick on him at school. A progressive school principal who promoted a safe school culture and security in the halls has managed to protect Francois from much of their abuse.

The same level of accommodation he experiences at school is also found in his community where he plays ice hockey as a defender. Even though the other boys won't pass him the puck (he's unable to see it), he has found a niche for himself in a sport that is important to boys his age in his neighborhood. Fortunately, he's big enough to defend his zone.

While almost all his time is spent in activities with individuals without physical disabilities, he socializes with other children with visual impairments at a day camp during the summer. There, he has assumed a leadership role as a mentor to younger children who, just like Francois, are trying to be as independent as they can be.

Francois also has access to the services of a social worker who helps him and his family advocate for resources, though the family has made little use of professional help except to secure school-based support for assisted learning. Though the family is working class, their community is fortunately quite rich with services and recreational opportunities that they can access themselves. It's this matrix of supports at home, in school, with peers, and in the wider community that have made it possible for Francois to cope so well with his disability.

Not all children are so lucky. Many end up in counseling for problem behaviors that result from the stigma that comes with being perceived by others as different; still others seek professional help to find strategies to realize their full potential. Francois teaches us to pay attention to a child's social ecology and the role good resources, case management, and advocacy play in optimizing a child's psychosocial development. Sometimes, it seems, those are the best mental health interventions.

Complex Navigations

Francois is certainly one of the fortunate ones who is able to navigate to what he needs. Many children are far less resourced. Citing a number of US reports, Marsali Hansen and her colleagues (Hansen et al., 2004) estimate that two thirds of children who need mental health services do not receive them. Others have estimated the number to be as high as 80% (Kataoka, Zhang & Wells, 2002) with Latino and uninsured youth being the most likely to be ignored by mental health care providers. Among the minority of children who do receive services, coordination of the systems of care that are supposed to be put in place for them is seriously lacking (Ungar, Liebenberg & Ikeda, 2012). Navigation to counselors that have the resources to help children become more resilient when they have physical disabilities like Francois, have been exposed to potentially traumatizing events, or when mental disorders like Fetal Alcohol Spectrum Disorder, Attention Deficit Hyperactivity Disorder, and depression are present in their lives, are complicated by the many different service silos with their many competing mandates. For example, among children with serious emotional disorders (SED) that require mental health interventions, only 40% of these children receive treatment from the mental health sector, while the others receive counseling through their schools, departments of child welfare, or juvenile justice systems (Wood et al., 2005). The result is a patchwork of services that prioritize different problems as the focus of their interventions (substance abuse may be the focus in one setting, learning disabilities, family dynamics, delinquency, and attachment issues may get attention in others) (Ungar, Liebenberg & Ikeda, 2012). For the child navigating to access the services he needs, it can feel like service providers have opened a bag of M&Ms and scattered them on the floor. Depending where the client is standing he may get a red, green, or blue candy, regardless of whether that is the color he wants or needs.

In the past few decades, we've come to understand a little better young people's patterns of multiple service use across systems of mental health, education, health care, juvenile justice, and child welfare (Farmer et al., 2003). In one longitudinal study involving 1,420 American youth using services, 45% were clients of more than one service sector (Malmgren & Meisel, 2002). These studies tell us that even among those children who do get service (even excellent services like Multisystemic Therapy [Henggeler et al., 2009] and Wraparound [Copp et al., 2007]), long-term benefits are unlikely unless the treatment is consistent and sustained. While children may engage with their mental health care providers episodically (meaning they agree to treatment during a crisis or when their psychosocial development is proceeding through a difficult transition like changing schools or peer groups) file reviews across systems of care suggest that over time young people with complex needs will access mental health counselors over and over again (Ungar et al., 2012).

It is interesting that different gateways into mental health services provide different rates of referral to other services. Here again, a child's navigation through multiple systems is not a matter of the child's motivation, but instead depends upon the way services are coordinated. Where the child starts his "career" as a client will decide the service providers he gets referred to, if he is referred at all. To illustrate, Arlene Stiffman and her colleagues (Stiffman et al., 1997) interviewed 792 youth from juvenile justice, education, primary health care, and child welfare services recruited from the waiting rooms of each service. The sample of mostly African American youth aged 13–17 showed that regardless of which service the youth were waiting for, many showed signs of depression, problematic substance use, and suicidal ideation. Of the youth with mental health problems, however, only about half were receiving services for their mental health problem specifically. *The rates varied depending on the service where the child was waiting and the child's diagnosis.* Health sector interviewees reported the lowest mental health service rates, while the juvenile justice sector reported the highest.

This means that different services are better or worse at helping children navigate their way to the resources they need to nurture and sustain mental health. Many of the young people in those waiting rooms were not being made aware by their service providers of the many possible services they could access. Not surprisingly, it is the gatekeeper's assessment of the child's needs that is most likely to determine referral (Stiffman et al., 2000).

For mental health counselors, these patterns of complex need and service silos mean that it is up to us to not just help children learn new coping strategies or work through the after-effects of early trauma; we must also facilitate children's navigations to resources, including psychological and social services. If we don't, children become poorly served, or served by systems that offer help more by chance than design. Good case management, building bridges to multiple coordinated services, and advocating for access *are* important mental health interventions that help children and their families navigate effectively.

Of course, there is an affective component to navigation too. As we navigate, our attachments to those close to us along the way evoke emotional reactions. These emotions influence how we think about our problems, their solutions, and our behavior. Emotions exert a large influence over which resources we think we want and our motivation to get them.

When it comes to helping clients navigate, there are 10 skills that counselors use who are effective at helping clients like Francois and their families succeed as navigators.

10 Navigation Skills

The following are examples of the types of questions one asks when helping children and their families identify and access resources. The questions are designed to open conversations that explore how young people can become effective navigators in contexts where there are few resources that are realistically available. My assumption is that counselors are still mostly office-bound. Few of us have the luxury of becoming our client's full-time case managers. That doesn't mean, however, that we can't change our practice and help clients explore the strengths and barriers to well-being that are part of their social ecologies.

As you review the following questions, try integrating them into your practice regardless of the approach you currently use. For example, a counselor I know who likes CBT broadens her conversations with her clients to include an assessment of cultural factors that will influence the process of change and its sustainability over time. A friend of mine who is a narrative therapist looks at the very concrete barriers a child experiences when standing up to problem behaviors. And a colleague of mine who is a psychiatrist at a local children's hospital has shown me that psychopharmacological interventions work better if we understand the meaning children and parents attach to taking medication and the potential stigma that goes along with it. With few exceptions, all therapeutic approaches benefit from more focus on the social ecologies that facilitate (or thwart) positive developmental outcomes.

A Word on Language

Before we begin, though, a word on language. The questions I've listed here are just guides to the kinds of questions we could ask. When I look over transcripts from my interviews with young people and their families, I rarely see such nicely-worded questions, nor do I see questions that are so difficult to understand. For example, when I use a question template like "Of the resources you said you needed, which are realistically available?" with a young person like Francois, I adapt my wording to look like this: "Francois, at school, can you get the extra one-on-one support from the Learning Support Worker? Is that person really available, at a time and place where you can get to them without making it too obvious to the other kids that you need extra help?" As you can see, the way I ask my question is matched to the cognitive capacities and contextual norms of the child. Complete transcripts of interviews throughout this book give you an idea of what these questions look like when used in actual counseling sessions.

My experience tells me that questions are only useful if the attitude one brings to an ecological practice acknowledges the complex multisystemic nature of people's problems. Without a sincere appreciation of our clients' cultural values, their atypical solutions, and a willingness to honestly consider counseling a poor substitute for people's natural support networks, these questions can be experienced by clients as condescending or manipulative. Beware! When we ask these questions, we must sincerely believe that solutions are mostly to be found in people's social ecologies. *Individuals are not to blame for the strategies they use to cope in contexts that deny them choices.* When I get myself sorted out and have the right attitude for the work I am doing, I encounter little or no resistance from young people and their families to the interventions we design together.

1. Make resources available.
The counselor helps the client identify the internal and external resources that are available.

Practice questions:

- Of the resources you said you needed, which are realistically available?
- Which resources can't be used, even though they are available?
- What has it felt like in the past trying to use the resources that are available?
- Are there (internal and external) resources we should discuss later? Ones you think it would be good to look for?

2. Make resources accessible.
The counselor discusses how the client can access the resources that are available.

Practice questions:

- Of these resources that are available, what are the steps we can take to reach them?
- Have you had the experience of trying to make use of a resource in your family, school, or community and encountering problems? What happened? Who or what made accessing resources difficult? Who do you blame for the difficulty you experienced?
- Who has helped you in the past to access the supports you needed to succeed?
- If you've mostly had to fend for yourself, what strategies did you use to get around the barriers you faced?

3. Explore barriers to change.

The counselor discusses the barriers to change the client experiences, and which resources are most likely needed to address which barriers.

Practice questions:

- What things inside you and outside you stop you from making changes in your life?
- When you think of a specific problem, which barrier is causing the most problems?
- If that barrier wasn't there, would you be able to make the changes you want to make? Would you feel hesitant, afraid, or maybe anxious about making the changes you want to make?

4. Build bridges to new services and supports.

The counselor discusses with the client the services and supports that the counselor is familiar with and her or his role as a bridge builder to help make new resources available and accessible.

Practice questions (for the counselor):

- What solutions to the client's problem can you help make happen?
- Are there resources that you know about that could help the client?
- What can you do to help make these resources available and accessible to the client?

5. Ask what is meaningful.

The counselor explores with the client which resources are the most meaningful given the client's context and culture.

Practice questions:

- Of the things you need to change, which do you feel most strongly about? Which change would be the most helpful?
- What resources/experiences do you need to have to be able to show others you've changed?
- In your context/culture, how do people go about solving problems like the one you are experiencing?
- Are there unique strategies to cope that you, your family, or your community typically use for the kind of problem you have?

6. Keep solutions as complex as the problems they solve.

The counselor explores solutions that are as complex (multisystemic) as the problems they address.

Practice questions:

- What else will need to change to make this solution sustainable?
- Is the solution you're trying working well or does it need to be changed?

7. Find allies.

The counselor explores possible allies who can help the client access resources and put new ways of coping into practice.

Practice questions:

- Who will help you get what you need to change/cope with this problem?
- Will you have to ask them for help, or are you expecting them to volunteer?
- Who in your family, among your friends, or in your community has coped well with a similar problem? What advice can they give you?
- Who will notice the changes you're making? Will that be a good or bad thing, to be noticed?

8. Ask whether coping strategies are adaptive or maladaptive.

The counselor helps the client explore whether the solutions she/he/they are using to cope in challenging contexts are adaptive or maladaptive, how well they are working as solutions, if they make sense to the client and the client's friends and family, and the consequences to the choices the client makes.

Practice questions:

- Are the solutions you're trying bringing more advantages than disadvantages?
- What is it about the solutions you've tried that you like? Dislike?
- What do you hear about the solutions you've tried? Do people think you make good choices, or bad choices?
- How well do others understand why you make the choices you do? Does anyone understand how difficult it is to find other solutions?

9. Explore the client's level of motivation.

The counselor discusses with the client her/his/their level of motivation to implement new preferred solutions.

Practice questions:

- How motivated are you to make these changes?
- What would make you more motivated?

10. Advocate.

The counselor advocates with, or on behalf of, the client, or shows the client how to advocate independently to make resources more available and accessible.

Practice questions (for the counselor):

- What can you do to help the client succeed? What personal contacts or resources can you make available and accessible that are ethical to share?
- Have you asked the client what you could do as their counselor that would be most helpful? Have you let them direct your work together?
- Have you asked others what they can do to help the client?
- Have you shown the client how to advocate for themselves, practicing the skills required?

Case Study: Julia

Variations of these 10 navigation questions were important to the success of the clinical work with Julia who is much like other 13-year-old girls. She wants friends, to feel special, and to balance her dependence on her mother with her need to make decisions for herself. For Julia, navigating through normal developmental phases is, however, much more difficult because of her status as a recent immigrant from Brazil. Julia, her parents, her ten-year-old sister and seven-year-old brother left Brazil 18 months before she was referred to counseling. Her parents separated shortly after they moved, leaving Julia's mother, Angela, to support the family alone. Reluctantly, Angela moved the family into a low-rent neighborhood with a high rate of crime. Angela worries about her children being unsupervised in the community, but can't afford to move elsewhere nor decrease her work hours at a dry cleaning business.

With little supervision, a dangerous neighborhood to find safety in, and few opportunities to feel as good about herself as she did when she was younger, Julia has been hanging out with older boys, many rumored to be members of local gangs. She is also struggling to maintain her grades at school and admits to having begun to use drugs and alcohol. Angela asks the guidance counselor at Julia's school to refer Julia to a drug and alcohol counselor for treatment.

In the following transcript, Angela joins Julia and her counselor, Bryan, a colleague of mine, for their third meeting. The meeting takes place in a drug and alcohol treatment center for youth. A video of the full interview is available online.[1] The abbreviated transcript is a good example of how Bryan explores Julia's patterns of navigation to the resources she needs to feel good about herself, make friends, and compensate for the emotional turmoil that followed her move to a new country and her parents' separation.

To show how the 20 principles of a social ecological practice, along with the 10 navigation skills, and the 10 negotiation skills (discussed in more detail in the next chapter) work together during counseling, I've annotated the transcript below with process notes (my thoughts on what is occurring during the intervention) to identify when specific principles and skills are being used. If you need a reminder of what each principle means, or a complete list of the skills, you can find these in Chapter 3. My choices are sometimes arbitrary as any single intervention could reflect many principles and skills.

Thinking back to the self-assessment tool that you completed in Chapter 1, you can use that same tool to evaluate the counselor, Bryan's, adherence to a social ecological model of practice as he works with the family.

Bryan: And you remember when we were together the last time we talked about harmful involvement? And the definition that we used at that time was if you, if you use drugs or alcohol or gamble in a way that's causing harm in your life . . . Julia: It's not causing anything . . . Bryan: . . . that's harmful involvement. Julia: . . . any problems.	In his efforts to engage Julia in the counseling process, Bryan accepts Julia's explanation that her poor grades are not the result of her drug and alcohol use. It's important to him that he understands how she sees her problem and to position her point of view and her mother's side-by-side. His goal is to neither defend Julia, nor to support her continuing to use illegal substances. In the process he opens a door to understanding the *meaning* Julia attributes to her school problems and use of drugs.

Angela: I think it does cause problems. It is causing problems for you.

Julia: It doesn't.

Bryan: It doesn't cause any problems at all Julia?

Julia: Sometimes in my grades but I don't think it's because of drugs. I don't like it so I don't . . .

Bryan: Okay.

Julia: . . . push myself to learn.

Bryan: Right, and how does drugs or alcohol cause a problem with those, with those subjects?

Julia: I don't know. I think I always had problems with that subject so . . .

Bryan: These are not your favorite subjects so that's why you're having . . .

Julia: . . . Yeah. I don't like Science and English, so I don't push myself to learn it. That's why my grades are low.

Principles that are observed:

Principle #1: Julia's definition of the problem is explored.

Principle #7: Bryan explores internal and external barriers to growth.

Principle #10: Bryan identifies Julia's strengths and coping strategies.

Principle #20: Bryan does not try to convince Julia to comply with rules like attending all classes.

Skills being used:

Navigation Skill #3: Explore barriers to change.

Navigation Skill #8: Are coping strategies adaptive or maladaptive?

Negotiation Skill #1: Explore Julia's thoughts and feelings about the problem.

Negotiation Skill #2: Julia's context is explored.

Negotiation Skill #4: Julia's voice gets heard.

Angela: But there, your grades were better. It's getting worse and worse, even if you don't like it, you don't like them.

Bryan: They were, they were better before the last three months?

Angela: Yes.

Julia: But it's just those . . .

Angela: Yes.

Julia: . . . subjects . . .

Angela: Yes, even in Brazil it was better.

Julia: . . . but the other ones are not bad. They're good. It's just those subjects. See even she knows.

Bryan: Yeah.

Julia: Yeah.

Bryan: Yeah. They were better, when in Brazil, or they weren't?

Angela: Yeah they were better.

Bryan: Julia?

Angela: Your grades were better.

Julia: Yeah, but it's English here so, sometimes . . .

We learn that Julia believes that her low grades are a consequence of having come to a new country and being educated in English. While Angela remains convinced that Julia's marks could be better if she wasn't hanging out with her friends and using drugs and drinking, Bryan's intervention helps show that Julia sees her problem differently. The conversation decenters the focus of the session from Julia and her problem behaviors to the challenging context that makes achieving good grades difficult. While her motivation to change may not be high, Julia makes it clear that she believes good grades are not possible because of her lack of fluency in English.

Principles that are observed:

Principle #1: Julia's definition of the problem is explored.

Principle #7: Bryan explores internal and external barriers to growth.

Principle #9: Even as Bryan assesses the problem, the intervention sustains Julia's engagement.

Skills being used:

Navigation Skill #3: Explore barriers to change.

Navigation Skill #6: By focusing on aspects of Julia's life

Bryan: So sometimes it's, it's difficult because of the, the new language.

Julia: Yeah.

seemingly unrelated to her drug use, Bryan pays attention to the complexity of Julia's life.

Negotiation Skill #2: Julia's context is explored.

Negotiation Skill #3: Julia shifts responsibility for her poor grades to her changing context and language problems.

Negotiation Skill #4: Julia's voice gets heard.

Bryan: Right.

Angela: And she just think about hanging out with her friends and . . .

Julia: That's not . . .

Angela: . . . it is true. It is so . . .

Julia: It's not.

Angela: Okay . . . but what I'm worried is, with a people she's hanging out and using drug with. That's my concern. And I think they are bad guys. They are involved with these with gangs and . . .

Julia: You . . . you don't even know.

Angela: I know. I know your friends, of course, I know your friends.

Julia: You, you don't know them.

Angela: Yes, but, I feel. I don't feel that I can trust them. Bryan, I'm sorry but I have a lot of concerns about the people that she's hanging out. They're boys, I think they are involved in gangs . . .

Julia: You can't say that . . .

Angela: . . . you know . . .

Julia: . . . you don't know . . .

Bryan: Uhmmm.

Angela: . . . I know them.

Julia: . . . it's not true . . .

Angela: We live in a community . . .

Bryan: Right.

Angela: . . . it's a poor community, and I've heard there are a lot of traffic, drug traffic here . . .

Bryan: Uhmmm.

Angela: . . . so they might be involved, and that's my concern.

Bryan: Right.

Julia appears to have found a peer group that accepts her and provides a way to distance herself from her mother. Her delinquent peers are a resource that she experiences as both *available* and *accessible*. Though it is a resource that may also bring with it danger, Bryan doesn't focus on the problems as much as how her pattern of peer relationships has been a source of support. Being with those peers is a maladaptive behavior with long-term consequences, but Julia is clearly portraying her choice of peer group as an *adaptive* solution to the challenges she faces right now.

Principles that are observed:

Principle #2: Bryan asks Julia how she uses the resources available to her.

Principle #16: Bryan uses what he understands about resilience to avoid pathologizing Julia's coping strategy. He asks simply what her and her friends do when together.

Principle #17: By not assuming Julia's peers are problems, Bryan may be able to help her find those peers who could offer support without jeopardizing Julia's safety.

Skills being used:

Navigation Skill #2: Bryan is gathering information on what resources are accessible to Julia.

Navigation Skill #7: Bryan is helping to identify potential allies.

Negotiation Skill #4: Julia insists she be heard and Bryan helps her by giving her opportunities to express herself. Bryan also gives Angela space to express her concerns.

Angela: They're not a good influence.

Bryan: So you're worried that they might be.

Angela: Yes.

Bryan: Right. So, Julia, I wonder if you can tell me a little bit about how you spend your weekends with your friends, what do you do?

Julia: Umm . . .

Angela: What do you do with them?

Julia: . . . hang out.

Angela: Huh?

Julia: We hang out.

Bryan: Yeah.

Julia: Yeah.

Bryan: Yeah.

Angela: Yeah, but . . .

Julia: That's what everyone does . . .

Bryan: Is it the whole weekends like Friday through to Sunday you're with your friends . . .

Julia: Yeah. it's the . . .

Bryan: . . . that your mom's concerned about?

Julia: . . . weekend. I don't have anything to do.

Bryan: Okay alright.

Angela: But I don't know exactly what they do when they hang out. You know that's what I'm worried. What do they do when they hang out? I don't know what do you do? Do you just talk or do you have . . .? Do you drink or do you use . . .?

Julia: Yeah.

Bryan: Do you ever go to their houses to visit them and do they come to yours?

Julia: Some . . . no they don't . . .

Angela: No they, no they don't come at home.

Julia: Eu to falando, meu [Now it is my turn to talk]. They don't come home. I go to their houses.

Bryan: If there was things to do together Julia, you'd be home more?

Julia: Umm.

Bryan: You'd try to be a home a little bit more?

Julia: Maybe.

Bryan: Yeah? That . . .

Angela: Yeah. I . . .

Bryan: . . . that's something that we could work on?

Julia: Maybe.

Angela: I don't know what can I do for her because, she, she never hear me. Sometime I ask her, oh yes we can go to a movie or . . .

Julia: I do.

Angela: . . . you can stay here, yeah, and you could stay here help me with you know to help me at home. Or help with her brother and sister, and you know, stay at home with the family but she prefer to hang out with them.

Julia: Yeah. It's funner.

Bryan: Why do you . . .

Angela: She said it's funny.

Julia: Fun.

Bryan: Fun. Yeah.

Angela: It's fun. They have, but I think she could have fun with healthier things.

It may not be a terribly profound reason to explain Julia's motivation to spend time with her friends, but it is meaningful, nonetheless. Julia experiences her time with her friends as "fun." The problem with offering Julia a substitute peer group is that Julia perceives herself as having few opportunities to find other peers or create other equally exciting recreational opportunities for herself. Her mother's solution is for Julia to stay home and help care for her younger siblings. It's no surprise that Julia rejects this option as it does not solve the problem of finding ways to have fun appropriate for a 13-year-old. In Julia's *complex* social ecology, what can Bryan do? Invite Julia to stop using drugs and change peer groups? Who would she have fun with? While Julia's problem may appear to have a simple solution, the complexity of Julia's life is going to require a multisystemic intervention that not only addresses patterns of individual drug use and the psychological factors that contribute to it, but also changes Julia's social ecology to make new resources *available* and *accessible*. In the next passage (taken from a little later in the transcript) notice the way Bryan sequences his intervention, moving from individual risk assessment to a discussion of the ecological factors that are the real danger facing Julia.

Principles that are observed:

Principle #2: Julia explains a strategy she uses to find "fun."

Principle #4: Bryan and Julia talk about which coping strategy is most meaningful to Julia.

Principle #8: Rather than following Angela's lead and seeking to understand Julia's deeper motivations for being with her friends, Bryan focuses instead on the very functional way Julia's friends get her what she needs.

Skills being used:

Navigation Skill #8: Bryan helps Julia assess what she gets from her relationships with youth who use drugs and whether these relationships are adaptive.

Negotiation Skill #5: Bryan sets up the interaction so that Julia's problem becomes one of a search for resources like friends and fun, rather than drug abuse, a problem that Julia is not ready to discuss.

Negotiation Skill #9: Bryan conveys respect for Julia's solution (though will challenge it later).

Bryan: Okay. So just let me review with you Julia what I understand has happened up till now. In terms of your drug use and other concerns. If I get it wrong though, please correct me as we go along. Is that Okay? Okay, so you told me over the last number of weekends you used somewhere between two to three beer, two grams of marijuana you shared with about four friends. Is that correct? Yeah.

Julia: Yup.

Bryan: And that's normally how your drug use occurs on weekends?

Julia: Yeah.

Bryan: Okay. And the guys that you're hanging with, the guys and girls that you hang with, they all use drugs and alcohol?

Julia: Yup.

Bryan: Some more than you though. And that you told me that some of these guys are in trouble with the law sometimes. They do things that, and the law gets involved.

Julia: Yeah, some of them.

Bryan: Yeah?

Julia: Yeah.

Bryan: Are, are any of them involved in gangs?

Julia: I don't know. I think some of them but not all of them and I don't go with them.

Bryan: Okay, so you're not involved with them when they're doing kinda gang-related activities. You're not part of that.

Julia: Yeah.

[. . .]

Bryan: Well I hear two things though, Angela. I hear your concern that she may be in danger, and when around these guys because of the behavior,

This is a wonderful example of showing Angela that her daughter is actually not committed to becoming involved in a gang or increasing her drug use. In fact, Julia portrays herself as thoughtful and her choices reasonable. She resists getting into more serious trouble while taking advantage of the opportunities afforded her through her peer group. The conversation also shows a girl who is fully engaged in the therapeutic process. The intervention can now shift focus and look for other available and accessible resources for Julia that can be substitutes for the time she spends with delinquent peers.

Principles that are observed:
Principle #5: Bryan and Julia talk about Julia's coping strategies and how she keeps herself safe.
Principle #9: Bryan is both assessing Julia's drug use and engaging her in the work of evaluating the effectiveness of her coping strategies.
Principle #10: Bryan focuses attention on how Julia keeps herself safe and her strategies to avoid criminal activity.
Principle #18: Bryan identifies Julia's drug use pattern, suggesting that this is a significant pattern of use.

Skills being used:
Navigation Skill #6: Rather than asking Julia to stop using drugs, Bryan focuses on the complex patterns of recreational use and relationships when Julia is with her friends.
Negotiation Skill #5: Listen closely and one sees Bryan helping Julia create an identity as a responsible young woman trying to make good decisions for herself.
Negotiation Skill #10: When Bryan invites Julia to talk about how she avoids delinquent acts, he gives her the chance to perform her identity as a responsible adolescent.

that they're doing. But I hear another thing too, which is that Julia is watching for when it's maybe unsafe, and she's doing something. She's acting on that information. She's removing herself. I'm still a little bit confused about what, what you like about this group that you hang out with. What is it that the group does for you? What do you do for the group? What does the group do for you?

Julia: I don't know. They're my friends.

Bryan: They're your friends and they've been your friends for how long again?

Julia: Since I moved here.

Bryan: Since you moved here. Yeah. Do you go to the movies at all or like theater movies?

Julia: Yeah.

Bryan: Yeah. Okay. Good. That sounds like fun.

Angela: But I don't know where she finds money for do that.

Bryan: Okay.

Angela: I don't know.

Bryan: So can you help us with that Julia? Where does the money come from?

Julia: They pay for me.

Bryan: They pay for you.

Julia: And I don't know where they get the money. They just pay for me.

Angela: So that's why I'm worried.

Bryan: Fair enough.

Julia: Correct.

Bryan: So, they like you, they want you to be with them. They pay your way. Is there any expectation, do they have any expectation from you, having given you the money?

Julia: I don't know.

Angela: So you know, I think they have.

Bryan: Well, but, let's see if there's, let's look for the evidence.

Angela: Okay.

Bryan: Umm, so have they asked you to do something that you'd be uncomfortable about?

Julia: Uhmmm.

Bryan: So there hasn't been?

Julia: Maybe the gang things but I don't do it so I don't care.

Bryan: Okay. So you just tell them "No"?

Julia: Yeah.

Bryan: Ahh, and do you have friends that you're really close to?

Julia: In Brazil I, Yeah.

Bryan: 'Cause I understand there's been lots of changes since you've come from Brazil.

Julia: Yeah.

Bryan: And can you talk a little about what those changes have been?

Julia: I stopped dancing. That's a big change, 'cause I used to dance a lot.

Bryan: How often were you dancing at home?

Julia: Twice or sometimes three times . . .

Bryan: Wow.

Julia: . . . and for an hour and a half or two hours. No, ballet and tap dancing together was, three hours I think.

Bryan: Wow. That's a lot of work.

Julia: Yeah.

Bryan: Yup. But you enjoyed it?

Julia: Yeah.

Bryan: Yeah. And are you still interested in those activities?

Julia: Yeah. I'd like to go back to dancing classes but my mom can't pay for it, so.

Bryan: Yeah. And how do you feel about that?

Julia: Bad.

Bryan: Yeah. Yeah. And do you talk to mom about . . .

Julia: No.

Again, the focus of intervention is on more than just Julia's problem behavior. The focus shifts to what resources she needs and how she finds them. Bryan helps Julia and Angela to realize that Julia's changed behavior reflects changing circumstances, not just a bad attitude or a flawed personality.

Principles that are observed:

Principle #6: Bryan's intervention makes it clear that Julia might make other choices if she had access to other types of recreational opportunities.

Principle #16: It is very clear that Bryan's questions follow from those that came before. He continues to talk about which resources are accessible as required by the model.

Skills being used:

Navigation Skill #3: Bryan finds out more about why Julia is unable to have fun in ways that don't involve delinquent peers.

Navigation Skill #9: Bryan assesses Julia's interest in becoming involved again in dance.

Negotiation Skill #3: Julia explains that she can't dance because her mother can't pay for classes. Responsibility for change is shared with her mother.

Negotiation Skill #6: Dance is developed as a viable alternative for Julia.

Bryan: . . . What else has changed?

Julia: Umm. My dad left us.

Bryan: Yeah.

Julia: Yeah.

Bryan: Is that something that surprised you?

Julia: Yeah.

Bryan: That was a big surprise. It seems that it's very difficult to talk about dad, very painful. Is there anything that I can do to make it easier to talk about what, what's happened?

Julia: No.

Bryan: And, and do you ever talk to your mom about how you feel about your dad?

Julia: She calls him asshole all the time.

Angela: But he is . . .

Julia: And he drinks a lot.

Angela: . . . but he is an asshole . . .

Julia: You don't need to . . .

Angela: . . . he is . . .

Julia: . . . talk about it.

Angela: . . . he. Yeah. But you have to talk about that, Julia. We came here with him. He left us here. We're alone here, do you, Ele é um idiota [He is an idiot].

Julia: Mas voce nao precisa ficar falando disso [But you don't have to be talking like this].

Angela: But he is. And I have to talk about that. Okay.

Bryan: And so for you Julia, how do you get breaks from away from all of this stuff with dad? What do you do for yourself? Are your friends helpful for you in that way?

Julia: Yeah, they're fun to be with.

Bryan will return to this issue of Julia's father again later, but to sustain the focus for this meeting, with Angela present and to fulfill their contract to find ways to keep Julia safe, he avoids trying to resolve differences between Angela and Julia regarding Julia's father. Doing so will need more time and an explicit agreement to talk about this issue further. In the meantime, Bryan continues to focus on alternatives for Julia to experience fun.

Principles that are observed:

Principle #1: Bryan provides a space for Julia and Angela to disagree about Julia's father (negotiate different descriptions of his behavior).

Principle #12: Bryan has changed slightly the focus of the contract, but it is done with Julia's permission. They are no longer talking about her drug use, but about the loss of resources she had to manage in a new country without resorting to hanging out with dangerous peers.

Principle #15: Bryan's tone and focus suggests concern for Julia.

Skills being used:

Navigation Skill #7: Bryan explores how much Julia's father can be a resource (ally) for his daughter and how much Angela may oppose any contact.

Negotiation Skill #1: Bryan talks with Julia about her feelings relating to the losses she's experienced.

Negotiation Skill #8: the conversation leads into new possibilities that are alternatives to drug use for Julia, including dance lessons, her father, and new peers who might more closely resemble her peers back in Brazil.

Later in the session Bryan starts a discussion with Julia about whether she might be interested in participating in dance classes offered by the municipality at a reduced fee. They may not be the very best classes, but they could provide Julia with access to another way of experiencing fun, connecting her to a new peer group, and best of all, provide her a powerful identity as a dancer among her peers. If it worked, that identity as a dancer (something her delinquent peers respect) might be a powerful (and socially acceptable) alternative to drug user or gang member. Bryan and Julia also talk later about Julia's feelings toward her father and a plan was developed to bring them together without Angela.

What characterizes all this work is both its clear focus (preventing Julia from further exposure to the risks associated with drug use and delinquent peers) and Bryan's willingness to play multiple roles. He is at times a cognitive behavioral therapist doing harm-reduction work with Julia, then her advocate, coaching her and Angela on how to get subsidized dance classes. Along the way, he builds bridges to the resources he knows are available in his community. His interventions work because they address the barriers that are very real in Julia's life and seek solutions that are multisystemic and complex.

Thinking about this complexity can make counseling daunting. But as the transcript shows, the actual flow of the conversation is quite simple. Bryan remains focused on Julia's description of her problems and the solutions she prefers. He focuses on ecological factors as much, or more than, Julia's individual patterns of behavior and he looks for ways to change the structures that make Julia's choices reasonable adaptations in a risky environment.

It is a strategy that addresses what we know helps children avoid gang involvement. For example, in his research, Michael Chettleburgh (2007) shows that a gang can become (as it was starting to become for Julia) a better society than the one given to youth who are disadvantaged. Considering what is currently happening for young men and women on the margins of society, Chettleburgh writes, "By our actions and by our decisions, [we] have produced street gangs. When he is faced with a future flipping burgers at McDonald's for minimum wage, a troubled home life, an absent dad, a crime-infested community and stifled dreams, the pull of a gang and all that it offers may be just too strong for a young man" (p. 41). Gangs, he notes, are bad solutions for young people in bad circumstances. We should fear their cause, not their outcome. As Chettleburgh explains, "No child is born a gangster; rather, he or she is shaped into one through a confluence of many factors to which they are exposed over a dozen-plus years" (p. 237). Those factors include the police, courts, social services, business, and government. The good news is that solutions are doable: conduct research to know the extent of the problem; mobilize the community to focus on early intervention; train and support parents; provide after-school programs; support a youth center; create economic opportunities; get serious about mentoring; reach out to at-risk youth; invest in alternative school programs; promote social marketing and public awareness; target gang suppression activities; enhance community policing; revitalize social housing; invest in mental health services; evaluate and disseminate funds to target what works. These are all great strategies that help young people navigate to alternatives that offer substitutes to gang involvement.

Several of these interventions are reflected in Bryan's work with Julia, albeit from his position as her drug and alcohol counselor. What Bryan knows, and what the research shows, is that the problems Julia experiences are not just inside of Julia. The best solutions are those that will shape the world around her.

Navigations in Context

The context in which navigations take place offer access to many and varied types of resources. Not all resources, however, are equally important to a child's success. Nor can any one resource be enough to solve all the problems for a youth with complex needs. For example, among immigrant youth in the United States, identification with the values of their culture of origin and their parents' approach to discipline (whether it has adjusted to dominant cultural norms) can have a profound impact on the likelihood first and second generation young people will become involved in delinquent behavior (Beckett et al., 2006). Resources are like this. It is seldom enough to help a child navigate to just one. Multiple resources create a cumulative effect and combine exponentially. One resource is good, two is much better, three is wonderful, and four have the potential to have an exceptionally large impact on a child's life.

The problem with helping children navigate is even more challenging if we think about how fluid a child's social and physical ecology is over time. We know that resilience and child development both have temporal dimensions. The child changes physically and cognitively with each passing year. Her world also changes over time, providing different opportunities for self-expression and new rules and expectations. One need only think of the changing styles of clothing worn by adolescents, or the expectations placed on them to marry, go to war or prolong adolescence, all possibilities extolled as virtuous over the past 60 years. It is the same for personal qualities like self-efficacy. A child may easily locate experiences of personal power and control in one context or at one developmental stage (many elementary school children seem to be quite confident), only to have their beliefs about their ability to influence their world undermined later. To illustrate, the rambunctious child may be admonished by her more traditional parents for being unladylike once she reaches puberty (Benight & Cieslak, 2011). Understanding how to help a child navigate effectively requires that a great deal of thought be given to the child's changing, and potentially challenging, context.

Chapter Summary

In this chapter I've shown how complex young people's navigations can be when they are looking for the internal and external resources they need to change problem thoughts, feelings, and behaviors. As one of the most important forces for change in the lives of vulnerable children and youth, service providers need to consider whether the provision of service is done in ways that are intentional and most likely to meet children's needs or haphazard and disjointed.

Good counselors help young people and their families navigate through challenging social ecologies by using ten skills that make it more likely young people find the resources they need to thrive. These skills, as the case study of Julia shows, are embedded in a seamless process of intervention. An effective counselor, like Bryan, remains focused on helping his client navigate to substitute resources that are available, accessible, and meaningful. The counselor ensures that solutions are complex enough to sustain change. He pays attention to the adaptive quality of maladaptive, atypical solutions to problems that marginalized children use to cope in dangerous social ecologies, and he advocates on behalf of clients, helping to create opportunities to access resources which, in the process, motivates clients by instilling hope for a better future. Of course, the counselor's work is supervised by his agency and community, both of whom may want him to focus more on individual problems and leave the case management and advocacy work to others. In Chapter 9, we'll explore this problem more, looking at the things that are necessary to make it possible for counselors to work ecologically.

The principle of navigation, however, reminds us to *both* help people experience a personal sense of efficacy while also addressing the structural challenges that prevent people from accessing the supports and services that can help them realize their potential. As we've seen, helping young people and their families navigate is always easier when they play a role in defining their problems and solutions.

Note

1 This dialogue is transcribed from one of a series of videos that are used to train counselors. Parts of the transcript have been edited in order to shorten the dialogue and focus attention on aspects of Julia's patterns of navigation. The full video of the interview is available online at the author's youtube channel. Please go to: www.youtube.com/MichaelUngarPhD.

Questions to Help People Navigate

Navigation Skills		Questions
Navigation Skill #1	**Make resources available** The counselor helps the client identify the internal and external resources that are available.	• Of the resources you said you needed, which are realistically available? • Which resources can't be used, even though they are available? • What has it felt like in the past trying to use the resources that are available? • Are there (internal and external) resources we should discuss later? Ones you think it would be good to look for? *Add your own questions here:* • •
Navigation Skill #2	**Make resources accessible** The counselor discusses how the client can access the resources that are available.	• Of these resources that are available, what are the steps we can take to reach them? • Have you had the experience of trying to make use of a resource in your family, school, or community and encountering problems? What happened? Who or what made accessing resources difficult? Who do you blame for the difficulty you experienced? • Who has helped you in the past to access the supports you needed to succeed? • If you've mostly had to fend for yourself, what strategies did you use to get around the barriers you faced? *Add your own questions here:* • •
Navigation Skill #3	**Explore barriers to change** The counselor discusses the barriers to change the client experiences, and which resources are most likely needed to address which barriers.	• What things inside you and outside you stop you from making changes in your life? • When you think of a specific problem, which barrier is causing the most problems? • If that barrier wasn't there, would you be able to make the changes you want to make? Would you feel hesitant, afraid, or maybe anxious about making the changes you want to make?

Add your own questions here:
-
-

Navigation Skill #4	**Build bridges to new services and supports** The counselor discusses with the client the services and supports that the counselor is familiar with and her or his role as a bridge builder to help make new resources available and accessible.	• What solutions to the client's problem can you help make happen? • Are there resources that you know about that could help the client? • What can you do to help make these resources available and accessible to the client? *Add your own questions here:* • •
Navigation Skill #5	**Ask what is meaningful** The counselor explores with the client which resources are the most meaningful given the client's context and culture.	• Of the things you need to change, which do you feel most strongly about? Which change would be the most helpful? • What resources/experiences do you need to have to be able to show others you've changed? • In your context/culture, how do people go about solving problems like the one you are experiencing? • Are there unique strategies to cope that you, your family, or your community typically use for the kind of problem you have? *Add your own questions here:* • •
Navigation Skill #6	**Keep solutions as complex as the problems they solve** The counselor explores solutions that are as complex (multisystemic) as the problems they address.	• What else will need to change to make this solution sustainable? • Is the solution you're trying working well or does it need to be changed? *Add your own questions here:* • •

Navigation Skill #7	**Find allies** The counselor explores possible allies who can help the client access resources and put new ways of coping into practice.	• Who will help you get what you need to change/cope with this problem? • Will you have to ask them for help, or are you expecting them to volunteer? • Who in your family, among your friends, or in your community has coped well with a similar problem? What advice can they give you? • Who will notice the changes you're making? Will that be a good or bad thing, to be noticed? *Add your own questions here:* • •
Navigation Skill #8	**Ask whether coping strategies are adaptive or maladaptive** The counselor helps the client explore whether the solutions she/he/they are using to cope in challenging contexts are adaptive or maladaptive, and the consequences to the choices the client is making.	• Are the solutions you're trying bringing more advantages than disadvantages? • What is it about the solutions you've tried that you like? Dislike? • What do you hear about the solutions you've tried? Do people think you make good choices, or bad choices? • How well do others understand why you make the choices you do? Does anyone understand how difficult it is to find other solutions? *Add your own questions here:* • •
Navigation Skill #9	**Explore the client's level of motivation** The counselor discusses with the client her/his/their level of motivation to implement new preferred solutions.	• How motivated are you to make these changes? • What would make you more motivated? *Add your own questions here:* • •

Navigation Skill #10 **Advocate**
The counselor advocates with, or on behalf of, the client, or shows the client how to advocate independently to make resources more available and accessible.

- What can you do to help the client succeed? What personal contacts or resources can you make available and accessible that are ethical to share?
- Have you asked the client what you could do as their counselor that would be most helpful? Have you let them direct your work together?
- Have you asked others what they can do to help the client?
- Have you shown the client how to advocate for themselves, practicing the skills required?

Add your own questions here:

-

-

CHAPTER 5

THE SECOND SET OF SKILLS: HELP CLIENTS NEGOTIATE

Sir Albert Aynsley Green, England's first Children's Commissioner, understands children and their need to distinguish themselves from adults. In a jest aimed at schools that had banned adolescents from wearing hoodies (cotton sweatshirts with hoods that hide the child's face), he told me, "The fastest way to get the kids from wearing hoodies is to have the wrinklies wear them." It's a friendly reminder that children negotiate with their peers and the adults in their lives (the wrinklies) for a powerful sense of individual and collective identity. If their teachers started wearing hoodies, I would imagine teenagers would quickly find some other way to show us that they are different.

Clinically, clients do exactly the same thing, bringing to counseling problems negotiating access to the resources they need to experience well-being, including the right to be seen by others as capable, competent, caring, and unique. In the last chapter we discussed techniques to help children, youth, and families navigate better. Navigations only work, however, when they succeed at increasing a client's access to relationships, a powerful identity, experiences of power and control, social justice, material resources, social cohesion, and cultural roots (the seven factors associated with resilience that I discussed in Chapter 1). When it comes to access, however, it's a child's family, community, and institutional gatekeepers who decide which resources the child gets, when, and in what quantity. In these negotiations, children (and adults) with complex needs are too often silenced.

Even an individual quality like self-esteem needs genuine opportunities to be experienced (Dumont & Provost, 1999; Swenson & Prelow, 2005). The school that does not accommodate a child's ADHD, a family who berates a child for being uncoordinated, or a coach who won't put a child on the field, deny a child access to a valuable resource, the chance to feel talented and perform those talents in front of others. No amount of certificates that name the child as the "Student of the Day" is ever going to replace more genuine opportunities for a child to make a meaningful contribution to the welfare of others and, for the briefest of moments, be the center of attention for the right reasons rather than the wrong ones.

Discursive Empowerment

Any clinician who has offered her help to a recalcitrant youth knows that making a service available and accessible doesn't necessarily lead the young person to embrace the opportunity he's given. I was naïve enough to think so early in my career until several well-intentioned efforts to engage youth living on the street and juvenile delinquents in secure custody showed me how quickly I could be "fired." What we offer as clinicians must be meaningful to the young person. It must be culturally relevant and supported by a value system that says this resource for this child at this time provided in this way is a good thing (Lerner, 2006).

The process of negotiation introduces clinicians to postmodern innovations in counseling that have shown that people's worldviews are co-constructions (Flemons, Green & Rambo, 1996; Gergen, 2001). By this I mean we all participate in the collective conversations that define our world. Should a 10-year-old child be responsible for cooking dinner for his parents? There are few places on earth where parents would say this is appropriate except in conditions where (a) both parents are required to work outside of the home and the family is living in poverty and (b) where the adultification of a child is necessary because one or both parents suffer from a mental or physical illness (Burton, 2007). In both instances, the child will experience no ill-effects from his role as caregiver to his caregivers if he receives recognition for his contribution from both his family and his community (Godsall et al., 2004). Contrast this situation with a different family where the child is simply treated badly, like Cinderella, made to do chores the parents should do but are too lazy or mean to do themselves. There is an elaborate dance that takes place to decide what appropriate parenting practices are, a dance in which children, families, child welfare workers, and broader social and political actors all participate. Together we create a discourse, a conversation that defines our world for us. In that discourse we are both subjects and actors, told what to do while all the while talking back and telling others what we think should be accepted as normal (Madigan & Law, 1998; Ungar, 2004).

Discursive empowerment, then, is important to clients during counseling. While young people are looking for the seven factors associated with resilience, how they go about their search and what each factor looks like when it is experienced is always a matter of negotiation. An extreme example from the world of child soldiers helps to show the uniqueness of children's patterns of negotiation, a uniqueness which is also seen among gang members, bullies, and delinquents who are asked to change their troubling behaviors. Ishmael Beah (2007), a former child soldier, wrote about his experience escaping from the rebels in Sierra Leone and then enlisting with the army at age 14. Remarkably, he was upset when he was demobilized by aid workers. Instead of welcoming his chance to become a child again, Beah describes in his memoir the anger he felt when his gun was taken away and how much he wanted to return to his army unit. He had been proud to play an important part in attacks on the rebels who had killed his parents. Beah's experience as a soldier, while condemned internationally, was respected by his peers and many adults in his community. Demobilization, much like leaving a gang or being asked to stop hanging out with delinquent peers, puts a child in an awkward position. The one powerful identity he has is stripped away. Along with it go relationships, a sense of personal and political efficacy, maybe even the security that comes with being armed and dangerous. What is offered (typically education and a "normal" life as a child) is seldom seen by the young person as a powerful substitute for what he already had.

Closer to home, and as I showed in Chapter 2 through the example of Colin and his mother Becky, a parent can yell at her child "Stand up for yourself" and her meaning will still be unclear unless I fully understand the family context. Though it might sound obvious what the parent means, I'll argue that as the family's counselor I have no idea what the parent meant to say, no more than I could understand Beah's experience of demobilization. My job must always be to ask what "stand up" means to this family living in their context and with their culture and values. To promote social justice, it is very important that we counselors bracket our own biases, paying attention to how we are different from our clients because of our life experience, gender, sexual orientation, race, class, or ability (Chung & Bemak, 2012; Sue & Sue, 2003).

There are many ways that we can become trapped in thinking that we know best what the client needs when we really don't. Good negotiators are good listeners, humble enough to acknowledge what we don't know, sensitive enough to pay attention to contextual and cultural differences between us and the people with whom we work. The skills required to help empower young people to effectively negotiate for solutions that are meaningful to them is the focus of this chapter.

Case Study: Roberta

Roberta's mother, Christina, and father, David, had Roberta when they were still in high school. Christina's father, Shane, adopted his grandchild, and he and his second wife, Pamela, raised Roberta as their own, with Christina as Roberta's older sister. The situation remained relatively stable until Roberta turned 10 years old. That year, Pamela died four months after a terrible car accident that had left her severely disabled. The family was forced to move to less expensive housing, and Christina insisted on telling Roberta who her mother really was. Reluctantly, Shane agreed to let the secret out. Roberta responded by becoming more and more isolated from her family, remaining in her room for long periods of time and avoiding the awkwardness of making friends at her new school.

Shane loves his daughter and has tried to help her adjust to her status as his grandaughter, but his work hours have changed and he doesn't return home until 10 P.M. on weeknights after his shift as a security guard at the mall. His new girlfriend and her 8-year-old son have moved in with him and Roberta. More people in the home haven't made things any easier for his grandaughter who, when I met her, described an overwhelming feeling of sadness that was like an aching "tightness" across her chest. A short, skinny child, Roberta says she'll only eat dinner when her father gets home from work. The oddness of the situation has meant Roberta gets far less sleep than she needs and looks physically emaciated. She's often too tired or sad to attend school, something that worries the school social worker.

Meanwhile, Roberta's biological mother, Christina, has had three more children with David. They live a short drive away, though Roberta is seldom invited to come over. Roberta still doesn't understand why Christina was so insistent that Roberta be told who her real parents are but doesn't seem to want to spend any time with her.

While there is little conflict at home, the school signaled the case to the community mental health clinic where I worked because of Roberta's depressive symptoms. Although they attended sessions together, Roberta refused to let Shane bring his girlfriend or to have Christina and David join us during sessions.

I approached the work in a way that gave Roberta the most say possible over her situation (something she had not often experienced). I asked her first about the effectiveness of her coping strategies that kept her connected to her grandfather (who she refers to as her dad) and isolated from others. I used the 10 navigation skills I introduced earlier, as well as the 10 negotiation skills which are the focus of this chapter, to help us identify the resources Roberta experiences as most meaningful. We also eventually talked about the trauma and sense of loss that followed Pamela's death and the disclosure of Roberta's mother's identity. Before I did all that, however, I positioned Roberta within a complex social ecology and tried to understand what she most valued as solutions to the rejection she was experiencing. These negotiations for her definition of the problem and its solution led to some very creative ideas for how to cope with her feeling depressed and not attending school regularly.

Michael: When does the tightness decrease?

Roberta: Usually when I hear dad come in the house. Then it feels less.

Shane: I want to be home more, but this job is what I've got right now.

Roberta: I understand that.

Michael: Then you come out of your room?

Roberta: Yeah, and go and sit with my dad when he has dinner.

Shane: I always go up and see Roberta first, and change.

Michael: So Roberta wants to be with you, people who love her. The isolation isn't necessarily what she wants. [They both nod agreement.] Then, I'm curious, Shane, what kind of contact did you have with your father growing up?

Shane: My dad? He was in the military so I never saw him much. It was my mother who did everything with us kids. But Roberta doesn't have her mom [referring to his second wife, Pamela].

Michael: Did you ever do things with him?

Shane: Yes. But mostly when he was dying. My mother died 8 years ago and so when my father was dying of cancer back in 2008, I went and spent time with him every day for two years. Roberta came with me sometimes. I was even paid as his home support, so he wouldn't have to go to hospital. The military had some program for that.

Michael: You're telling me that you really put yourself out for your father?

Shane: And then again for Pamela. It's not been easy to hold a job. With Pamela, Roberta, and me we were at home a lot. She took two months off school while her mother was sick.

Michael: Roberta, you too, you really sacrificed to be there for your mother?

Roberta: I helped as much as I could. Dad did most of it.

My work focused on trying to understand the family's way of relating. I made no assumptions regarding how much time Roberta and her father should be spending together, but did believe that, first, Roberta wanted to spend time with her father, and second, there was a strong commitment within this family to look after each other. It was this value system that became the basis for generating solutions. They were, after all, comfortable with a level of enmeshment that might make others feel constrained. Working with what they told me, I suggested that Roberta come out of her room and make her father dinner once a week. Shane was surprised by the suggestion since his girlfriend did the cooking, but I pointed out that he had been modeling for his daughter for years the way family members should look after one another. It was time that Roberta took some control over what happened in the family. Roberta liked the suggestion. Over the next month she cooked dinner twice. Her father taught her how to make his favorite meal, the southern style pork chops that they both loved.

Slowly, Roberta began to eat more regularly and was willing to talk to Shane's girlfriend when they were both at home. Her sleep was still far too little to allow her to function well at school, but she was attending more often. She realized that if she didn't her father worried and in a home where people sacrificed for each other (and had shown it through the care they'd given to Pamela before her death) Roberta was more than willing to do her part to make the family work.

Each of these interventions fit with what the family valued. Because they were meaningful, it was easy to motivate people to participate. These solutions, however, were not necessarily reflective of values I held. A child staying up late at night to cook dinner for her father? It was an odd solution but one that worked because it gave Roberta access to many of the experiences that helped her cope with the losses she'd experienced.

With some success helping Roberta do things that made sense to her, our next conversation considered whether she could negotiate a better relationship with Christina and David, her biological parents.

Michael: When you go over for a visit with Christina and David, and their children, would you say that people put themselves out like your father and you do? Do they agree to pick you up and drive you over themselves, or make you feel special?

Roberta: Not really. They always complain about money. Like my mother gave me five dollars and then she asked dad for it back. It was just for food.

Shane: Christina's like that. I don't think Roberta is all that welcome there. Unless I take the bus and go with her, to get her there, they'll never come and get her even though they both have a car and I don't.

Michael: So, if I'm understanding, you both have this value in your home that you do things for people, but it's different for Roberta's mother and father.

Roberta: I think they're really selfish.

Instead of talking about Roberta's depressive symptoms as an individual problem, we shifted the focus to Christina and David. Clearly, they were the ones with the problem, not Roberta. Once we began to look at Roberta's world as comprising two types of people, those who were devoted to her and those who were selfish (her word), Roberta began to see her father's girlfriend in a very different light. Not only was she happy to look after Roberta while Shane was at work, she volunteered to buy Roberta school supplies and clothing out of her own money. Roberta had never considered that her father's girlfriend, someone she'd only known for a year, could show more concern for her well-being than Christina and David. Roberta stopped asking to visit her biological parents so often and slowly found ways to come out of her room and be part of her new blended family.

Two Types of Negotiation: Being Heard, Being Seen

Being Heard: Negotiations are, at their most mundane level, about ensuring people are *heard* when decisions are made about their access to resources. Roberta hadn't been heard very often over the years. She'd had no say over her abandonment by her biological mother, her adopted mother's death, where she lived, nor her father's work hours. What Roberta could control, however, was when she went to bed, how often she went to school, when she ate, who she played with, and of course, contact with her father after he came home from work. It might seem odd that I didn't focus my intervention on getting Roberta to go to school more often, her grief following her grandmother's death, her resentment toward her biological parents, her need to sleep more and eat better or find new friends. What would have been the point? None of these goals would have been what Roberta wanted, at least right away.

Listening to Roberta and faithfully negotiating with her to set the goals for counseling meant I had to suspend my biased perception of the right solutions to Roberta's problems. Not that I was entirely silent. I came up with the idea for Roberta to cook a meal for her grandfather. That intervention, though, was a calculated risk. Once I understood what Roberta was looking for (the security of attachment to a parent), and what she and her family valued (taking time off work and from school is a pretty good barometer of how important commitment is to people in this family), it was much easier to fit the intervention to the context.

Being heard also means ensuring that interventions are provided in ways that make sense to clients and match the resources they have (Dodge & Coleman, 2009; Weine et al., 2012). At its most basic, good negotiation means clients can afford counseling. But that's not all. Even when made affordable, good counselors also do what they can to meet their clients' expectations for a service that:

- Is available at a convenient time (Why do so many counselors working in settings like schools or hospitals so seldom meet with parents during the evenings? All too often it is financially and socially vulnerable parents whose children need help. They are also the employees with the least flexibility and the most punitive rules when it comes to taking time off work without losing pay).
- Is respectful of a client's comfort with self-disclosure (That's not something many cultures are comfortable with).
- Doesn't insist on clients signing consent forms or having everything they say written down or tape recorded (For families who have immigrated from countries where there were dictatorships or war, something as simple as signing a piece of paper can be perceived as dangerous).

These accommodations to the client's needs for a safe, convenient environment tell the client, especially children, that they matter (Chung & Bemak, 2012).

Being Seen: The second kind of negotiation is a little more complicated. It is negotiation for discursive power, meaning the right to influence the way we are *seen* by others, and to have our descriptions of the world (what things mean to us) valued. Is Roberta a truant child or a child struggling to find a way to remain connected to her family? Likewise, is a child who acts impulsively a delinquent or a survivor of child sexual abuse with signs of fetal alcohol syndrome for whom impulsivity is normal behavior? It is important to understand that there is competition for control over the everyday language that shapes our experience (Madigan, 2006; Parton, 2002). In discourses, there are always winners and losers.

Roberta and her grandfather seemed to be competing with Christina and David over what it means to be a family. For Roberta and Shane, it was all about selfless service to others. For Christina and David, it was about what's good for individuals. During counseling we negotiated for an acceptable definition of family, privileging (giving voice to) the description of selfless devotion to others that Roberta, Shane, and Shane's girlfriend reflected through their actions. If counseling worked, it was because the secure attachments that were provided to Roberta were those that she valued most (we heard her when she told us what mattered most to her) and those that made her feel respected by others. Rather than feeling unloved because Christina rejected her, my goal was to help Roberta feel secure in her belief that she is a special person who gives to others, and that her problem is really the flawed capacity of some family members to *be more like her.*

This skill of negotiation is evident in many approaches to counseling. For example, Selekman (2006) describes a stress busters group he started for suicidal, depressed, and self-harming adolescent girls. Rather than victimizing them with labels or individual treatment, he created an eight-week psycho-educational experience that drew on the girls' expertise. He started with the premise that the girls' behaviors were coping strategies that made sense to them. Selekman made the girls their own therapists, then encouraged them to become peer helpers to others who were struggling with the same kinds of stress. By having these young women perform as responsible helpers, Selekman created an all-important condition for successful negotiations: recognition from others for how the client prefers to be seen. The strategy was therapeutic because it changed a master status (Brown, 2004), a sociological concept that explains which aspects of our identity rise to prominence. Whereas these young women were previously seen as mentally ill, Selekman's intervention transforms the perception of the mentally ill into the mentally competent. A social ecological practice helps clients do the same: discover a new collective self that is seen by others as worthy of their respect.

10 Negotiation Skills

Just as there are 10 navigation skills, there are also 10 negotiation skills. While I've presented these two lists sequentially over two chapters, in clinical practice counselors use both sets of skills at the same time, asking about resources and their meaning in ways that are continuously interwoven through conversation.

Many of these negotiation questions share similarities with other solution-focused, strengths-based, postmodern, social justice, and feminist therapies. The difference here is that they are closely linked to goals for navigation. For example, in the previous chapter I asked my client to find new coping strategies that required new resources like relationships, social justice, and cultural roots. Those navigations are unlikely to succeed or motivate a client to act unless the resources we agree to look for are those the client finds meaningful. Many therapists intuitively know this. Far fewer, however, ensure that the goals they establish for counseling are: (a) reflective of what the client wants to achieve, even when her goals appear maladaptive or viable only in the short-term and (b) contextualized, understood as constrained by very real social, political, and economic factors.

Helping a child negotiate for the resources required to put a new coping strategy into practice is an overtly political act. Is there any good reason to offer the child who is bullied lessons in assertiveness and self-esteem if she is likely to be hurt again? At what point do we affirm a child's atypical behavior like truancy as adaptive and take responsibility for changing the child's social ecology before we ask the child to change?

1. Explore thoughts and feelings.
The counselor explores with the client thoughts and feelings about the problem that brought the client to counseling.

Practice questions:

- What do you think the problem is?
- Do others see the problem the same way?
- Do you agree or disagree with how others see it?
- How does it feel having this problem?
- How do you feel about how others see you when the problem is a part of your life?
- How has having the problem influenced the story you tell about yourself?

2. Look broadly at the context in which problems occur.

The counselor and the client explore the context in which problems occur, how problems are defined by others, and the social, economic, and political conditions that sustain problems.

Practice questions:

- When is the problem bigger/smaller?
- When is it more/less influential?
- In what context does it change?
- Which relationships add to the problem, and which make it go away?
- Culturally, what do people who share your culture say about this problem?
- What social, economic, and political conditions make the problem more likely to occur? Which make it less likely?

3. Explore who has responsibility for making change happen.

The counselor and client discuss who has responsibility to change patterns of coping that are causing problems for the client, and/or for others in the client's life.

Practice questions:

- Who has responsibility for making changes?
- Who would notice change if it did occur?
- Are solutions within the control of the client? Under the control of others? Or both?

4. Make the client's voice heard.

The counselor helps the client's voice be heard when she/he/they name the people and resources necessary to make life better.

Practice questions:

- What would you find helpful to deal with this problem at this time?
- Who do you want to listen to you when you suggest solutions?
- How much are you listened to when you tell people what the problem is and the best solutions?
- What services and supports would help? Have you ever been given access to these? How much say over their design and delivery have you had?
- How would it feel accepting help from others?

5. Consider new names for old problems.

When appropriate, the counselor may offer different names for a problem, and explore what these new descriptions mean for how the counselor and the client will work together.

Practice questions (for the counselor):

- What other ways could we describe this problem?
- Which of the seven factors (associated with resilience) need to change to make your life better?
- How would others in your life describe the problem? What words would they use?

6. Find a description of the problem that fits.

The client chooses one (or more) new descriptions of the problem that fit with how she/he/they see the world.

Practice questions:

- Do any of the ways of describing the problem that we've discussed fit with how you see it?
- If we use that description of the problem, what does that mean for our contract to work together? What will we need to add or take away?

7. Find resources the client values.

The client and counselor work together to find the internal and external resources the client says she/he/they need to put new solutions into practice.

Practice questions:

- Of the seven factors that relate to doing well, which do you think are most important?
- Which get solved by having the problem?
- Are there other ways to get the problem solved (using one or more of the seven factors)?
- Which solution would make the most sense to you? To others in your life?
- Which solution would people most criticize? Would you agree or disagree with them?

8. Expand possibilities for change.

The client experiences possibilities for change which are more numerous than expected.

Practice questions:

- If we put these new strategies into practice, what personal strengths/assets/resources would you have that you don't have now?
- To put these strategies into practice, what resources from your family/school/community/neighbors/government, etc., would you need?
- How do you feel about the options we've discussed? Overwhelmed? Wanting more?
- The choice you've made to fix the problem, is that still your best choice?

9. Performance

The counselor and the client identify times when the client is performing new ways of coping and discuss who will notice the changes.

Practice questions:

- How will others know you've changed? What will they see? What will they hear about you?
- How will it feel once you've changed?
- What's the new "preferred" story you'll tell about yourself?
- How will you get others to tell that same story about you?

10. Perception

The counselor helps the client find ways to convince others that she/he/they have changed, or are doing better than expected.

Practice questions:

- How can we convince others that you've changed?
- Who will be most reluctant to acknowledge that you've changed? Who can we ask to help convince people that you've changed?
- Will people think better of you, or worse, once you've changed? Whose opinion counts most?

Case Study: Brian

My colleague, Alison, used many of these negotiation skills in her work with Brian, a 16-year-old young white man who has been living in a shelter for homeless youth for two months. A video of this interview is available online.[1] Brian's youth worker, Ben, is concerned that Brian isn't attending classes regularly and referred Brian to Alison, a therapist working with a community-based organization that provides outreach, shelter, employment, and counseling services to youth-at-risk. If Brian doesn't go to school or find a job, he can't stay at the shelter. Brian left home after years of ongoing conflict with his mother and father. His parents complained, he said, that he would likely end up in jail just like his father's brother.

Brian has witnessed a great deal of family violence while growing up. His mother, Janet, and father, Alfred, fight constantly, though Brian is not hit "very often," and almost never in the past year since he hit his father back. His father has been previously charged with assault of his mother after a neighbor called the police. Brian's father separated from his mother when he was five, but came back to the family three years later. Recently, Brian has been seeing less and less of his father who works as a construction worker in Alaska. Brian left home shortly after turning 16 years old, saying he didn't want to live at home any longer. He insists he won't return.

Brian is the oldest of three siblings. His 12-year-old brother, Jason, and 10-year-old half-sister, Susie, whose mother had an affair with Brian's father while his parents were separated, also live with Alfred and Janet. Susie came to live with Brian and his family when her mother married another man.

Brian has had several encounters with the law resulting from having a hunting knife on school property, vandalizing school property with his friends, and possession of drugs (marijuana). He is also sometimes bullied at school.

When Alison and Brian meet, Brian is in grade 10 and at risk of failing his school year because of repeated absenteeism. He is on an Individual Progress Plan and gets extra help from a teacher's aid for math and English. He has been diagnosed with ADD.

I've included below excerpts from two interviews, the first between Brian and Alison, the second with Janet, Brian, and Alison that explores what would need to change if Brian is to return home. In both excerpts, Alison uses many of the ten negotiation strategies listed above, though her questions are never as neat and tidy as I presented them earlier.

Once again, to help show principles and skills applied to practice, the following transcript is annotated with process notes. Specific principles and skills that are used are identified. As in the last chapter, my choices are somewhat arbitrary. Interventions often reflect several principles and skills at the same time. A few of the most evident are described.

Excerpt One: Brian and Alison

Alison: I'm just gonna let you know what Ben told me.

Brian: Yeah.

Alison: But then, I really kinda wanna get from you what your experience of it was like.

Brian: Yeah.

Alison: So what? From Ben's point of view, you'd been missing some school . . .

Brian: Yeah.

Alison: . . . and the house is getting kinda worried about how much school you're missing. You look kinda surprised by that. Brian, tell me from your point of view, like what's, what's . . .?

Alison begins the session by being transparent about what she has heard from Ben about Brian's behavior. The strategy helps to engage Brian in a more forthright conversation and signals to him that the information Alison has about him is just a story that others tell about him. She wants to know how he sees his problems and what he considers possible solutions.

Principles that are observed:

Principle #1 and Principle #14: By Alison letting Brian know what she knows, she sets the stage for Brian to negotiate with her what his perspective on the problem is too.

Skills being used:

Navigation Skill #7: Alison positions herself as a potential ally, without suggesting Ben is aligned with her against Brian.

Negotiation Skill #9: Brian is given the opportunity to change how his workers see him. Why is he not attending school? Is that perception accurate?

Alison: . . . It's more enticing to go hang out . . .

Brian: Yeah.

Alison: . . . with your friends. When you compare how it feels to hang out with your friends . . .

Brian: Ummm.

Alison: . . . compared to how it feels to be overwhelmed by what's expected of you in English class . . .

Brian: Yeah.

Alison: . . . how does it stack up?

Brian: Well . . .

Alison: It sounds like such an obvious question but . . .

Brian: Yeah.

Alison: . . . I'm really interested in what you're . . .

Brian: I'm kinda thinking about it, but

Alison suggests that Brian expand his audience so that others see him the way he wants to be seen (as a young man who is trying to learn). Alison also pays attention to Brian's definition of the problem (school work is difficult for him, but he's not lazy). She wonders if his coping strategy, truancy, protects him from threats to his self-esteem. Notice as well the way Alison compares Brian's two experiences, being in class and being with his friends. She doesn't judge one strategy to be any better than the other, but she does acknowledge that Brian is putting his residential placement in jeopardy by not attending school. She eventually suggests that Brian advocate for himself and explain to his shelter workers his experience at school. If they understand his coping strategy better, they may tolerate his truancy more or be more patient with him when he gets poor grades. If this works, Brian will be able to challenge his workers' negative perception of him with a redefinition of his behavior as "trying."

I'd probably say hang out with friends.

Alison: Yeah. Okay. Okay. What're you, what's your sense right now, about what the house understands the reasons are for you missing school? Like, what does the house think right now?

Brian: Probably just that I'm not trying.

Alison: Ooh. Okay, and, and what do you think about that? Is that, is that, really kinda what's happening? Is it that you're not trying?

Brian: No.

Alison: This stuff's kinda snowballing for you. You know, so you're missing art class, and you're missing English class, and you're telling me some reasons why and it's not just . . .

Brian: Yeah.

Alison: . . . it's not, just 'cause whatever, or you're being lazy, you know, and, there might be, we don't know yet 'cause we'll talk to Ben about this. There might be, an impression at the house, that it's 'cause you're not trying hard enough.

Brian: Okay.

Alison: And then, you also said to me. That there's lots of ways that you do try hard . . .

Brian: Yeah.

Alison: . . . and, you know, I think that's also, like really interesting stuff. And do you think that also might be something that, would be good to have a discussion with Ben about the ways that you do try hard?

Brian: With Ben, well, I guess if that would really help with the house.

Alison: The other thing that Ben did let me know was you got suspended for a day last week because you brought

Principles that are observed:

Principle #3: Alison and Brian discuss how staff at the residence see Brian and his coping strategies.

Principle #9: While Alison is engaging with Brian, she is also doing the work of helping him begin the process of negotiating a better description of his behavior.

Principle #20: Alison does not try to make Brian go to school: she simply explores his experience of school.

Skills being used:

Navigation Skill #8: Alison begins the process of exploring whether Brian experiences his way of handling school as positive or negative.

Negotiation Skill #5: By Brian's experience being described as trying hard rather than school refusal, a new definition of the problem and its solution is suggested.

Negotiation Skill #6: Brian appears to accept this new description of his way of coping.

Just like their discussion about truancy, Alison again explores with Brian his definition of what carrying a knife to school means. It's interesting that for Brian the knife a knife to school. Can you tell me about that?

Brian: I guess when you state it like that it does sound really harsh but I mean yeah, I don't know how to really explain it to a lot of people because most people just come up to me, and, well they all see it like, "Were you gonna go stab somebody?"

Alison: Right. Okay.

Brian: And, just, I've been asked like "Is someone picking on you? You gonna get back at them?"

Alison: Yeah.

Brian: That kinda thing.

Alison: Can you tell me a little bit more, Brian, by what you meant by bringing the knife, and, and, like, just give me the details 'cause I don't really have a sense of what is this knife, and, how come you have it, and, what was, what was that about . . .

Brian: It's just a little pocketknife, but, I mean . . .

Alison: Okay, what's that knife mean to you, what's, how . . . Is it something that you value?

Brian: Nope, a lot of people have them, well, I include myself in that, just, you feel better, like, safety . . .

means "safety" even though authorities interpret it as a threatening behavior. While Alison never tells Brian that bringing a knife to school is a good thing (which would be unethical and contrary to her own values), she does encourage Brian to explain his behavior in ways that make sense to him. Her intervention decenters the problem, suggesting that it is the lack of safety at school which is at least some of the problem, not just Brian's way of protecting himself.

Principles that are observed:
Principle #2: Brian's use of the knife is one way he finds safety.
Principle #4: The discussion doesn't suggest it is a bad strategy, but instead one that is meaningful (at least for now).
Principle #14: Alison does a wonderful job of maintaining a nonjudgmental stance.

Skills being used:
Navigation Skill #5: Alison asks whether carrying his pocketknife is valued/meaningful to Brian.
Navigation Skill #6: The solution of carrying a knife is understood as part of a response to a complex social ecology where Brian feels unsafe.
Negotiation Skill #1: Brian's feelings about his behavior are discussed.
Negotiationg Skill #2: Alison pays attention to Brian's context and the danger he experiences.

Alison: . . . Ah, yeah. I'm wondering, if, is it linked at all, to those times that you told me about, when we first met, about what you, what was going on with your dad, and, when you saw your dad's violence, is that, were those times, were, did you keep yourself safe somehow in those times?

Brian: I guess there were some situations like that, I mean, not recently. I mean, he's never around anymore.

Alison: Yeah.

In this section, Alison masterfully links Brian's need for safety from bullies when at school to his experiences at home with his father. This is new for Brian and he seems very engaged in the conversation. Notice that it is Alison who makes this connection for Brian, but the connection is made based on the information she and Brian have been gathering together over time.

Principles that are observed:
Principle #8: Alison doesn't explore the trauma of Brian's past experience of his father but instead focuses on how that experience has affected his choice of coping strategy (using a knife to remain safe).

Brian: He used to a lot more when I was younger, but, at school, I mean . . . I do run into people like my dad, a lot. I don't know. Kids in the hall and stuff, I mean, well, if you're looking for an actual circumstance like, a concrete example, like, that I mean . . .

Alison: Yeah. Has there been any lately?

Brian: I don't know. If someone called me idiot, it would just bring back days of my dad.

Alison: Really, if someone called you an idiot or did someone call you an idiot?

Brian: Yeah, did.

Alison: Okay.

Brian: That's, like the first one I can think of right off the bat where it kinda triggers memories like that.

Alison: Yeah. Makes sense to me. Right.

Brian: Yeah.

Alison: Like, if that's the, you know, something that reminds you of all that stuff that you went through with your dad, like often you know, I've heard other youth say to me that they really hate when they get called stupid especially, if it reminds them of stuff, or, especially in school where they're struggling a little bit.

Brian: Yeah.

Principle #10: Alison helps Brian to see that he has had to cope with his father's violence in the past, and why he might be feeling he has to use the threat of violence to keep himself safe now.

Principle #16: Alison brings with her some understanding of why children use delinquency to cope. That knowledge informs her work as she introduces a possible explanation for Brian's behavior. Principle #20: Alison does not yet worry about getting Brian to stop taking a knife to school.

Skills being used:

Navigation Skill #5: Brian's knife-carrying behavior is described as functional (for now).

Negotiation Skill #6: Brian's acceptance of the link between his experience at school and home shows that Alison's intervention fit with Brian's perception of his behavior.

Work like this can change our perception of a troubled youth from the source of the problem to a child using reasonable coping strategies in dangerous situations. Later, Alison requests a meeting with Brian and his mother, Janet, to explore possible new ways to keep Brian safe, address his need for permanent housing, and change his experience at school.

Excerpt Two: Brian, Janet, and Alison

Alison: Brian and I decided that it would be helpful to ask you, invite you into a meeting to come and talk to us. Brian you, you've talked to me about, you know, one of the hardest things for you at home is when your dad's on the scene and that's a time when there seems like there's a lot of tension. And you've used the terms like people are kinda, umm, you know, on edge.

Brian: Bugs me when we fight. I don't like it. It's worse when he's around. Yup.

Alison: And that's when the fighting is bigger between you and your mom . . .?

Brian: Yeah.

Alison: At that time right? And Janet you kind of noted to me, you agreed, you agreed with that, that things seem to be a lot more stressful when Alfred's home. But also, you also have some concerns that this is sort of an ongoing thing between the two of you as well. Did you relate to anything that Brian was saying about kind of sometimes the fear that he feels around Alfred's anger, and, the worry that and concern that he has for your safety? Was there any part of that you kind of went, "Yeah, you know I kind of understand that"?

Janet: Of course, and you have to understand that I've been with Al for many years.

Alison: Hmmhmm.

Janet: And I know better than anybody how much he cares about his family, and how much he wants to do what's right. Al's always had a hard time controlling his temper.

Alison: Hmmhmm.

Alison provides Janet with Brian's perception of the family pattern of communication that makes it difficult for him to be at home. In this way, Alison (with Brian's permission) elevates his voice in the family discourse that defines the problem that prevents Brian from living at home. Notice, however, that Janet excuses Al's behavior by saying this was how he was raised. The result is two competing definitions of the problem. Despite the lack of empathy Janet shows for what Brian has experienced, the session with Alison begins a process that will help Brian better position his point of view in conversations about the family's problems.

Principles that are observed:

Principle #1: Alison opens space for Janet to describe her understanding of the problem (she minimizes the violence in the home).

Principle #5: Brian's safety at home is discussed.

Principle #6: Alison introduces the idea that Alfred will have to change if Brian is to come home.

Principle #13: By including Janet in the session, Alison is exploring whether she will be a support to Brian if he transitioned out of the shelter and back home.

Skills being used:

Navigation Skill #4: Alison is exploring whether Janet will be an ongoing support to her son.

Negotiation Skill #3: The responsibility for the violence (and Brian's homelessness) is explored.

Negotiation Skill #4: Alison helps raise the volume on Brian's voice, explaining to Janet his experience of the violence, while also having her voice in the room.

Janet: He was brought up in a, at a time when people didn't think about those things. We didn't have anything to help us with, with things and you know, he was beaten with a belt for God's sakes. At least he just uses his hand with you. I mean it's not, it's just not the same as it was for us. You don't understand.

Alison: I'm hearing that you know, that you're saying in many ways, that you know you're handling this situation in the best way that you know how. Today we're not looking at just looking at one option. It may be that you know where Brian is 16, it may be that you two end up in a relationship with each other that's better if he doesn't live at home. It may be that we end up that it's okay if he goes back home, but if it can't become safe, and really, it's not your responsibility to make it safe. It's Al's responsibility. And if that can't happen, then you know, maybe another solution, we look at some other solution . . .

Brian: I've lived by myself the last two months, and I've had a lot more time to myself, and I'm not living around you. I'm not living around dad. I'm not living around the whole environment at home. I've got just myself and I'm telling myself what to do. And it's worked out for me for the most parts so far. I don't have anyone calling me stupid . . .

Janet: You're not stupid . . .

Brian: . . . being put down.

Janet: . . . and I've never called you stupid. Your father does not have the vocabulary to be able to say what he really means. You, don't apply yourself. You don't try . . .

Before the conversation becomes a repeat of the arguments at home, Alison interrupts. Her strategy is to give the family a different experience of themselves during counseling and shift the conversation towards helping Janet empathize with how Brian feels at school and at home.

Notice that Alison has made two unconventional interventions: she has suggested that the problem is not Brian's and that it really is Al's responsibility to change and she has opened the possibility that going home is not the best option for Brian. Typically, therapists work to reunite families. In this case, though, Alison pays close attention to Brian's description of his experience at the shelter. Though he is "homeless," he is safer there and exercising his independence, all factors that contribute to resilience.

Principles that are observed:

Principle #2: The idea that living in a shelter is a way to maintain a safe connection between Brian and his mother is discussed.

Principle #11: It is clear that the contract is about where Brian lives. Relational dynamics are discussed, but only in regard to their influence on the fulfillment of the contract.

Principle #13: Even as they do the work of sorting out where Brian will live, attention is paid to his transition after counseling and whether Janet will maintain a supportive relationship with him.

Skills being used:

Navigation Skill #2: There is a focus on whether the shelter (and home) are resources available to Brian and sustainable.

Navigation Skill #6: An easy solution would have been to have Brian go home; a solution that is sensitive to the

Alison: Janet.

Janet: . . . you never have tried. It's . . .

Alison: Janet can I just, is it okay if I just interrupt for a second just, I just want to just take a minute, if you don't mind Janet, to, I just want to go back to something that Brian said that really sort of stood out for me as important. And it was that when he said how you know there was way less arguing when his, when his dad is not there, and that he also mentioned too, and it really stood out for me, that no one's calling him stupid. I'd really like to know a little bit more about what you think that would feel like to him, to him to have his dad call him stupid?

Janet: Al needs to change I probably even need to change but it's not just us.

Alison: Right.

Janet: He needs to try.

Alison: Right.

Janet: He needs to be a part of . . .

Alison: Yeah.

Janet: . . . the world . . .

Alison: Yeah.

Janet: . . . and our family.

Alison: Okay. Is that the first time you heard your mum say that your dad needs to change?

Brian: Yeah.

complexity of the situation is that he lives in the shelter and visits his parents whenever he feels safe.

Negotiation Skill #3: Responsibility for Brian's homelessness is shifted from Brian to his father.

Very little of this intervention has focused on identifying the cognitive processes that impair Brian's functioning. While that work will follow later, in this series of interviews, Alison helps Brian negotiate for solutions to his problems that make sense to him. He is encouraged to take advantage of the supports and challenges provided by his social ecology, including unconventional pathways to success available to him by living at a shelter.

Negotiating Definitions of Hidden Resilience

It would be easy to overlook the coping strategies children like Roberta and Brian use to maintain a sense of coherence in their lives. Though their strategies appear maladaptive, they show signs of hidden resilience, a capacity to navigate and negotiate in unconventional ways.

In my clinical work and research, I have observed two ways that resilience is hidden (Ungar, 2004). First, and as the examples above show, children may resort to atypical or risky behaviors to cope in environments that threaten their psychosocial development. A teen like Roberta who isolates herself in her room may be trying to draw attention to her feelings of rejection, or simply experiencing the isolation as easier to deal with emotionally than being among peers at school and family members at home whom she doesn't trust. Likewise, Brian's truancy, carrying a weapon to school, and living in a shelter are all atypical ways of coping, but remarkably sensible once we ask Brian to explain his experience of domestic violence and bullying.

The second way that resilience is hidden occurs when patterns of coping are culturally embedded, meaning that they make sense in one cultural context but not in another (Bell, 2011). Consider recent immigrants to countries like the United States and Canada who hold to the patriarchal values of their previous communities. While we may criticize a family for bringing with them patterns of behavior unacceptable in their new community, we make this judgment at the risk of overlooking some of the temporary benefits the family experiences. Those values they've brought along may actually sustain a sense of family cohesion during a challenging time of transition (Cruz-Santiago & Ramirez-Garcia, 2011). This is tricky terrain to find a solid footing on. On the one hand, as counselors, we can appear to be condoning misogynist or homophobic attitudes by not confronting them, while on the other we may destabilize a family system that needs all the stability it can find during a tumultuous period of change. In these complex negotiations there are seldom easy solutions.

Frankly, my own personal values aside, families I've worked with who are experiencing this transition between cultures seem to benefit from adherence to their heritage culture and the conservative values they sometimes bring with them as long as the harm they cause to others is minimal *and slowly challenged*. Research has shown that mental health is preserved when first generation immigrants demonstrate greater attachment to their cultures of origin (Hansson et al., 2012). Fortunately, children of later generations will develop a third culture that amalgamates the best of both their heritage cultures and the values of the dominant culture into which they've moved (Beckett et al., 2006). Many of the troubling patterns of coping we might observe during the first few years following immigration may later be changed or softened as dominant cultural values contribute to new values that are co-constructed.

We might, therefore, think of a child as having to negotiate her way across two different psychological spaces: a cultural space and a consciousness space. The cultural space includes a child's values and beliefs (Rogoff, 2003); the space of consciousness is the child's awareness of her values and the child's perception of her capacity to change them (Brown & Rodriguez, 2009). Both spaces shape the stories a child tells about the resources they need to be healthy. In contexts where the social ecology a child inhabits is threatening, a child's adaptation may be socially undesirable but function well enough for a child at risk. For example, when racism pushes African American youth to the fringes of society, consciousness of how they are treated may ignite a powerful story of resistance that is performed through their dress, language, hairstyles, and even attitudes toward violence or getting an education (American Psychological Association Task Force on Resilience and Strengths in Black Children and Adolescents, 2008; Dotterer, McHale & Crouter, 2009). These acts of resistance to cultural hegemony (non-conformity) can actually protect mental health even while they expose children to other types of risks.

Whether culturally embedded or simply atypical behavior, we only see hidden resilience when we fully appreciate the context in which young people navigate and negotiate for resources, and the barriers they face to behaving in more conventional ways outsiders consider socially acceptable.

Fragile Identities in Fragile Social Ecologies

One of the most important reasons to help clients learn to negotiate better is the impact good negotiations have on identity. Through a carefully orchestrated series of interventions, Alison changed Brian's self-description (and his description by others) from a knife-wielding delinquent child who wouldn't attend school to a child escaping an abusive home, avoiding the insult of class-work that makes him feel stupid, and carrying a knife to keep safe. What looked like a vulnerable child became a child who was actually remarkably resilient in atypical ways in a toxic social environment.

As young people use various coping strategies they experience results that bolster their sense of self-worth, regardless of whether those patterns of coping are adaptive or maladaptive, socially acceptable or unacceptable, culturally relevant or those of the cultural outsider. Repeated use of negotiation strategies creates patterns to how children are seen by others close to them (like being feared on the playground, or needing to be monitored by their social workers in case they run away) (Swanson et al., 2002).

Of course, counseling, like children's other interactions in complex and potentially hazardous social ecologies, creates a safe space where identities are negotiated and performed. If therapy creates a context for the stories children tell about their lives that emphasize personal agency, motivation, victory, autonomy, and self-mastery, then these children are likely to be more resilient (McAdams, 2005), with powerful identities and fewer externalizing and internalizing problem behaviors (Schwartz, 2008).

As we've seen, children and young adults use a number of strategies to negotiate for identities in contexts where they are viewed by others as dangerous, delinquent, deviant, and disordered. For example, a group of young adults who participated in programs to treat early psychosis created for themselves identities as "normal" despite a diagnosis of a severe and potentially persistent mental illness. In her interviews with 17 such young people, Shalini Lal (2012) showed that young adults engage in narrative practices in which they: (1) use language to distance themselves from their psychiatric labels; (2) de-emphasize their identification with the label; (3) embrace the label and crusade for control over how others treat people with mental illnesses; (4) abstain from taking up the label in the first place, remaining objectively curious but uncommitted to becoming a "patient" with a problem.

Counseling can provide a forum in which the meaning that one attaches to an experience of early psychosis is negotiated. Far from being passive victims of the disorder, youth can be active negotiators to maintain positive identities for themselves. Their success, however, is contextually dependent and closely related to a young person's ability to negotiate. In Lal's study, she noted that young people living in a shelter for homeless youth did not experience the same access to specialized treatment programs that youth living with their caregivers experienced even though the programs are publicly funded and available. Different programs in different contexts bring with them varying amounts of support for different self-definitions. When the youth lived at home and experienced more equitable access to programming, it was their time spent with supportive program staff that dramatically affected how capable they were at resisting negative labels. No surprise, then, that when we facilitate children's navigations into the services they need, they are more likely to be effective negotiators because of the people they meet. Good counselors are, of course, concerned with helping vulnerable children both navigate and negotiate effectively.

It is not always easy, however, to see negotiation strategies in isolation from one another. When combined, clients experience their knowledge of what they need as privileged, meaning they are heard when service providers, parents, teachers, and even government policy makers, make decisions that are supposed to be in children's best interests. Summarizing the impact of negotiation skills on clients, we can see four important processes that occur leading to changes in the client's thoughts, feelings, and behavior:

1. The counselor explores the process through which the client acquired her values (regarding gender, ability, human rights, the definition of success, happiness, etc.) and the identities that accompany the expression of each value.
2. The counselor and the client explore and challenge values that are no longer helpful, inventing new values that will, over time, become just as meaningful.
3. The counselor explores with the client what these new values say about the client as a person, and how they will influence how others see the client.
4. The client and the counselor advocate for changes to the client's social ecology so the client can be heard and seen.

A quick look back at Brian and Roberta and we see:

1. Alison asked Brian how he came to experience himself as "stupid" and how he has coped with that identity. Michael invited Roberta to reconsider whose values she liked most: her grandfather's or her mother and father's.
2. Alison invited Brian to consider his leaving home and school as an adaptive strategy, although one with long-term consequences. While truant and homeless, Brian no longer had to feel like a stupid child nor accept his father's abuse or threats of violence from bullies. He was finally old enough to take on a different identity, that of a responsible young man able to look after himself. Roberta, too, developed some new, atypical, coping strategies like cooking dinner for her father. But she also began to see herself differently, as a child who was actually loved by many, even if she still experienced neglect from her biological parents.
3. Brian began the slow process of considering whether his mother and father could see him as the competent young man he wanted to be. While he couldn't get his parents to see him differently, he could change how his shelter workers saw him. Through counseling, Roberta, too, began to be heard and seen by others as different. Rather than just a depressed child, her grandfather came to understand that Roberta wanted to belong in her family and keep him close. Once heard and seen, her behavior changed.
4. Alison helped Brian advocate for himself and convinced shelter staff Brian should remain in the shelter until he could transition to independent living. Going home became less and less of an option as Brian asserted himself in negotiations with his caregivers to get access to the resources he needed to succeed. For Roberta, the work took place during the clinical sessions with an increasing number of people coming to counseling to tell Roberta what she meant

to them. It was these opportunities for others to show Roberta how much they valued her that convinced Roberta she was not an unloved child.

Clients like Brian and Roberta who are helped to be heard and begin to have a say over the services and supports they receive will become much more effective negotiators for what they need. They will also become more resilient to future stressors, developing better capacity to look after themselves and access the people and institutions that can help them nurture and sustain their well-being.

Chapter Summary

As I've shown in this chapter, it is not enough to help young people with complex needs navigate to resources. If it was, we would only have to build drug and alcohol treatment programs, quality afterschool programs, foster homes, and hire special education teachers and children would flock to services. What we know instead is that even when services are available and accessible (for example, available at no charge) many children and their families resist interventions. Research and practice tell us that children, youth, and families navigate to the resources they need when those resources are offered in ways that they say are meaningful.

Note

1 This dialogue is transcribed from one of a series of videos that are used to train therapists. Parts of the transcript have been edited in order to shorten the dialogue and focus attention on aspects of Brian's patterns of negotiation. The full video of the interview is available online at the author's youtube channel. Please go to: www.youtube.com/MichaelUngarPhD.

Questions to Help People Negotiate

Negotiation Skills		Questions
Negotiation Skill #1	**Thoughts and feelings** The counselor explores with the client thoughts and feelings about the problem that brought the client to counseling.	• What do you think the problem is? • Do others see the problem the same way? • Do you agree or disagree with how others see it? • How does it feel having this problem? • How do you feel about how others see you when the problem is a part of your life? • How has having the problem influenced the story you tell about yourself? *Add your own questions here*: • •
Negotiation Skill #2	**Context** The counselor and the client explore the context in which problems occur, and the conditions that sustain them.	• When is the problem bigger/smaller? • When is it more/less influential? • In what context does it change? • Which relationships add to the problem, and which make it go away? • Culturally, what do people who share your culture say about this problem? • What social, economic, and political conditions make the problem more likely to occur? Which make it less likely? *Add your own questions here*: • •
Negotiation Skill #3	**Responsibility** The counselor and client discuss who has responsibility to change patterns of coping that are causing problems for the client, and/or for others in the client's life.	• Who has responsibility for making changes? • Who would notice change if it did occur? • Are solutions within the control of the client? Under the control of others? Or both? *Add your own questions here*: • •

Negotiation Skill #4	**Voice** The counselor helps the client's voice be heard when she/he/they name the people and resources necessary to make life better.	• What would you find helpful to deal with this problem at this time? • Who do you want to listen to you when you suggest solutions? • How much are you listened to when you tell people what the problem is and the best solutions? • What services and supports would help? Have you ever been given access to these? How much say over their design and delivery have you had? • How would it feel accepting help from others? *Add your own questions here:* • •
Negotiation Skill #5	**New names** When appropriate, the counselor may offer different names for a problem, and explore what these new descriptions mean for how the counselor and the client will work together.	• What other ways could we describe this problem? • Which of the seven factors (associated with resilience) need to change to make your life better? • How would others in your life describe the problem? What words would they use? *Add your own questions here:* • •
Negotiation Skill #6	**Fit** The client chooses one (or more) new descriptions of the problem that fit with how she/he/they see the world.	• Do any of the ways of describing the problem that we've discussed fit with how you see it? • If we use that description of the problem, what does that mean for our contract to work together? What will we need to add or take away? *Add your own questions here:* • •

Negotiation Skill #7	**Resources** The client and counselor work together to find the internal and external resources the client needs to put new solutions into practice.	• Of the seven factors that relate to doing well, which do you think are most important? • Which get solved by having the problem? • Are there other ways to get the problem solved (using one or more of the seven factors)? • Which solution would make the most sense to you? To others in your life? • Which solution would people most criticize? Would you agree or disagree with them? *Add your own questions here*: • •
Negotiation Skill #8	**Possibilities** The client experiences possibilities for change that are more numerous than expected.	• If we put these new strategies into practice, what personal strengths/assets/resources would you have that you don't have now? • To put these strategies into practice, what resources from your family/school/community/neighbors/government, etc., would you need? • How do you feel about the options we've discussed? Overwhelmed? Wanting more? • The choice you've made to fix the problem, is that still your best choice? *Add your own questions here*: • •
Negotiation Skill #9	**Performance** The counselor and the client identify times when the client is performing new ways of coping and discuss who will notice the changes.	• How will others know you've changed? What will they see? What will they hear about you? • How will it feel once you've changed? • What's the new "preferred" story you'll tell about yourself? • How will you get others to tell that same story about you? *Add your own questions here*: • •

Negotiation Skill #10 **Perception**

The counselor helps the client find ways to convince others that she/he/they have changed, or are doing better than expected.

- How can we convince others that you've changed?
- Who will be most reluctant to acknowledge that you've changed? Who can we ask to help convince people that you've changed?
- Will people think better of you, or worse, once you've changed? Whose opinion counts most?

Add your own questions here:

-

-

CHAPTER 6

THE THIRD SET OF SKILLS: INTEGRATE THE FIVE PHASES OF COUNSELING

Once we are thinking ecologically, there is no way to get around the complexity of the five phases of counseling (engagement, assessment, contracting, work, transition) and the many different stakeholders who must become involved. Each person or institution we introduce into the clinical work, whether actually present during a session or simply discussed, becomes another part of the multiple systems that must be engaged, assessed, and have their needs represented in the contract for service. They become part of the work, and if we're successful, a support for the client's smooth transition out of counseling.

This reliance on others throughout the counseling process is an important aspect of the work of an ecologically-oriented therapist. It builds on the radical position now taken by "deep ecologists" (who are focused on how natural ecologies sustain themselves) that each element of an ecosystem has as much value as any other (Naess & Jickling, 2000). To an ecologist, the slug in our garden is as important as the human who gardens. After all, without the slug the complex processes that lead to plant pollination and a healthy physical ecology for plant growth are made vulnerable. It is the same for children and youth. A safe school policy, a bus driver who greets the child by name, a grandparent who asks the child to visit, and a smorgasbord of other opportunities combine to offer children and youth what they need to thrive. Counseling is most effective when it acknowledges this complex weave of associations and supports. Alone, the counselor cannot be effective any more than a gardener can succeed without the complexity of an entire ecosystem to grow her plants.

If we borrow this understanding of ecology as a complex system we come to a very different model for clinical intervention. Why work with the delinquent directly when we can coach a janitor to be the young person's inspiration for change? If ten sessions into our work with a young woman who is at risk of abusing intravenous drugs and contracting HIV she identifies the mother of her drug-dealing boyfriend as someone whom she trusts, why wouldn't we reboot therapy and engage the boyfriend's mother in family counseling? Every part of a system has the potential to be important to a change process.

This means that the tidy five-step process of therapy cannot be easily controlled. New information is constantly changing the resources that are available and accessible to protect children and help them grow. It's for this reason that the five phases overlap when using an ecological approach to intervention. It's also why I called the fifth phase transition. Other models of intervention sometimes refer to the end of therapy as termination, which makes sense if therapy is about what the clinician does with the client rather than what the client needs to sustain change in the less than forgiving social and physical ecologies that exist beyond the counselor–client relationship. If the clinical work stops, then the process we call counseling ends too. That needn't happen if we rely less on professionals and more on people's natural supports. When every phase of our intervention helps us to consider options for sustainability, then we are much more likely to consider the contribution that a janitor or a boyfriend's mother can make to resolving a young person's problems. These other people can be powerful forces for growth if we look at them in the right way and consider them when we engage, assess, contract, work, and transition. They are the client's powerful allies who continue to pursue the goals of counseling long after the counselor leaves the stage.

Phase 1: Engagement

It's one of the ironies of clinical practice that very nice people who are very good at forming relationships with others become counselors who then struggle to engage with their clients because their communication becomes weighted down by what they think they are supposed to say. Many counselors, when starting out, are so afraid of doing something wrong that the magic of what they used to do before they were trained gets lost. Let's first, then, begin with advice from Mary Catherine Bateson (2008), a family systems researcher and daughter of Gregory Bateson, the father of human cybernetics. Mary Catherine Bateson tells us, "For better or worse, I always say what comes into my head." It's that genuineness that makes counseling feel like a friendly, albeit focused, conversation. Duncan, Hubble and Miller (1997) view the process of engagement as the dethroning of themselves as experts, "courting" the client to join them in an embarrassingly simple process of finding the client's strengths and making the changes that are important to them. The counselor takes the lead creating this space because counseling is such an unnatural space in which two or more people encounter each other. A good process of engagement reassures the client that this new relationship will be focused on their needs and respect the broader social ecology from which they come.

For example, when Perry and Thurston (2007) reviewed programs that provide sexual health information to adolescents, they found that the services that encouraged young people to bring along their friends and sexual partners were the ones most likely to engage youth. In cases where the young people were already sexually active, condoms were provided. Both strategies show respect for the client and demonstrate concretely an appreciation for the world in which the client lives. Need condoms? Service providers have them. Need information about sexual health? Makes sense to include the young person's partners and peers who are going to reinforce both negative and positive behavior.

When we think about engagement ecologically, then we are also going to appreciate that clients live in complex social ecologies that influence their decision to come to counseling, even when counseling is mandated by a court or other administrative body. When McKay et al. (1998) studied intake procedures at a children's mental health center, business as usual was a 20–30 minute intake call during which basic information on the child and the child's problem was gathered. Next, a brief assessment was done to see if there was a good fit between the child and the mental health center's programs. McKay and her colleagues changed this interview for new intakes to help caregivers invest in the counseling process by looking at their part in the child's problems and anticipate barriers to counseling, such as negative past experiences with therapists. Another group of potential clients received these extended intake phone calls and contact with a therapist who had received eight hours of specialized training in client engagement. During that training, the counselor learned how to clarify expectations regarding the helping process, develop a collaborative relationship with the client, get down to practical concerns quickly, and address barriers to counseling. Not surprisingly, families that received the briefest intake calls stayed in counseling the shortest period of time (5 sessions); those that received the longer phone calls were likely to stick with counseling a little longer (5.9 sessions); those that received the longer phone calls and the services of a therapist trained in engagement skills lasted an average of 7.3 sessions.

Examples like this teach us that the first meeting counts, especially when the therapist pays attention to more than the client's motivation. The more our first contact meets people's needs as they define them (think negotiation) the more likely they are to sustain contact with a service provider. That means clarifying from the very beginning the role of the counselor, the agency, and the intake process so that clients are certain they are getting the right service for the problem they've identified. Too often, however, first sessions become part of complicated assessments that meet the needs of agencies but do little to engage the client. Echoing the same argument, Mark Smith and his colleagues (Smith et al., 2011) showed that when social workers work with involuntary service users, "formal social work procedures, such as professional-dominated meetings, dense reports and risk assessment forms, hinder user engagement at the level of front line practice . . . If social work is to develop user engagement in a way that is meaningful for the 'users' involved, then these systems should be drastically reduced, revised and simplified so that they support relational working, rather than undermining it" (p. 1463).

One way to counter this tendency toward overly bureaucratizing the engagement phase of clinical work is to create a collaborative relationship that makes counseling transparent. This is extremely important to a social ecological approach to counseling. Because there is likely to be lots of information shared with the counselor, it is best to make counseling transparent from the start. If I as the counselor know something about a client because I read it in a case file or discussed the client with another professional, then I must make sure the client knows exactly what I know. Only when I am working with different family members and they are all my clients will I keep secrets (even then, I prefer we negotiate a way for anything I know to be shared). Transparency builds trust and avoids the insidious pathologizing that takes place when professionals talk among themselves and characterize a client as dangerous, delinquent, deviant, or disordered. I prefer to start a process that builds resilience by ensuring the client has access to all the same information I have, including her assessments and what others say about her. After all, our goal will eventually be to change the client's experience well beyond the confines of my office. How can she do that if she isn't aware of the labels she carries?

When we think ecologically about engagement we also consider aspects of who we are as counselors, the physical spaces we occupy, barriers (and bridges) our agencies erect that affect access to services, and our verbal and nonverbal communication. None of these are free of the politics of class and culture. All are vested with meaning. Is our clothing so different from our clients' that they perceive the potential for class bias? Will they believe us when we say, "I understand"? Then again, could our differentness be a comfort? Are we seen as someone beyond the world of our clients, an individual who can bring the perspective of an objective outsider? What will behaviors like extended periods of silence or eye contact mean to clients from different cultures where, for example, it is considered rude for lower status individuals to look directly into the face of higher status ones? Will our offices intimidate? Should we expect children to sit in chairs or will we join them on the floor?

Pondering these questions, we are likely to change what we do to make it easier for clients from challenging social ecologies to engage. It is never, however, just up to us. For example, Landau,

Mittal and Wieling (2008) created ARISE (A Relational Intervention Sequence for Engagement) that works with a person's natural supports to motivate the person to enter counseling. The focus on the therapist is decreased in favor of the influence family and friends can exert. Engagement proceeds through three steps. Step one, the counselor or another professional tries to engage the client, usually someone with a mental health problem or addiction. When that fails a level two intervention follows. The professional caller works through the client's network of concerned others to convince the client to come to counseling. If there is still no progress, the client's natural supports enact consequences for the client to convince her she needs help. There is a firm commitment and follow-through that compels the client to address her problems.

I like the approach mostly because it lets us counselors off the hook. I don't have to be the one with the magic wand who will somehow convince my client to attend sessions. Nor am I left to do my work all on my own. Right from the very beginning, I have the support of the client's network of concerned individuals. The client's transition out of counseling, as well as the support I'll need to conduct a thorough assessment and to be creative in how I work systemically, are all problems solved from the very beginning of the engagement phase with the client. When it is a collaborative process, the surprising experience for many counselors is that even involuntary clients are appreciative of the help offered (Smith et al., 2011). Research has shown that people appreciate help navigating and negotiating, even from service providers they are mandated to see. That appreciation, however, depends on whether the clinician is able to focus on the client's needs as the client defines them. In the negotiations for a service contract where counseling is forced on the client, good counselors always seek the fulfillment of both the client's goals and the service provider's, never just one or the other.

Phase 2: Assessment

An assessment should be for the benefit of the client, not the counselor. If that sounds obvious, it can often seem that the questions that are asked and the process through which assessment takes place gather information that the client doesn't value. I like to think of assessment as a collaborative search for what are meaningful explanations for a client's problem. As the therapist, we can suggest useful places to look and helpful metrics upon which to base our assessment (for example, is the client scoring high on a depression inventory?), but whenever possible, an assessment should be transparent and inform work the client wants to do.

The only exception is mandated treatment. When asked to perform a parenting capacity assessment for the court, or a predisposition report for probation services, our assessments may be driven more by the third-party client than the individual sitting in front of us. Who are we really working for? As long as that is made clear, and the goal is to provide third parties with the information they need, then even these assessments can be done collaboratively. I routinely include a few paragraph synopsis that clients themselves help me write to ensure that my reports reflect the clients' voices as well as my own.

At the heart of this process is an opportunity for a client to define her problem in ways that make sense to her. "I'd go to school if my high school had a daycare so I could take my daughter with me," says the teenage mother of a 9-month-old. "I'd stop stealing cars if someone gave me a real job," an adolescent boy tells me while in custody for the third time. I needn't always agree with my client's assessment of their problem, but their self-assessments always give me clues to what we can work on together. The young mother wants her education and an advocate for services for her child. The adolescent boy would like to earn money legitimately if he could. With regard to my assessment, both are telling me a great deal about what they value and their hopefulness for the future.

A comprehensive assessment should be of sufficiently wide scope, then, to address issues related to young people's navigations and negotiations. To understand navigation patterns, we need to know:

- What resources have been available in the past and present, and which are expected in the future?
- What coping strategies has the client used? Which, if any, were preferred?
- What are the barriers (internal and external) that the client faces to accessing the resources he needs?

To understand negotiations, we will need to ask:

- Of the coping strategies being used, which are the most meaningful?
- Which coping strategies fit best with the client's context and culture?
- What do these coping strategies mean to others who are important to the client?
- What labels does the client carry? Which are acceptable, and which would the client like to change?

Notice that I focus as much on problems as solutions. When I work with young people in very challenging contexts with complex needs, I have found that being Pollyannaish, focusing exclusively on solutions, and ignoring the very real social injustices and lack of access to resources they experience, results in my being quickly fired by my clients. It's as if they think I'm too out of touch to help them. That doesn't mean I focus exclusively on barriers to change, either. Barriers tend to figure most prominently, though, when I start working with a young person and her family.

I learned this sequence of moving from barriers to solutions from a colleague of mine in the field of education. A Principal at an urban school where children who were expelled from other schools went as their last stop before the street, he took a unique approach to his students: he believed they could change, but not alone. To sensitize his staff to the real barriers their students experienced, he arranged for educators to do home visits with the students they taught. It was an eye-opening experience for most that helped teachers understand why assignments weren't passed in and students fell asleep at their desks. What those teachers saw were often homes in disarray and parents struggling to survive. Suddenly, homework took on a new meaning. Where would a child do her homework, and who would be there to help her when she couldn't understand a question? These were the very real barriers these children experienced to achieving academically. With this contextualized understanding of the child's life, educators were better able to match solutions (like in-school supports) to children's academic needs.

An assessment that is contextualized can still capture intrapsychic aspects of functioning like motivation, self-esteem, cognitive function, attachment to others, and psychopathology. But it captures these individual antecedents of behavior in the context of the systemic dimensions of a child's life. At the level of the family, an ecological assessment examines the transgenerational transmission of values and behaviors such as substance abuse, school drop out, and the trauma caused by exposure to racism. The focus is as much on the collective story the family tells about itself as it is the individual child's role in that story. For example, a family that is wary of medications may have good reason to be skeptical of psychiatric interventions if a grandparent was treated badly inside an institution. Likewise, another family may express doubts about the value of a good education when all the parents have known their entire lives is exclusion from opportunities to succeed economically, regardless of whether or not they graduated from high school.

A good ecological assessment moves beyond the evaluation of specific factors to the assessment of interactions. We want to know why a child who appears defiant at home is compliant at daycare, or vice versa. Why does an early adolescent appear to be following in his older brother's footsteps when seeking out delinquent youth rather than following the role model of a cousin who excels at sports? Though beyond the scope of this book, there are numerous quantitative and qualitative assessment tools that can capture the diversity of coping patterns at multiple systemic levels.

I especially like visual representations that capture the inherent chaos of client's lives like genograms and ecomaps (for good examples, see Chapter 9 of Ungar, 2011). Both are drawings done collaboratively with the client to track relationships and themes. A good genogram looks a lot like a family tree with words and phrases next to people's names, ages, and their role vis-à-vis the client. If the client is wrestling with an addiction, then the genogram can be used to identify other members of his family who also struggled with a similar problem. Just as importantly, it can also tell us who resisted the pull into an addiction. Done well, a genogram provides insight into the nature versus nurture debate. Pictured are all the family members and the myriad of different coping strategies they've used. Why do some succeed and others follow predictable patterns of problem development? The visual representation can focus a conversation with the client and explore past, present, and the potential for future coping strategies. It can help to show where responsibility lies for observable patterns of behavior. Was it bad "genes," bad "luck," or bad "government" that made people the way they are?

An ecomap is another visual representation. I use a technique adapted from the work of Paolo Freire, the South American popular educator who worked with peasant laborers teaching them both literacy skills and conscientizing them to the reasons for their oppression (for example, exploitive landlords, greedy employers, corrupt governments). The ecomaps I do are not so dramatic but they do provide a visual representation of all the important relationships between clients and the individuals and institutions that affect them. For example, a foster child's ecomap would show the child at the centre of a tangled weave of lines connecting the client to child welfare services, social workers, mental health therapists, educators, school boards, government policies, and the state funding required for independent living when the youth transitions out of care. Where a genogram is all about family connections, an ecomap provides a snapshot of the many people and institutions that facilitate or constrain a client's navigations and negotiations for resources.

Interview guides and questionnaires approach assessment differently. These tools pose either open-ended questions or require the client to respond on a set scale, usually from 1–5 or something similar. Appendix 6.1 includes a list of many of the questions I use during the course of an ecological intervention to explore different aspects of a client's life. All the questions are never asked to any one client, but like all the other phases of intervention, assessment occurs incrementally over the course of treatment. Over time, a good many of these questions do eventually get answered. I have had new information emerge about a child's home just at the point of discharge from a residential program just as I've have a child tell me in our first session about the person who will take responsibility for supporting the child once our treatment ends. A good assessment tool provides the clinician with hints as to what to ask about multiple dimensions of the client's life. It is more, though, like a drawer of cooking utensils than a recipe book with detailed instructions for what to do next. The assessment tool in Appendix 6.1 is a systematic inquiry that includes:

- Demographic information.
- Problem-focused questions.
- Client's definition of the problem.
- History of the problem.
- Solution-focused questions.
- Support for solutions.
- Individual resources and barriers.
- Family resources and barriers.
- Community resources and barriers.
- The counselor's role in the community.

Instructions on how to summarize the results of the assessment and when to update results are also included.

The final set of assessment tools are standardized quantitative or qualitative measures that clinicians use to assess clients and the capacity of their social ecologies. When a comprehensive set of tools is used, capturing multiple aspects of the client's life and systemic interactions (for example, the relationship between parents and child, parents and school, school and child, etc.), an assessment can provide a reassuring picture of the risks and resilience a child experiences. These tools are, however, of limited use clinically unless one also asks clients to explain what the results mean to them. I'm as curious why they answered questions the way they did as I am about the tidy charts I can produce at the end of the assessment which show me graphically a child's strengths and challenges. For example, a 28-item measure of resilience (the Child and Youth Resilience Measure) that my colleague Linda Liebenberg and I have developed includes questions about individual, relational, and cultural strengths that have been shown to predict good mental health and behavioral outcomes across cultures (Ungar & Liebenberg, 2011). I am always amazed, though, that even simple questions such as, "I talk to my family/caregiver(s) about how I feel," "I cooperate with people around me," and "I am treated fairly in my community" can mean very different things to different children in different contexts. In some cultures, feelings are seldom discussed inside the family meaning that children score low on the first question but don't perceive their low score as a problem. Likewise, many delinquent youth who participate in antisocial behavior with their peers score high on cooperation, the second question. Meanwhile, boys and girls of different ages will differ somewhat in their perception of whether they are treated fairly, the third question. When using standardized measures in clinical practice it is highly recommended that you also include time to talk about what the questions mean to your client. This mixed methods approach to assessment helps us to contextualize findings.

Phase 3: Contracting

While all five phases of intervention are important, in my experience it is the clarity of the contract that best ensures progress is made toward the goals clients and counselors set. Most counselors are adept at engaging clients, doing whatever they can to make coming to counseling seem less frightening and the relationship with a counselor one of trust and commitment. Assessments are reasonably straightforward in that they elicit information, or, when done exceptionally well, create a life narrative for the client that includes both problems and solutions, initiates a process of self-reflection, and makes it clear that clients' lives are lived in complex non-linear relationships with others.

But contracting, that is something different. Most of the clinicians I supervise make one of two missteps during the contracting phase. The first is letting the client lead them from one crisis to the next, never clearly identifying the goals for counseling, nor the indicators of success. In such a state, the counselor may sustain a very engaging therapeutic alliance with the client but the work will be long and disjointed. It will be difficult to know what should be discussed, for how long, and what changes are the ones that signal therapy has succeeded and clients need to transition into other relationships.

The second most common error when contracting is to decide on a fixed contract, often signed, that is narrowly focused on the initial problem the individual client names (for example, "I can't sleep"; "My teacher says I'm a bully"; "My father abused me") and ignore broader systemic factors or new information that emerges during the assessment. When the focus of the clinical work becomes one obvious problem, it is difficult to think more ecologically. Clients, after all, seldom come to counseling with a deep and critical perspective on their problem. Foreclosing too quickly on what the client says she needs and the work that needs to be done will make the client–therapist interaction inflexible. There can be so much emphasis on a single problem that all the contributing factors are overlooked. A child who can't sleep may be worried about his parents' fighting and potential for divorce; a child who bullies may be embarrassed by a learning disorder; a child who has been abused may be more concerned with the stigma associated with her abuse and apprehension into care than the abuse itself.

Therapists who limit the scope of their work to fulfilling a contract in only one way also run the risk that they stop engaging new participants in therapy, or forget that the sustainability of their clinical intervention depends on how well the client later transitions out of counseling and back into relationships with other services and supports. A good contract is one that remains focused on the goals set by the client so that progress is easy to observe and measure, but doesn't get in the way of innovation and inspiration when new solutions present themselves at different systemic levels. Even if one begins by working with a child alone to help her modify her sleeping habits, it would be a shame not to also find a way to work with the parents if much of the child's explanation for her problem sleeping is the fighting she hears in the next room or the lack of structure around bedtime.

For these reasons, an ecological approach focuses attention on how to include a client's many natural supports in the very early phases of treatment. It is fairly easy to engage natural supports by extending them an invitation to attend a session (few refuse when the focus is on helping the client), or better, relocating a session to a client's home or school. Getting people in to see a counselor is relatively simple when compared to making sure the intervention includes the multiple perspectives on problems and solutions that are now present in the room. Counseling can stumble if the client and the client's natural supports disagree on what needs to change and why. When contracting with a client's family or community, it is crucial to view them as important sources of meaning that influence what the client believes about her problem and the solutions to it. In the circular patterns of communication (Tomm, 1988) that characterize families and communities, the questions counselors ask become a way for groups of people to discuss their competing perspectives. Multiple players will each have a different story to tell about the influence of the problem in their lives (White, 2007). That's a lot of helpful information with which to shape a contract.

Overt and Covert Contracts

Contracts can be overt or covert. The overt contract describes what the client says he'll do to change and what we as counselors will do to help. These can be verbal agreements but they are often written to satisfy the needs of the counselor's agency for a record of treatment.

My experience, however, is that no client has ever held back from doing anything he wanted to do just because he signed a contract with me that told him to do otherwise. If he was that compliant then he would likely never have been referred to me as he could have listened to the sage advice of those already in his life. Instead, I believe clients engage their therapists in covert contracts. They come to counseling with expectations for change and commit to doing whatever they can do to cope in challenging contexts. Their covert contract is what they do, rather than what they say. Sometimes the contract is no more sophisticated than that the client agrees to come back to another session and try to form a trusting bond with his counselor. All the other high-minded goals aside, the covert contract may be nothing more than learning to trust.

Ideally, we can see when people "vote with their feet" and engage or disengage from counseling. We can find mutually agreed upon goals, some out in the open, others more process-oriented and hard to define. If clients walk in the door, however, then they are usually ready to work on something that will make their lives better. The point of a good contract is that it lets everyone know what they are doing when the work is underway. For example, if I sign a contract with a young person to stop his self-harming behaviors and he comes back to see me a week later with new scratch marks on his wrists, I may become frustrated and think he has not fulfilled his end of the bargain. What I miss, however, unless I am thinking much more ecologically, is that the client came back! Here he is one more time looking to me for help and testing whether I'll abandon him like so many others. If I'm paying attention, I'll understand that our covert contract is to develop a sustainable trusting relationship at any price.

In such cases, we may not be able to name the specifics of the contract, but we may be able to behave like the contract is firm. I might simply compliment the young man on coming back to see me and express how glad I am to see he didn't harm himself any worse. Any good contract follows people's leads. Specifically, it restates the problem or problems that are the focus of the intervention. It is always preferable to name a problem using words that are meaningful to the client: the child who describes "giggles" may mean anxiety; the child who says he wants to stop being "angry" may mean he is frustrated with being teased because of a learning disability.

Phase 4: Working

The work phase is usually the longest phase as it is the point in counseling when change is accomplished in one or more of the following six areas:

- How clients behave, individually and in groups.
- The resources that clients experience as available.
- The resources that clients experience as accessible.
- The messages clients hear about the choices they make.
- The stories clients tell about themselves and others.
- How clients feel about themselves and their lives.

The work phase is the point at which the counselor uses the 10 navigation and 10 negotiation skills to facilitate changes in the way the client copes with challenges and the way the client's social ecology makes resources available and accessible. Change occurs at multiple levels simultaneously, whenever possible. For example, a 10-year-old girl who is struggling to change an unhealthy diet may come to see me for help to bolster her sense of self-esteem and develop the necessary social skills to expand her network of friends. She may also want to avoid the children in her neighborhood who tease her about her weight. The intervention will likely include conversations with a nutritionist at the children's hospital and networking with a neighborhood YMCA that has a program for adolescent girls that focuses on body image. Of course, research tells us that children have little success with weight loss or lifestyle changes unless there is coordination between the child's parents, school, and community supports (Pinhas-Hamiel et al., 2005). A change in only one support system is unlikely to cause sustainable change for the child. During the work phase, counseling becomes an opportunity to influence all of these different systems, including the girl herself. While the presenting problem is very individual, the solution is anything but.

No wonder, the nature of the work done during the work phase is usually quite complex. Though the goals are clear and good clinical work stays focused on the contract, the lives of people who live in very challenging contexts are too complex to offer a simple recipe for success. The counselor helps the client navigate and negotiate better, but separating the two processes can be like taking salt from water. Easy enough if you boil it down, but when mixed together they look like one and the same. Clinically, it is easier to show what an ecologically-trained counselor does during the work phase than it is to explain the microprocesses in isolation.

Phase 5: Transition

We've come a long way since individual psychotherapy was held up as the very best approach to treatment. Systems thinking, and now complexity theory and ecological models of practice are making individual sessions look underpowered as engines for change. As Rita Chung and Frederic Bemak (2012) write about their model of social justice counseling, "Given the challenges of daily life, globalization, changes, and transitions, it is clear that for mental health professionals and counselors to be truly effective, they need to move beyond their traditional role of providing psychotherapy and counseling. What may appear to be effective during psychotherapy and counseling is limited, since it is easily erased once clients leave counseling sessions and interact with the real world outside of therapy" (p. 40). It's a potent warning echoed by researchers (DuMont, Ehrhard-Dietzel & Kirkland, 2012; Harvey, 2007). When clients are confronting serious injustice and challenging, toxic social environments, the psychotherapist has an obligation to consider the client's transition back to the real world.

Why limit ourselves, then, to the motivational power of the counselor when a child's social ecology is rich in supportive others? Of course, those others also bring with them the potential to put a child down and thwart the child's progress. That too is fine if we see those negative patterns as opportunities to understand the child's world better. I would rather see the interpersonal dynamics that are holding my client back (and have the potential to propel the client forward) played out in my office in real-time than guess what the child experiences at home. At least then when the client looks at me, pleading with her eyes for me to understand her dilemma, there will be no doubt I've seen first-hand the barriers she faces.

From the moment of first contact, an ecological approach to counseling looks for the natural supports that can play a pivotal role in a client's success. Our goal is to put in place the resources required for clients to make smooth transitions toward new behaviors and later, to help them disengage from counseling. The better I am at providing my clients with access to significant others who know the changes my clients have made and can applaud my clients for making those changes, the more likely my clients are to sustain processes of change. Only a therapist who considers himself the engine of change would ever speak about the termination of counseling. Does the therapeutic work end just because we aren't there to do it? Most of the really good therapists I've had the honor to work with never terminate treatment. Instead, they recognize that it is the client who is responsible for change and time spent together in a therapeutic alliance is just one of the client's many sources of support critical to coping with complex problems (Blundo, 2001). As long as a plan is in place to support the changes that are made, those changes stand a better chance of being sustained through the client's relationships with others who will be there long after the counselor leaves.

There are many things we can do as counselors to make these transitions easier for clients. Among the most effective are:

- Show don't tell: Help the client to find opportunities to show others how she has changed. It's one thing to anticipate behavioral changes. It's another to actually advocate for a client to find work, a new school, or change her peer group. Each of these changes brings with it new opportunities to perform a different identity and to receive recognition from others for the better coping strategies the client puts into practice.
- An open door: Our offices can be places for others who have succeeded to tell their stories. These "outsider witnesses," as Michael White (2007) called them, can make transitions seem more manageable. They can also be supports to the client when a bond is formed, inspiring the client to carry the changes made during counseling out into the world beyond the clinic's front door.
- Transparency: What we do in counseling needn't be perceived as magic. Good counselors train the client's natural supports to look after the client as competently as the counselor (and often better). If, for example, we have managed to calm an anxious child in our office, there is no better person to share our techniques with than the child's parents, teachers, case aide, or an extended family member with whom the child has contact.
- Anticipate setbacks: It is unlikely that children make a change for the better once and never look back. We know from studies of resilience that positive developmental trajectories are always full of developmental hiccups. The child who has managed to cope with anxiety-provoking situations and develop a supportive group of peers in elementary school is very likely to revisit some of her earlier troubling behaviors when she transitions to junior high and is forced to change peer group and become more independent. By naming the possibility of impending problems and talking about strategies to cope (including turning to one's natural supports to revisit the work done during counseling), these delays in development don't have to become long downward spirals.

Counselors have many ways to make these transitions work smoothly. If sessions have been audio-taped or videotaped, reviewing them is a great tool to reinforce the changes that have been made. Even better if we share these videos with the child's new audience so that they can see how much the child has changed and reinforce new behaviors. A scrapbook that documents the new story a child tells about herself is also a powerful way to capture the changes that are being made. I love when clients bring to our final meeting, or a follow-up session, some artifact of their life like a photograph, newspaper clipping, or memento given them by a special adult in their life in recognition of the changes they've made. Letters of celebration work too. Writing a letter to a client after counseling ends is a useful way of documenting the progress the client made and encouraging her to use her natural supports when the next crisis hits. Likewise, simple celebrations during the final session or discharge from a program are always helpful ways to reinforce the new capacity the client has to undertake the transition the client is about to undertake. Case conferences can play their part too, especially when they become opportunities to review the client's progress and contribute to the celebrations.

Most effective, by far, however, is simply helping the client find a new space in which to perform her new coping strategy. To transition to junior high and make a new friend or not become anxious when riding a different school bus may seem small achievements for most of us. For the child who has performed uncomfortably earlier in life, a little success in the real world is going to be incredibly useful in reinforcing the changes she's made. If counselors have the luxury of reserving a follow-up session for later, the counselor too can be part of the child's transition team, reinforcing the changes the counselor sees the child sustaining.

With all these possibilities for smoothing client's transitions, it is remarkable that we sustain counseling longer than is necessary. A large study by Michael Barkham and his colleagues (Barkham et al., 2006) in Britain showed that for clients who left counseling with the agreement of their counselor (in other words, both client and their counselor agreed clinical goals had been met), 87.5% of those who left after just two sessions reported success. That number steadily declined the more sessions people attended, with only 61.7% of clients reporting success after 12 sessions. Of course, we could argue that people with more intransigent problems remain in counseling longer and may find solutions to problems much more difficult to achieve. However, there is also a suggestion in Barkham et al.'s study that more sessions don't always increase client satisfaction nor improve outcomes. Ecologically speaking, it may be better to transition clients back to their own natural supports as early as is feasibly possible.

In the following case example, I illustrate how a series of interviews with a mother and her daughter moved them toward a resolution of some long-standing problems. The case study is also useful as an example of how the five phases of intervention overlap.

Case Study: Christine and Tania

Christine was in her late thirties, though the black circles beneath her eyes and gray hair made her look ten years older. Her daughter, Tania, had just turned 16 years old. Tania's father, Christine's second husband, died of an aneurism two years earlier. Christine's eldest daughter, Pauline, was the result of a teenage marriage that ended before Pauline was even born. Pauline, who ran away at age 16, was 21 years old when I met the family, married and a mother. She wasn't close to Christine or Tania and seldom visited. Tania, meanwhile, couldn't wait to leave home and live independently like her sister.

Tania and Christine were referred to counseling at a prevention program operated by a service for homeless and street-involved youth. The referral came from Tania's school guidance counselor after Tania failed to attend classes for an entire semester. Tania had previously run away once and lived in a local youth shelter for a month. Everyone was worried that Tania would end up on the street permanently, without the supports she needed to make a successful transition to independent living.

It was a bleak picture that overlooked many of Tania's strengths. Despite her weakness academically, she'd held a job as a supermarket cashier for eight months before being fired when she lied about being ill. She also had a clear vision of her future. She wanted to be a hairdresser and knew that she could go to college at age 19 without having finished high school. As well, despite having lived on the street for many months, she had avoided developing a drug habit or getting pregnant, both risks that had affected many of her friends.

Of course, being at home brought with it risks as well. Christine moved her and Tania to the east coast five years earlier. A friend of Christine's, another single parent, had invited Christine and Tania to share a home with her. Christine found work as a supervisor at a call center that offered customer service for a large appliance maker. Christine liked to joke she's "Mrs. Fix-it" at work but hadn't a clue how to make things work better at home. When Christine and her friend got into a heated argument over chores and money, Christine and Tania decided it was best to move out on their own. They were given a subsidized apartment in a downtown low-rise housing development called the Project. They are one of the few families living there with a parent who is employed full time, though Christine's salary is so low that some months she and Tania are forced to use the food bank to get by. Adding to Christine's stress were problems in the housing development that is never safe day or night. Christine was constantly worried about her daughter going out alone and fretted endlessly about her and her daughter's safety.

My role, according to the guidance counselor who made the referral, was to salvage what I could of Tania and Christine's relationship, hopefully making it possible for Tania to stay with her mother until she turned 18 years old. I was also asked to help Tania reconsider her educational needs and encourage her to broaden her employment goals. I told the guidance counselor I'd do what I could, but was hesitant to commit until I'd met the family and heard what they each wanted to accomplish.

Session One

Though both Christine and Tania attended this first session, Tania made it very clear as she came into my office that "I ain't talking. You can ask my mother whatever you like, but I don't want to be here, and I'm only here because she threatened me that if I didn't come I wouldn't get a drive anywhere for the next month." I wasn't surprised, nodded, and agreed to the condition. After introductions and small talk, I asked Christine what brought them to this community.

Christine: My girlfriend invited me out here, said why don't you come out for a few years. She was someone that we did things together.
Michael: What happened to your friend?
Christine: What happened to my friend? Ha ha! She found a boyfriend out here and that changed everything. And she became quite different. And had no real time for me or Tania.
Tania: Come on, they had a big fight. Tell the truth why don't you. You always lie. Because they had a falling out.
Christine: Yes, we did have a falling out and that's why we don't spend time together.
Michael: Well, I know I can't ask questions of Tania directly, so maybe Christine, can you tell me what did Tania think of this, of the move here?
Christine: Well she was just little. So what could she say?

I stored this bit of information for later use, writing mom's words on the notepad I kept on my lap while we talked. What was becoming clear watching Tania and her mother interact was that Tania wanted to be treated as her mother's equal, speaking to her like she would a peer. Christine, meanwhile, was embarrassed by her daughter's outburst, and subtly reminded her that she was, and still is, her child and that it is Christine who makes the decisions for the family. Pausing to consider this dynamic, I was struck by how intensely Tania was negotiating with her mother for an identity as an adult. The conversation shifted to when Tania left home. Despite her reluctance to participate, Tania preferred to tell her own story rather than have Christine tell it for her. With her permission, I was happy to change the rules and ask her questions directly.

Michael: Did you go directly from home to the shelter? After you left your mother's?

Tania: I went to see some friends first.

Michael: Hmm, so what made it necessary for you to go to the shelter?

Christine: The way that happened is I kicked her out.

Tania: In the middle of the night she changed the locks, in the middle of the night, she locks me out all because she thinks I'm going to go off and be a prostitute because I have these pink pants, and get this, I just go out for a walk and then I come home and the locks are changed. So I go around the back door and no, can't get in there either. And then she throws a note out the upstairs window that says, "You can go to Chelsea's house if there is a bed available." No warning whatsoever. It was so horrible.

Christine: Sure it was horrible, but what else was I to do. She was still just 15. She wouldn't listen to me.

Michael: To get to that point, I'm guessing you must have been very frustrated. Both of you. Were there problems before you moved here?

Christine: No big problems, but let me put it this way, she was just turning 12 when we moved, and just before that Tania had just lost her dad. He died.

Tania: *(Yelling at her mother)* That doesn't have anything to do with this!

Christine: I think it has a lot to do with everything.

Tania: It had a lot to do with you, but nothing to do with me.

Christine: Well maybe that is the case, I don't know *(Christine changes the topic and Tania gnashes her teeth. After a moment, both calm down)*. But anyway, Tania never did very well at school. I never expected her to get good grades. I just wanted her to pass, but didn't want you to be too uptight. I wanted you to enjoy your school years, your childhood. So she just went through, just did what she needed to do to pass. Except in art, then she gets A's. She's very talented but hates when I say that. Then she started losing interest in school, her and her friends, they'd be wandering around, cutting class.

Tania: What? Are you talking about Wendy? She's like 2 or 3 years older than me and we'd be out playing basketball at the park, something productive.

Christine: Well Tania wasn't doing her schoolwork and there might not have been anything wrong but she seemed to have no interest in school.

Tania: You're making no sense. That was all during the summer. I wasn't supposed to have an interest in school during the summertime. You're crazy, that's what you are.

Christine: Anyway, there was this worry about her losing interest in school. I just thought if she moved to another school, that might help her be less distracted by her friends. And then when we got here Tania had a very hard time of it, being here. And we lived in the Project and of course once I realized what the Project was like, I knew this was going to be difficult.

Michael: So let me see if I'm getting the story here, at least how Tania might explain things. Tania didn't want to move, she didn't want to be kicked out. And she doesn't want to be told how her father's death may or may not have affected her. If I'm understanding, Tania, you're saying you haven't felt in control of your life for some time.

Because children tend to be less willing to engage in treatment of any kind, I prefer to err on the side of over-representing their points of view first. My hope is that it engages them by making counseling more meaningful. It also pays attention to one of the seven factors that children need to be resilient, a sense of personal efficacy. In this case, the strategy worked marvelously. Tania broke my initial contract with her and participated more than she said she would. My only disappointment was that I would have preferred to have had Tania speak in a civil manner and be heard rather than feeling that she had to be rude and abusive to get her mother to listen. With time, I changed that pattern, but at this point at which the above interview takes place, I just observed the pattern and used what I saw to inform my assessment of the family dynamics.

While I asked questions, I was also trying to understand not just Tania or Christine, but their interactional patterns, as well as their relationships with those outside of their family, including friends, their community, and institutions like school, the public housing authority, and Christine's employer. Each of these relationships provided information on the context and culture in which they lived. Each also provided resources, both useful and useless, that affected their well-being.

Finally, I received a lot of information about what each person meant when they spoke. Tania would tolerate none of her mother's suspicions that Tania is mourning the death of her father, nor that the girl is too young to make decisions for herself. Christine, meanwhile, appeared to be trying to play her role as parent as competently as she could and wanted others to see her in the same way. If Christine was negotiating with me for recognition as the caring parent, Tania was doing all she could to undermine that role and convince me she was a competent young woman ready to be on her own. In these negotiations I preferred not to take sides.

Having acknowledged Tania's version of the "truth" in the last piece of conversation, I next tried to help Tania hear what her mother had to say about her experience of their life together.

Michael: I hear you saying, Christine, that each strategy you used, was done to make things as best as they could be for your daughter. The moves, the way you let her relax at school, everything was, if I'm understanding, your way of trying to help her. Would you agree? (*Christine nods. I turn and address Tania*) Does that make at least some sense to you, that that was what your mom was trying to do?

Tania: I don't buy it. She came out for herself and now she's tried to convince everyone she's doing it for me, but that's not true.

Michael: So that's interesting, when you hear these stories of her trying to help you . . .

Tania: She's really trying to help herself.

Michael: Christine, you're also telling me Tania didn't do the things she would have had to do to help herself, like stay in school, and she probably never appreciated all that you were doing for her?

Christine: I don't think she ever realized what I'd done.

Tania: (*Changing the topic*) I think my mom thinks I'm so dumb. The other day she told me you can't reuse a condom. Like she thinks I'm so immature, like about day-to-day things I'm supposed to know nothing.

Christine: That's what she's always doing, criticizing me. (*Christine begins to cry*)

Tania: That's not criticism. That's just telling you like it is.

Michael: I'm a bit confused, you're 16, not 12, and out of school. Doing a lot of things we don't think of children doing. It's like I'm meeting an adult. And adults don't necessarily need their mothers to help them make decisions. It's as if you're telling me your life is under your control.

Christine: To a large extent, but if a person doesn't have her own money then her life really isn't under her own control.

Tania: I'm trying to get a job.

Michael: Sure, sure. Yes, that's important. But just in terms of how you each relate to each other, it does get to be a bit more . . . well, voluntary, doesn't it? You don't have to continue to live together.

Christine: Yes.

Michael: So, Tania, what brought you home? You were living in the shelter. I don't understand why you came back?

Tania: I was kicked out. Because I'd used up my days. I have to stay out for a couple of months before they'll let me back in.

Michael: So things at home, how are they day-to-day?

Christine: They're tense.

Tania: No they're not (*Laughing*). Except for the occasional time I ask her to come pick me up because I'm drunk. I've done that like three times.

Michael: And you call her.

Tania: Yeah, because I don't want to walk because we don't live in a very safe area.

Michael: That sounds like a very reasonable thing to do.

Christine: Oh yeah. It's a responsible thing. Mind you, there's other problems with her behavior, but that is, yes, responsible of her to call.

Carefully, I shifted the conversation to one in which Tania could be heard. Seizing the opportunity, she gives example after example of how she has made good decisions for herself, even if there remain many examples of ways she continues to place herself at risk. One cannot, however, understand Tania without understanding the culture and context in which she lives. Imagine a different context, one in a low-income country whose economy is based on agriculture and where children move much more quickly from childhood to adulthood, without years of adolescence. Commonly held beliefs which in my culture make us see young people as dependent and incompetent inform this conversation with Tania and Christine. Talking back to this understanding of childhood, I suggest that Christine and Tania are no longer mother and small child. Tania wanted a more peer-like relationship even though she is still dependent on her mother financially and in other instrumental ways such as helping to keep her safe late at night. Thinking about this as two intersecting conversations, I helped mother and daughter negotiate for a meaningful role for a 16-year-old in a stressed family (How independent can Tania become?). If Tania wanted to be an independent young woman she was going to have to do better than running from home and living at a youth shelter where there are more rules than she experienced at home.

My role, then, was two-fold. First, I needed to help Tania navigate her way to either work or school, both experiences which will convince others to see her as an adult. Second, I needed to see if I could heal the relationship between Tania and her mother, negotiating new roles for each as Tania matures. The remainder of our time together during this interview built on the themes that have emerged through our assessment of what each family member needed. While Tania's school may have been disappointed with me that I was willing to consider an atypical path to high school completion (dropping out, then completing high school as a mature student), Tania showed no resistance to working with me as long as I helped her convince her mother and guidance counselor that she was an adult who was ready to look after herself.

Michael: You went to school at St. Michael's? How did you do at school?

Tania: I didn't do very well at school. I just couldn't put up with the bullshit. The way I see it school is just a training ground for life. You learn to put up with bullshit. That's all. You don't need to know a bunch of little math equations. Stupid useless stuff I have no patience for.

Michael: You left in what grade?

Tania: Ten. I should have been in grade 11 but I never completed any courses. I'm going to get my GEDs [high school leaving credits] and become an esthetician, but I have to wait to do them until I'm 19. I even have the GED book. I've been studying it.

The conversation shifted away from conflict. Christine was upset with the school for expelling her daughter for missing classes. True, Tania stopped going to school, but Christine insisted that there were days when she had convinced Tania to attend but by that point the school had told her that unless Tania attended regularly, she was not to come to school at all. Tania was upset by this as she liked some of her teachers and wanted to stay engaged.

Christine: So she got kicked out in Grade 10. But I thought that's crazy, if my daughter wants to go to school even if she doesn't attend all the time she should be able to go. I even got our local politician involved. Tania wasn't even any trouble, or disruptive. But they insisted that she'd be holding the class back and said absolutely not. I just think that's wrong. I phoned the school board about it. But eventually I just gave up. They were all useless. I don't care if my daughter sits in the classroom and learns nothing, its better she's there.

Tania: No wonder I lost interest in school. Just listen to you. "I don't care if my daughter learns nothing."

Christine: That's not what I meant. I meant if you're not horsing around you should be there.

Michael: You never got kicked out for horsing around?

Tania: No, never.

Michael: Hmm, and have you been working?

Tania: Yeah, at Jamisons Pharmacy for eight months.

Michael: Oh yeah, okay. How did that go?

Tania: I got fired.

Michael: Oops.

Tania: She kicked me out and I didn't show up for a few days.

Michael: So you lost your job not because of your performance, but because you were living on the street.

Tania: Yeah. I was a cashier.

Michael: And you were able at 15 to hold down a job for 8 months.

Tania: Sometimes working like 30 hours a week.

Michael: How did you do that?

Tania: I just liked socializing with the people who worked there. The job sucked.

Michael: And what did you do with the money?

Tania: I'd pay $200 a month in rent, then the rest I'd get my nails done, stuff like that.

Christine: She came up with that all by herself, and as long as she was in school I didn't ask for it but once she dropped out then she paid me the money. And she did. She paid me every month. I thought that was perfect. That was showing a lot of maturity.

Michael: That's interesting because some families have trouble negotiating things like this, but you are both well ahead of other families. Most kids haven't by your age done so many responsible things.

Christine: Yeah.

In our continuing negotiations to define Tania as a young adult capable of taking responsibility for herself, I explored exceptions to the story of Tania as a high school drop-out with no future. It was becoming apparent that Tania hadn't completely disengaged from learning, just formal schooling. It was, however, very unlikely she would accept any intervention that put her back into a regular classroom. Instead, I needed to offer her a way of getting an education or employment that she would experience as meaningful. My questions continued to explore ways Tania could find the resources she needed, navigating to what made sense to her. No matter what my opinion of her plan was, in these negotiations I tried and let Tania be the expert on what she needed.

Michael: So Tania, you have a dream of what you want to become. An esthetician. So what would make the difference at home that would make it possible for you to stay at home and get your GEDs?

Tania: More trust at home. Not being followed down the street. She followed me down the street. It was my 16th birthday. I didn't want to be stuck at home. So I was meeting a friend that she doesn't like for whatever reasons. Just stubbornness. And I was waiting there on the street, not on the street corner, I was back by some bushes so no one would think I was a prostitute, and I could see her spying on me. Lack of trust. I don't even have a key to the house. That's what I mean. I have to leave when she's at work.

Christine: Just like it is at the shelter.

Tania: Not quite.

Christine: Maybe some of my rules are different but then nobody at the shelter cares about you like I do. Nobody would cry if you were found dead.

Michael: So Tania, you don't mind being at home but you just want a few changes.

Tania: She's always had such problems showing any trust in me. Like even when I'm on Facebook she'll go on and check who I've been speaking to. She's never shown me any trust.

Christine: There's a lot of danger being a teenaged girl online. You never really know who you're talking with, do you?

Michael: Do you still have a problem with this?

Tania: No, because she got rid of our computer.

Christine: No, here's what happened. We've had two break-ins. These kids kicked in our door and we had this beautiful computer system which I only bought because I had some money left to me by a woman who died who I knew. They took everything. The TV, the computer, my lovely jewelry. And they still haven't caught them. And I now have a steel door. But I wrote a letter to the police commission complaining about their response time. And the reason I kicked her out because, well she knows why.

Tania: She kicked me out because I was hanging out with this boy next door . . . and yes he used to hang out with these other kids in the area who were into gangs and breaking into houses and stuff, but he's not doing that stuff any more. But she doesn't believe me. She just tells me all the bad things about him. So I wasn't supposed to have any one in the house after the break-in, and I had him in and that's how I got kicked out.

There was a distinct shift in the conversation now. Mother and daughter were willing to discuss the real barriers to communication, including a lack of trust on both their parts. The challenge with a word like "trust," though, was that the meaning had to be negotiated. Tania insisted she was trustworthy, and that her mother was overstepping her rights as a parent. As the next passage shows, however, Christine had other more legitimate reasons to not trust her daughter.

Christine: That's exactly right. Tania was actually supposed to be going to work that day. She even said she didn't need a ride which is very unusual for Tania that she would walk.

Tania: I love walking. What do you mean?

Christine: Anyway, she refused the ride so I left then decided to come back and just see what was happening.

Tania: See what I mean, she doesn't trust me and she is always doing things like that, watching me.

Christine: Well when I got back to the house I was coming in the back door and could hear some male voice and Tania saying to him, "Give me my key" in a way that sounded like, to a mother, that he wasn't giving her the key. And then I walked into the foyer and there was this boy there, Clayton, who was still supposed to be on house arrest for holding a loaded gun to his uncle's head.

Tania: And haven't you heard a lot of positive things about him from our neighbor too?

Christine: I just thought, I want him out so I asked him to leave. Then the next day, it just kept on my mind and then I noticed Tania's key chain and no house key on it.

Tania: There hasn't been a key on it for a long time.

Christine: Anyway, I panicked and went to bed and just laid there wondering if Clayton had a key, or if Tania is so mad at me and comes home on Ecstasy, and what if she wanted to kill me and she and Clayton did something.

Tania: I wasn't on drugs.

Christine: That's when I said to Tania I can't live like this and asked her to leave.

Tania: And I'd said to her that was fine with me, only I was asking to not pay rent for a couple of months and save up my money and then leave on my own.

Out of fear for her safety, Christine was not willing to allow Tania to slowly navigate her way to independent living, but instead insisted she leave home prematurely. My explicit mandate was to prevent Tania from becoming homeless or leaving school. Sticking with my contract, I spent time talking about Tania's need for trust, Christine's fear, Tania's desire to work and eventually get more training, and the need to stabilize Tania's living situation. All these issues were linked. To accomplish these goals, I had to be attentive to how this family is different from others in the Project and Tania's paradoxical desire to drop out of school but still enter a college training course. In this strange pattern of navigation and negotiation, it would seem that helping Tania leave home and find work was not only our best option, it was also the one that would make both Tania and her mother most happy.

Michael: Well, let me see if I can pull this together. We could certainly work on getting more trust to be there between your mom and you Tania. *(Looking at Christine)* But I don't know if I can do that by making Tania change her friends or go back to school. *(Looking at Tania)* I'm going to have to assume that there are things happening on the streets that you know much more about than I can ever know and that you are making your life work for yourself as best you can. I'm going to have to rely on you to tell me and your mom how you keep yourself safe. And obviously in some ways you've been quite successful. You're 16 and have no drug problem, even held a job for 8 months.

Tania: I even had a job before I left school.

Michael: Hmm, so am hearing you both say that you would like to have some kind of relationship? No matter where Tania is living.

Tania: I never said I wanted to end our relationship.

Christine: Well, yeah, I just want Tania to know I care about her very much and am just so worried about her. *(Crying)* It's all my fault. Her dropping out of school.

Tania: I keep telling her, "You don't need a lot of education to be successful." If you're smart with your money. There are lots of people, like the guy who owns Virgin records. You can be very rich without school. Even a high school drop out can do okay.

Michael: So you need your mom to leave you alone more, to trust you. And she would if she wasn't so afraid what was going to happen. When I'm working with a family, I try to find something we can work together on. If I'm getting it, Tania, you want more trust and Christine, you would find it easier to show Tania more trust if she was doing something productive with her time. Like working.

Christine: Yes, I've said that to her. I want her to do something better with her time. Then I'd trust her. Give her a key, anything.

Tania: I want to work.

Michael: So we're all on the same page. We all want the same thing *(Both nod)*.

To be able to say, "We all want the same thing" is about as good as it gets during the work phase of counseling. If the client appears to be navigating toward what she wants (and that includes all the clients who have joined the process) and the client's voice is front and center in the negotiations regarding which resources will be accessed, when and how, then the counselor can feel reasonably optimistic that progress is being made. Though Tania and Christine were still far from certain what their relationship would look like, we were at least working together to explore options. Imagine I had worked with Tania alone. It would certainly have been possible to advance the goals of therapy except I would always have been at a distinct disadvantage to understand why Tania's mother was so determined to lock her daughter out. The emotional traps that each lay for the other would also have been largely invisible. Is Tania upset about her father's death? Or is it Christine who is still recovering from a violent relationship and feeling traumatized by her daughter's obstinate behavior? Just as our collaborative assessment would continue to inform our evolving contract, so too would the specific focus of our work keep changing. Tania's independence and her relationship with Christine would, however, remain the overarching focus of our time together.

How Many Sessions is Enough?

An ecological practice can be brief or not. While I find most young people prefer to engage in counseling in short seasons, much like my favorite television shows, I also find that a successful phase of six to ten sessions usually predicts the child returning later if they encounter more crises that are beyond their capacity to handle. By that point, we've hopefully had enough success together to inspire confidence that a few more sessions could be helpful when life stressors pile up.

Overlapping the phases means that even a relatively short few sessions, or a single session, can have an impact. One way, though, to estimate how long counseling is likely to be required is by considering the questions in Exercise 6.1.

EXERCISE 6.1

Estimating the Duration of Counseling

How many risk factors does the client face?	*Few risks*	*Many risks*
• If many, then the complexity of the clinical work is likely to increase.	− _____ + (Fewer sessions)	(More sessions)
How severe are the risks the client faces?		
• The more severe one or more risk factors are, the more time will be required to find solutions.	*Less severe* − _____ + (Fewer sessions)	*More severe* (More sessions)
How many of the seven resilience factors are available in the client's life?	*Many available*	*Few available*
• The more there are evident during the assessment, the fewer clinical contacts are likely to be needed.	− _____ + (Fewer sessions)	(More sessions)
How many of these are accessible?	*Many accessible*	*Few accessible*
• The more available these factors are, the less the counselor will be needed.	− _____ + (Fewer sessions)	(More sessions)
How motivated is the client to find new coping strategies?	*Motivated*	*Less motivated*
• The more motivated the child, the fewer sessions will be required.	− _____ + (Fewer sessions)	(More sessions)
How easy will it be to change the client's social and physical ecologies?	*Easy*	*Difficult*
• How open are individuals and institutions that control the client's psychosocial resources to changing how they interact with the client?	− _____ + (Fewer sessions)	(More sessions)

How much say does the client have over how her/his/their problems are understood, and the solutions that are most meaningful?

- When a client has a louder voice in defining problems and finding solutions, it takes less time to find better coping strategies.

Has a say   *Has very little say*

– _____ +

(Fewer sessions)   (More sessions)

If the client does start to change, will there be sufficient support to make those changes sustainable?

- The more supports, the easier to transition out of counseling.

Sufficient support   *Little support*

– _____ +

(Fewer sessions)   (More sessions)

Five Phases in One Session

A detailed transcript like that between Tania, Christine, and myself shows the way the five phases of intervention overlap smoothly. As the conversation unfolded, it became increasingly clear what the specific resources were that Tania needed to transition to independent living. It wasn't easy finding them. She had all but destroyed her mother's confidence in her ability to be home alone or hold down a job and was refusing to consider any case plans other than: (1) leave home; (2) find a job; (3) get her GEDs; (4) enroll in college to become an esthetician. Our work together became helping her to consider each step of this search for independence and how she'd convince others that her plan was a sensible one. While I was doing that, I was circling backwards and forwards, always conscious of whether Tania and Christine felt engaged in the therapeutic relationship, snooping out new information to make my assessment more detailed, renewing our contract, and of course, considering who would be there for Tania when she transitioned to independent living and counseling ended.

Case Study: Christine and Tania Six Weeks Later

Six weeks later, we held our fifth meeting. By that point, Tania was positive about the changes that she was making and Christine had responded by agreeing to give Tania more responsibility. The problem of how to transition Tania to independent living, though, continued as she was still too young to live entirely on her own.

Tania: I got a job. At the Burger Captain.

Michael: Great.

Tania: My first shift is today.

Michael: So this is all good news. But let me ask Christine, is your daughter doing less of something that troubled you, besides getting the job?

Christine: Well she is . . . I don't know if I should say this with Tania around, but I just feel that I've had to limit myself so much in what I say to her to keep her at home that I haven't been able to parent her the way I think I should parent a teen [*Crying*] and I'm just tired of that, of not doing what I should be doing. Of being quiet, of all the things around our home that I find very disrespectful.

Michael: So around the home the last two weeks, even with Tania looking for work, things for you have still been bad?

Christine: Well there's so many levels of disrespect.

Tania: Give examples of me disrespecting. What? Of me not folding towels? Of little things like that?

Christine: Well yeah, like she'll take a towel from a pile in the closet and when she does she just rips it out from the pile and the rest all fall down and it just shows me the work I do is not appreciated [*Crying*].

Tania: Oh go on with you [*Rolls her eyes*].

Christine: I don't deserve it. I've taken it for years. And I can't take any more. Tania thinks it just a small thing, but it's not.

Michael: So these things add up, the accumulation of things makes it difficult for you. And yet I'm also hearing that when you hold back, it makes it easier for your daughter to be in the house, so that you can influence and parent her?

Christine: Yes, but I think the time has come, I mean she's not at the same point in life she was when she was at 14. Maybe it's time for her to go get her own place and have things her own way.

Tania: Okay, so let me not pay you rent, and save it up so I can get my own place.

Christine: Maybe it's time for her to move out.

Tania: Fine.

During this phase of work, we wrestled with at least two issues: First, what does "respect" mean to Christine, and how does she expect her teenage daughter to behave? Second, when would Tania be ready to live on her own? In this exchange we continued to hold to the original contract, though Tania's reluctance to move out and Christine's growing insistence her daughter leave home changed our contract slightly with regard to when Tania would transition to living on her own.

Over the next few sessions we explored what Tania needed to do to show she could act responsibly and convince her mother to treat her more like an adult. We also addressed safety issues around the house, and during individual sessions Tania and Christine's experiences earlier in their lives when Christine was being physically abused by Tania's father and later, working as a prostitute to make enough money to support her and Tania after Tania's father died.

Tania: I'm letting you know I don't want to be here. I had to come, right.

Michael: What made you come? It's great to see you, and I'm glad we'll have a chance to talk this through.

Tania: I came because mom is like, "You agreed to do this if I let you live here" [*In a whiney voice*].

Christine: When I took her back in August, she said she'd agreed to go to counseling.

Tania: But if I'm leaving January first, then I don't see the point of it anymore.

Michael: Well let me explain what's going to happen here for this meeting. Christine, you had a plan last time we met. January first, you'd give Tania six weeks to make the transition to her own place. She'll be 17. It's young, but with some help, Christine thinks you can do it.

Christine: Yeah.

Michael: And what about you, Tania?

Tania: I don't know. I don't even want to talk. Talk to her.

Michael: Well to clarify, it has always been before a crisis and you're out. This time we talked about planning for this transition to independent living very purposefully. My worry was that your relationship with your mom would all of a sudden just break apart. Whoosh and that would be the end of it. No place to go, no plan, no job, no money. And that's not a safe place to put you in. So has it worked any better in the last week, without the pressure to leave right away?

Christine: No.

Tania: Excuse me, like we haven't fought or anything for the last week.

Christine: [*Laughing nervously*] I don't consider that working.

Tania: We were talking just fine the other day. You're such a liar. Don't even talk if you're going to lie. She may not be happy with me and that's her own problem, so I don't want to hear her expressing herself to me. I'm fine with her just being quiet.

Michael: So could you see yourself staying longer than January then?

Tania: I'm okay with leaving.

Michael: Do you have a plan?

Tania: I'm going to the shelter.

Michael: Hmm, the shelter is only temporary.

Tania: A month, and if you have a job it can be extended.

Michael: Wait, I'm confused. And I'm having a little problem understanding this. I thought that you wanted your own room, own job, own life. Own plan.

Tania: Yeah, I have a plan, it's different from the shelter, but I don't want to be here and I don't want to talk about my plan either.

Michael: Can your mom help you to make that plan work?

Tania: No, she can't help. She can just stay out of my life.

Michael: I don't hear your mom saying she wants to control your plan, just offer assistance to make this transition easier for you. Living in the same house isn't working. You don't have a key, no freedom, the relationship is withering. And you aren't feeling safe in your own home. It's not working. The relationship is dying.

Tania: Good.

Tania was obviously hurt that her mother wanted her to leave. Our work shifted again as we negotiated independence for Tania and tried to preserve the mother–daughter relationship. The contract remained stable, but there was a need to keep Tania engaged in counseling despite the hopelessness she was feeling.

Eventually, Tania left home temporarily and lived in a shelter, but she maintained contact with her mother and two months later, returned to live with her again. This was not a typical solution to parent–teen conflict, but in this case, given the unique challenges facing this family, the solution was a good one.

While the work with Tania and Christine honored the original contract (helping them find a way for Tania to become independent and for mother and daughter to maintain their relationship), it was difficult to not express my own bias as a therapist and want them to remain living in the same house while they worked through their conflicts. Sadly, even when Tania began to change and make concessions, Christine became afraid that her daughter would not sustain her new behavior. She insisted Tania leave. The situation was complicated by the fact that there was a shelter to which Tania could go. That external resource made it possible for Christine to abdicate her responsibility as Tania's parent. That is not the shelter's fault, but it does remind us that external resources influence how people cope with adversity.

Once again, all five phases of intervention are evident in the dialogue. Engagement with both mother and daughter always felt precarious as Tania was constantly threatening to stop attending sessions. Our assessment was ever ongoing, with more and more information helping to explain the at times erratic behavior of both Tania and Christine. The contract was reviewed frequently to ensure that I didn't slide off topic and further upset anyone. The work was focused on finding the best possible ways for us to fulfill the contract, even if negotiating independent living for a 17-year-old seemed odd to me as the counselor. When I finally asked if Tania could stay at home until she turned 18 years old, that was my bias coming through, though both Tania and Christine seemed comfortable with the suggestion. And of course transitions were being anticipated, especially when I did what I could to maintain continuity in the mother–daughter relationship.

As a model of practice, working ecologically promotes this fluid style of work. Notice, though, that the content of the work phase could have been entirely different without affecting any of the other phases of intervention. For example, a therapist focused on family dynamics might have worked more on communication patterns between Christine and Tania. A narrative therapist might have externalized Tania's problem behavior, or the conflict between mother and daughter. Attachment-oriented work may have focused on the traumatic losses each person has experienced and the impact of these on their ability to connect with one another. A feminist or post-structuralist therapist may have been more concerned with the politics of gender and the feminization of poverty. They may have asked Tania about her choice of future career or looked deeper at the family's experience of male violence and the continuation of that violence in their neighborhood.

Regardless of which model of work is used, engagement, assessment, contracting work, and transition phases are attentive to the broader social forces that shape what brings people to counseling and what they will experience after counseling ends. The plan of treatment with Tania and Christine had a feeling of being open-ended, negotiated, and contextually responsive. If Tania continued attending it was likely because she felt that her solutions were being given full consideration. She wasn't being forced to go back to school or stay at home. The focus was seldom on suppressing Tania's disordered behavior, but instead emphasized our building on her capacity and desire to look after herself. In her own unique way, Tania is resilient, having come through an abusive home, endured many moves, the death of her father, and life in a dangerous neighborhood. While most adolescents would not experience living in a shelter as stabilizing, in Tania's case, this atypical living situation could actually be desirable. After all, if given all she'd experienced, her mother saw messing up a stack of towels as justification to have Tania leave home, then life in a shelter might just be an intelligible alternative to coping in a context where Tania felt she had few options to be a normal kid.

Fidelity to the Approach

Fidelity to an ecological approach (by that I mean how well the counselor adheres to the principles and practices that are likely to produce the best results through an ecological model of intervention) should always show seamless continuity between the five phases of practice. While this principle of overlapping phases of treatment appears simple enough, disrupting linear processes of counseling that move from one phase to the next is difficult. Sadly, we are trained to think about processes of change as sequential and under the control of the therapist. Instead, as Bell (2012) suggests, a more "post-conventional" view of intervention is needed, one that is attentive to "wholeness, interdependence, interconnectedness, diversity and broader community context" (p. 420). In such a complex terrain, it's near impossible to think that an assessment can be over and done with, or that contracts won't change as clients come to understand their lives as situated in wider social discourses, susceptible to the vagaries of socio-economic forces and the shifting politics of privilege (Who gets respect and who is marginalized?). In practice, this means the difference between telling a 16-year-old teenager like Tania to live at home and obey her mother and appreciating the reasonableness of negotiating her path to independence much earlier than is typically expected.

Interventions like this that work well and keep clients engaged don't just happen randomly. As I've shown, there are intentional strategies we can use as counselors to help clients navigate and negotiate effectively. We know an intervention is successful when it helps to make children and families more resilient. The greater the fidelity to the model shown in this chapter and the previous two, the more likely an intervention is to be successful.

Summary

In this chapter, I've used a detailed case example to illustrate the overlap between the five phases of intervention. An ecological practice focuses attention on changing both the client and the client's social ecology in a non-linear fashion and promotes the continual anticipation of what the client will do after counseling ends. While many other approaches to working with children, youth, and families are also effective, my goal here was to show that adding ecological principles to one's practice can make clinical work more engaging and outcomes more sustainable in complex social ecologies.

APPENDIX 6.1

Collaborative Assessment Guide[1]

PART ONE

Client Name:

Counselor:

Referral Source:

Employment/Education Status:

Date(s) of Assessment:

Contacts (people included in this assessment):

Client Demographic Information

- Where do you live?
- With whom do you live?
- Who do you consider your family?
- How often have you moved in the past year? Five years? Lifetime?
- Do you have any important cultural affiliations?
- Are there any important ways you identify yourself that I should know about? (If the client identifies characteristics such as sexual orientation, ethnicity, race, a disability or special ability, national identity, or affiliation with a particular religious group, and says these are important, this should be noted.)
- Have you experienced any developmental challenges? Has there been any significant life events that caused problems with normal developmental tasks (events that influenced attending school, making friends, getting work, forming an intimate relationship, etc.)?

PART TWO

Problem-focused Questions

- What brings you to counseling now? What situation would you like to see changed?
- What patterns in your life, either individually, or as part of your family and community, would you like to change?
- How do you explain the problem that has brought you to counseling? What is it about this problem that causes it to influence your life?

Client's Definition of the Problem

- How would you describe the problem from your point of view?
- Do others agree or disagree with how you see the problem?
- What do these others think about the problem, and your ability to cope with it?

History of the Problem

- Explore the history of the problem across generations.

  - Who else that you know has been affected by this problem? Family members? Peers? Members of your community?
  - What ways have you (and others in your family or community) tried to solve similar problems before?
  - Have you had previous experience solving a problem like the one that has brought you to counseling?

- Explore the history of the individual's experience of the problem.

  - How has the problem affected you?
  - How has the problem affected others?
  - What's helped you in the past cope with the problem?

- Explore individual coping strategies used in the past and present with other problems.

  - What are some of the ways you have solved similar problems?
  - What do you think about these coping strategies?
  - Are they possible solutions for you now?

PART THREE

Solution-focused Questions

- Explore solutions the client has tried in the past, or is using now, to cope with the problem.

  - How well are they working?
  - What are the good things about the solutions you're using?
  - Are there any disadvantages to your coping strategies?

- Explore coping strategies used by others in the past and present.

  - What are some of the ways other family and community members solve similar problems?
  - What do you think about these others' coping strategies?
  - Are they possible solutions for you too?
  - Are you the same or different from other members of your family? Your community? Who do you resemble most? Who do you resemble least?
  - How would the people you most respect in your family and community handle the challenges you face?
  - Who would be an ally in standing up to the problem?
  - Who would be against you if you tried to fix the problem? How do you explain their behavior?

© 2015, *Working with Children and Youth with Complex Needs: 20 Skills to Build Resilience*, Michael Ungar, Routledge

- Explore the identities that follow each possible solution.

  - How do people see you most days? At home? At school? At work? In your community?
  - If you didn't have this problem, how would people see you? Would this be better or worse for you?

Support for Solutions

- Consider past problems the client has experienced and the solutions that she/he/they have tried.

  - What do others close to you think about the way you've solved problems?
  - What do they think about you now and your ability to survive and thrive?
  - What would they say if you tried to solve problems in the same way you did before?
  - What would they say if you tried to solve problems in a different way?
  - Looking back at your family history, has anyone else struggled with a similar problem?

- How were they seen by others?
- Was their problem seen as a problem at the time?

PART FOUR

Individual Resources and Barriers

- Comment on general aspects of the individual:

  - Motivation to change.
  - Self-esteem.
  - Cognitive functioning.
  - Ability to attach to others.
  - Psychopathology (personality disorders and organic dysfunctions of the brain related to behavior and learning, like Attention Deficit Hyperactivity Disorder, etc.).
  - Capacity for insight and reflection.
  - Social competence.
  - Problem-solving.
  - Sense of humor.
  - Attribution style (internal or external locus of control).

- Identify aspects of resilience related to individual functioning.

  - Relationships:

    - What is the quality of your relationships with others?
    - How large, or small, is your social network?
    - Who are the most significant people among your close relationships, and what do they provide?

- Identity:

  - How satisfied are you with your personal identity (the way you see yourself, or are seen by others)?
  - Do you have a sense of purpose in life? Please explain.
  - What are your personal strengths and weaknesses?
  - What are your personal values and beliefs?
  - Do you have a positive identification with a particular social group, spiritual system of belief, occupation, or nation?

- Power and control:

  - Can you care for yourself?
  - Are you responsible for others?
  - Do you experience personal efficacy (the ability to change your world)? Political efficacy (the ability to effect social policy)?
  - Can you access resources that support your sense of well-being when you need them?

- Access to material resources:

  - Do you have enough food?
  - Are you safe?
  - Do you have access to education? Medical care and medication? Housing? Employment? Financial assistance?

- Social Justice:

  - Do you have a meaningful role in your community?
  - Do you experience social equality? If not, please describe your experience of marginalization or oppression.
  - Do you have opportunities to make a contribution to the welfare of others? How do you do this?

- Cohesion:

  - Do you have a sense of spirituality and/or a connection to a religious organization? Please describe the connection.
  - Do you feel you belong in your family, school, workplace, and community?
  - Do you seek help from others?
  - What do you wish for in the future? Are you optimistic or pessimistic about what will happen?

- Cultural adherence:

  - Are you aware of your culture and the customs and practices associated with it? How do these make you feel?
  - How tolerant are you of others' differences?
  - If necessary (serious challenges are suspected, or service mandate requires assessment), explore

with individuals aspects of their mental status with a focus on specific observations related to the following factors.

- Willingness:

  – Is the client able to engage with a counselor?

- Appearance:

  – Is the client's dress, level of nutrition, hygiene, or other aspect of his/her physical appearance of concern?

- Consciousness:

  – Is the client sufficiently alert to be in counseling?

- Psychomotor behavior:

  – Are any of the client's movements of concern (explosive, withdrawn, fidgeting, etc.)?

- Attention:

  – Is the client distracted or attentive?

- Speech:

  – Is the client's speech disturbed, coherent, or otherwise a cause for concern?

- Thinking:

  – Is the client thinking clearly and able to sustain a conversation (or are his/her words fragmented, slurred, confused, etc.)?

- Orientation:

  – Does the client know where he/she is and what day, season, year, it is?

- Affect:

  – Is the client feeling odd in any way that causes concern (anxious, disgusted, guilty, etc.)?

- Insight:

  – Is the client able to reflect on his/her condition and why counseling has been recommended?

- Intellectual impairment:

  - Does the client show signs of intellectual impairment?

PART FIVE

Family Resources and Barriers

- Prepare a genogram to capture important family details, as well as the history of problems and solutions across generations.
- Assess the individual's family system's patterns of interaction.
- How much change has your family experienced recently? Over its entire history?
- Are there significant life events that affected you and your family (like adoption, major dislocations, incarceration, violence)?
- How have changes in your family structure (like the birth of a child, divorce of parents, death of a grandparent, etc.) affected your family's ability to cope or meet people's needs?
- What is the quality of the relationships between people in your family?
- Which relationships are working well?
- Which are strained or challenging?
- How is affection shown between family members in your family? When and where is it shown?
- What are your family's plans for the future?
- What are your family's daily routines? For example, when do you eat? And who attends meals?
- Are there any significant health concerns that affect your family functioning?
- How much contact occurs between you and your extended family? Is this a source of support or problems? Please explain.
- How much contact occurs between your family and its community, such as children's schools, your neighbors, or the police?
- How willing, and able, is your family to change patterns of interaction that may be associated with the problem that brought family members to counseling?
- Explore both the family's mutually-held values and beliefs, and those areas where there is disagreement.
- Which family members are most likely to be close?
- How do people share what they believe across generations? Is this helpful or unhelpful to you and others in your family?
- How do different groups of people in your family (subsystems like those of siblings, or a child and adult with a close emotional connection) support each other?
- How do people's expectations of each other influence the behavior of individuals and of your family as a group?
- How do individuals in your family who pay more attention to one another exclude other family members?
- Are these subgroups within the family a source of strength, vulnerability, or both?
- If more than one family member was seen by the counselor, comment on the interactions that were observed. Then ask the client:

  - How do you explain what I observed? Would you say these interactions were positive, negative, or both? Please explain.

- How do the patterns of family interaction that I saw affect problems?
- How do patterns of family interaction that I saw help support solutions?

- Explore whether the family has a dominant story it tells about itself. Ask the client:

  - In your own words, how would you describe your family and the life you live together?
  - If you wrote a story about your family, what would be the title?

PART SIX

Community Resources and Barriers

- Explore important details of an individual's or family's interactions with their community, as well as the history of problems and solutions employed by others with similar challenges in the community.
- Assess patterns of interaction in the community that support solutions or cause problems for the client:

  - How have recent or past changes in your community affected its ability to support you?
  - Are there significant events that have added to the community's resources or threatened its ability to help?
  - What is the quality of the relationships between people in your neighborhood? Community? Which relationships are working well? Which are strained or challenging?
  - How is support shown between community members? When and where?
  - Are there any significant threats to your health related to being a part of your community?
  - How much contact occurs with elected officials, or government personnel who have responsibility for providing resources to your community?
  - How safe is your community? How clean and orderly is it?
  - How willing, and able, is your community to help you find new solutions to persistent or acute problems?

- Explore both the community's mutually-held values and beliefs, and those areas where there is disagreement.

  - Which community members are most likely to be supportive of you?
  - How do people in your community share their values across generations? Is this helpful or unhelpful to you?
  - How do people's expectations of each other in your community influence people's behavior?
  - How does your community help build bridges of inclusion, or exclude those the community doesn't like?

- If a member of the client's community (family friend, teacher, work colleague, etc.) is seen in counseling, comment on the interactions that were observed.

  - How do you explain what I observed? Would you say these interactions were positive, negative, or both? Please explain.
  - How do these patterns of interaction help or hinder finding good solutions to problems?

- Does the community have a dominant story it tells about itself?

  - What title would you give to a story about your community?

- Explore the external barriers facing individuals and families in their communities.

  - Income:

    - Do you have enough money to meet your basic needs?
    - How do you experience your economic status in relation to those around you? Do you feel poor, wealthy, lucky, stigmatized?

  - Housing and shelter:

    - What do you define as adequate housing?
    - Does your housing match your capacity for independent living? For example, are you dependent on others when you'd rather be independent?
    - Is you housing adequate and safe?
    - Is your housing structured in ways that encourage neighbor-to-neighbor communication?

  - Education and Employment:

    - Do you have adequate education and employment opportunities?
    - Are there support services to help you make the transition into educational institutions or employment, including guidance counselors, placement services, and retraining support?
    - If you are a vulnerable learner or employee, is support provided that is appropriate to your needs?

  - Health care:

    - What health care services have you used over time?
    - Which health care services have been lacking?
    - What are the barriers to you accessing health care and who is working to address these?

  - Social networks:

    - How accessible are networks of like-minded individuals and those who share beliefs and behaviors similar to yours?
    - What infrastructure, like parks and associations, help to address your marginalization?
    - What does your community need that could help people know each other better?

  - Recreation:

    - Are recreational facilities and programs in your community accessible to those with limited financial means and mobility challenges?
    - How inclusive are the services offered?

- Transportation:

  - Can you navigate your way around your community?
  - Is transportation affordable and accessible?
  - Is public transit seen as a resource to the entire community, removing stigma from those who use it?

- Legal assistance:

  - Do you have access to representation in legal matters?

PART SEVEN

The Counselor's Role in the Community

- How much does the counselor himself/herself know about his/her client's community? A counselor can ask himself/herself:

  - Do I share any resources, or am I aware of specific supports, that may be helpful to my client?
  - Can I share these without breaching the boundaries of professional practice? How?

- How much does the counselor himself/herself understand his/her client's culture? A counselor can ask himself/herself:

  - What do I need to learn more about to understand and appreciate my client's culture and context? (It's recommended that counselors ask their clients for help answering this.)

PART EIGHT

Assessment Summary

- In the client's own words, capture as much as possible the client's perspective on her/his/their problem and the possible solutions she/he/they would like to pursue. Pay particular attention to the words the client uses and what they mean to her/him/them.

  - Are the problems other people see in your life problems for you? Please explain.
  - Are the solutions other people have suggested acceptable ways to solve the problem (that brought you to counseling) as you've described it?

- Explore the client's expectations for change.

  - How much do you expect counseling to help?
  - What has been your previous experience working with a counselor?

- Summarize the client's most important navigation strategies.

  - What resources have been most available in the past?
  - What resources are most realistically available now?
  - What resources are most realistically accessible to help you change?
  - Of the coping strategies you've tried, which, if any, are still preferred?

- Summarize the client's most important negotiation strategies:

  - Which past ways of coping were most meaningful?
  - What has this coping strategy meant to you? Has it been valued or criticized by others?
  - What words would you use to describe your most common way of coping? Is using this language helpful or unhelpful?

- Summarize for the client:

  - The significant problems you have identified are _____. Have I understood you correctly?
  - The solutions you've proposed (if identified) are _____. Have I understood you correctly?

Updating the Assessment and Contract

- Be sure and leave time in later sessions to update this assessment as new information becomes available.
- Before formulating any case plan, contract or suggesting an intervention, invite the client to comment on your understanding of the problem and its many possible solutions.
- Integrate into the contract new information as it becomes available.

Note

1 Adapted from: Ungar, M. (2011). *Counseling in challenging contexts: Working with individuals and families across clinical and community settings.* Belmont, CA: Brooks/Cole.

CHAPTER 7

PERILS AND PITFALLS OF BEING A COUNSELOR

In the previous chapters, I've discussed techniques that counselors use to make their practice more ecological. These techniques depend on the counselor's sincere belief that the client is an equal partner in the clinical work. It's not good enough to invite the client into a process of negotiation when we secretly believe we know best what the solution to the client's problem is. When I train therapists, I'll sometimes hear the comment, "The counselor is just manipulating the client." It can certainly look like that from the outside. But negotiating with a client to help him navigate effectively, changing contracts so they make sense to the client, relying on the client's natural supports as substitutes for counseling after the clinical work ends, none of these strategies are tricks to speed the client toward compliance with what the counselor wants. The cynics among us may think that, but my experience is that intervening with young people in ways that accept the complexity of their social ecologies requires humility. A right attitude is the beginning to a successful intervention.

That doesn't mean counselors ignore client's self-destructive behaviors. A client's choice of navigation and negotiation strategy can evoke strong emotions in the counselor. While it is possible to act professionally with every client, there will always be clients in our practices who upset us, or evoke in us a parental concern that makes us wrongly think we can solve their problems. In the therapeutic relationships typical of an ecological approach, both the client and the counselor are thinking, feeling parts of complex social interactions.

That means the client, too, is just as susceptible to personal demons. No matter how sincere the counselor, a client with a history of bad counseling experiences is likely to smell a bad odor in the therapy room, whether it's there or not. No matter what the counselor does, the client will resist treatment out of fear of being made vulnerable again. In these and so many other ways, the client and the counselor are actively shaping their mutual experience of the therapeutic relationship.

Though less visible during the clinical process, the counselor's employer, the community of professional therapists with whom the counselor is a member, and the wider community in which client and counselor live are all participants in the clinical encounter too. Navigations in hostile environments or bureaucratic gridlocks caused by agency procedures are going to thwart even the best case plans. Negotiations in contexts where the client is thought by others to be incapable of making good decisions, or where gatekeepers to resources are simply apathetic to the client's needs, can shape a client's motivation to change. As one of my clients once told me, "Why bother being good if nobody notices that you've changed?"

The Counselor's Use of Self

Because a social ecological intervention requires the counselor to be aware of these clinical stumbling blocks and the broader social factors that influence the client, clinical practice tends to become very reflective. Ideally, as counselors, we recognize how our experience is both similar to and different from that of our client. Our work should be a series of intentional decisions: what we think, say, and ask our clients to do. The client's behavior and the environment in which he navigates and negotiates is bound to evoke in us strong feelings, whether of disbelief ("It can't be as bad as he says"), frustration ("Surely, change is easier than he makes it out to be"), or even pity ("He's so cute, he doesn't deserve what's happened to him"). An ecological model makes counselors masterful at helping clients move through a process that opens new opportunities. It does not make us experts on what clients need to solve their problems.

Head and Heart

Our work is both head and heart. While many of our interventions to help clients navigate and negotiate are cognitive, focused on what clients think and how they behave, their emotional reactions to solutions play a critical role in the likelihood of their success. It is much the same for us counselors. It is not enough to know what to say: a successful therapeutic alliance depends on how we feel about the client and our attitude toward change. If we honestly think the client is mostly responsible for his problems, then our questions about the client's access to resources, the barriers he faces, and the natural supports which he needs to transition out of counseling will all sound insincere. I've seen newly-trained counselors ask questions about the client's social ecology for half an hour, then conclude with, "And what can *you* do to change?" Certainly, clients share responsibility for change, but unless they are the perpetrators of violence (think of an adolescent who is abusing his parent), then we as counselors need the compassion to understand the client's experience of living in a world where he perceives few opportunities for meaningful adaptation.

To illustrate, I recently worked with a mother of three boys who brought her youngest, who was 13 years old at the time, in for counseling. He had recently witnessed his 21-year-old brother shoot and kill his 17-year-old brother. In one tragic moment, the 13-year-old lost one brother to a bullet, another brother to jail, and his mother to PTSD that kept her from looking after him or working outside of the home.

While I could empathize, I also found it frustrating that the younger boy was quickly drifting into the same pattern of behavior that had put his eldest brother in jail for life. Even when Jonathan, my client, was willing to do more than grunt yes or no during our scheduled sessions, our conversations still went nowhere. If I asked him about his truancy, delinquency, or even his preferred future (which he once told me was jail or death by the time he turned 18 years old), our process stalled. After two weeks of this nonsense, I switched my focus. Instead of asking Jonathan about his problem behaviors, I asked him to tell me about the intensely good times that he remembered having with his brothers before the eldest dropped out of school, got into serious trouble and was forced to leave home. His answers weren't what I expected. Jonathan spoke passionately about how he used to feel that he belonged in a family that protected him. Though he was hesitant to admit it, he now felt very vulnerable and alone. His delinquency had become his only source of real strength. "Nobody messes me with when I act like my brother," Jonathan confided quietly and on the verge of tears.

I knew nothing of his experience first hand, but I could sense his loss. In the quiet of our time together, the best intervention I found was to simply help Jonathan remember that he had once felt loved. Our work became navigating our way through his emotional turmoil. There was little else we could do, and little else Jonathan could control that would make his life at home any better. He was now on his own, parenting his parent who thankfully had long-term disability insurance to pay the bills. When I told Jonathan he seemed trapped and that I could understand why he felt powerless to make any changes, he began sobbing and told me, "It's always been like that."

His father had left the family when Jonathan was a small boy. They'd moved several times before his mother had found adequate employment doing the accounts for a home cleaning service. The three boys mostly looked after themselves. Jonathan had never felt he had much say over anything he did or anything others did to him.

As we continued to meet, Jonathan began to find inspiration in his motivation to exercise whatever power he had to make his own decisions. He began to do better at school and refused to spend his time after school looking after his mother. He found his own extra-curricular activities and met people who hadn't heard stories about his older brother. He moved the furniture in his room. He insisted his mother let him buy a pet rat. Four months after we began meeting, Jonathan stopped attending our weekly sessions. When I phoned to see if I could help, he said little, but I could practically see him shrug at the other end of the line. There was no need, I could tell, for more talking. He had found new places to belong and was relying on himself to make his world feel secure.

Emotional Drain, Emotional Charge

There are many aspects of an ecological practice that can be emotionally draining for the counselor. Interventions are most effective when they force counselors to decenter themselves and their expertise. It can be difficult, though, to remain focused on the fact that counseling is not about what the counselor wants, though the counselor, the counselor's agency, and the wider community may have a stake in the work a client contracts to do. For example, a sexually-abusive 14-year-old may not willingly consent to treatment, leaving his therapist and the courts no other option but to mandate a secure placement. Even in such a restrictive context, what the young person needs, what is available, and who decides what service is given and what is denied, are all part of processes of navigation and negotiation that form the basis for good clinical intervention.

Sometimes, though, the emotional work that needs to be done is entirely for the counselor to do, not the client. In the case of one boy with whom I worked who had mild cognitive delays and had sexually assaulted a two-year-old whom he had babysat on many occasions, the solution to his sexual offending was not directly related to treatment for his abusive behavior. He most wanted a friend his own age; he wanted the bullying to stop at school; he wanted to do better at school; he wanted to feel like someone loved him. He had thought the little boy whom he had abused could help him solve some of these problems. He had never meant to harm him nor get himself in trouble. Our goal, then, became to pursue the external resources he had named (a friend, safety at school, better grades, and the attention of a caregiver) and focus very little on the sexual offending. It made sense, though the nature of the offence bothered me. The disregard the boy had shown for the feelings of his victim were difficult to accept, even if I could understand that I was expecting too much of the boy to feel otherwise.

While aware I was sometimes ignoring the boy's goals for counseling, I occasionally spent a session doing a more cognitive behavioral intervention related to the boy's perception of his victim's willingness to engage with him sexually. That work was much more successful the more I helped the boy realize his own goals for counseling. As the counselor, the challenge I had during treatment was staying focused on the boy's context and the way it marginalized him rather than the experience of his victim. While the boy was still the perpetrator, I had to force myself to think about the boy as a victim too and help him find the resources he needed to stop what would surely become a pattern of offending. When I managed to experience this cognitive flip, the work became far less draining and much more emotionally rewarding.

A case plan like that does not affirm the boy's lack of responsibility. It simply acknowledges the barriers to growth the boy experiences because of his complex needs. A counselor's effective use of self means avoiding the traps of arrogance and omniscience when helping clients find solutions that will work for them. Therefore, though objective measures of success are important to assess clinical outcomes (for example, Does an adolescent return to school? Does a younger child show fewer signs of anxiety? Does an early adolescent decrease her sexually precocious behavior?), clinicians who work ecologically are just as concerned with whether individuals meet the goals *they* themselves find the most meaningful (for example, Is the adolescent safe at school? Is the anxious child feeling securely attached to a non-custodial parent? Is the early adolescent being given manageable amounts of responsibility to make her own decisions?). The next case study illustrates what I mean.

Case Study: Adam

Adam, who had just turned 15 years old when I met him, and his divorced mother, Catrina, lived within ten blocks of my house. Though my own children were at the time close in age to Adam, and I knew the streets he walked and the school he attended, his mother's perception of our neighborhood was very different from my own. To her it was an extremely dangerous neighborhood that justified her protective parenting practices. Adam didn't think his neighborhood was dangerous, nor did his friends. His father, Boris, didn't think so either. To work with Catrina, however, I couldn't let my personal beliefs influence our work. I had to at least try to see the world from her point of view, just as I was also trying to see it from Adam's. In this complex series of negotiations, we eventually found a way that Adam could get what he needed without his mother feeling she was jeopardizing her son's safety.

Adam's parents separated when he was four and his younger sister a year old. Just prior to the divorce, Adam's father had been removed from the home for verbally abusing Catrina and a minor assault (he'd thrown a rubber boot at her). The original referral for counseling came from Adam's school support worker. Though Adam had been performing well academically in junior high, he began to report lots of arguments at home and failed several math tests. Catrina had been a stay-at-home parent since Adam was born. The first time we met, she told me, "My babies need me." She maintains a middle-class lifestyle based on child support payments from her ex-husband, which makes it possible for the family to live in a comfortable neighborhood with tree-lined streets close to the city center.

According to both Adam and Boris, Catrina has always had strict rules for the children. Catrina explained this as reasonable since when she was younger, she was allowed to roam her neighborhood, got into drugs, and married her first husband in her late teens. He was also an abusive man. The couple divorced two years later and Catrina remarried in her mid-twenties. She was convinced that her first marriage was her mother's fault and that she should have had more rules growing up.

The family had seen two different counselors before coming to see me. Both advised Catrina to ease up on her controlling behavior. She'd refused, insisting Adam be home by 5:00 P.M. every weekday, and 8:00 P.M. on weekends. He was not allowed to go on sleepovers, nor was he allowed to bring his iPod home from his father's house because some of the music he listened to used "inappropriate" language. Adam was permitted exactly 60 minutes of television a day and no more, even if he asked to view a special sporting event like the opening ceremony of the Olympics or the final match of the hockey season. Catrina insisted that her rules helped Adam do well at school. The boy also played clarinet and was expected to practice for at least 45 minutes each day if he wanted his television privileges. "When he reaches university, then he'll appreciate me," Catrina said.

Adam reluctantly obeyed his mother's rules until several weeks before I met him. Trouble started the day Adam came home from school 20 minutes late. Catrina took away his television and computer privileges. Adam stormed upstairs to his room, on the way grabbing a few coins from a change dish by the front door and throwing them at a window. The window broke and Catrina called the police, fearing for her safety. Boris came over shortly afterwards and took the boy to spend the night with him. The police did nothing except recommend the family seek counseling.

Catrina thought Boris had undermined her authority. Adam, she said, should have been left in his room and the police should have done more to scare him. Catrina resents that Adam's father treats Adam very differently than she does. Adam can watch more television, studies when he feels like studying, and listens to any music he chooses when he's staying with his father. Adam would like to go live with his father full-time, but given that Boris travels for 10–15 days each month and is unable to provide a stable home for his son, a change in custody is not possible.

What stands out for me when I think back to my time with Adam is that he had managed to cope with his mother's rules in some intriguing ways. He played intramural basketball and football, not because he particularly liked these sports, but because Catrina let Adam stay out past his curfew any time he was in an organized activity. Adam often lied about his practice schedule so he could spend time with his friends. He also hid his iPod under his bed and listened to his music after he turned out his light at night. Many of Adam's behaviors resembled those of people who are institutionalized and resist the authority of the guards who watch over them. This feeling of being in jail, which Adam used to describe his experience of living with his mother, became a powerful metaphor during our sessions together.

Adam: I only see my friends at school. Except like tonight, she has to be out to take my sister to dance, so she'll leave me and I'll go to my friends.

Michael: I'm a bit confused. So nights she goes out, then it's okay for you to go out too?

Adam: Yeah, then she'll leave me a note and tell me when to be back and my supper. On those nights it's like she's a little less strict.

Michael: And where do you go?

Adam: My friends' house probably. They all live pretty close.

Michael: So when your mom's not there you have more freedom than when she is there.

Adam: Yeah, it's not like I sneak out. She actually leaves me a note . . . Right now I'm trying to do what she says. To follow the rules.

Michael: Do you have any solutions to this? Longer term? You're 15 now. I know that sometimes people have great ideas about how to solve this.

Adam: Well, I would just like, I want to find out her reasons. She's got to have some reasons for being so strict with me. She'll be like blank if you ask her a question. Like my dad asks her too, we'll go over together and she'll have nothing to say.

Adam's goal was simple: to get his mother to "lighten up" and have fewer rules, or at least rules that made sense. He insisted he'd never thrown anything else in the house and that he actually didn't mind most of his mother's rules. My next meeting began with Catrina alone. I thought it might be helpful to hear from her why she felt so afraid for her son's safety.

Catrina: So since their father was taken from our home, and I had nothing to do with that. But since then, when he was dragged from the home and then there was months of court proceedings and I had nothing to do with that, but since then, we felt that nobody could live with moving around all the time, with a week here or one day here and the next there. So we've had it so I have the children all week and their dad, when he's in town, every weekend. It's always been like that. I don't work. That's a choice we made when we had children. So after we divorced, I just kept at it. We never worked as a team. We'd be together if we could have worked as a team.

Michael: His dad was abusive? Would that have made it hard to work as a team?

Catrina: Well. . . it's not quite that because he was mostly just verbally abusive. Like Adam. Adam is just like his dad that way. He even looks like him. I even remember saying to Boris when Adam was in grade two, that this child is going to have problems. And Boris just said to me, well you wanted him during the week so you deal with him during school. By grade five we began having lots of problems. And I spent many days at the school with the teachers, counselors, with the principal trying to get someone to help me with this child who wouldn't do anything I told him to do, who wouldn't do his homework when I told him to do it, who was belligerent at home. But they kept trying to make me change. It was Adam who needed to change. I was happy to be the bad guy, well not happy, but willing to be the bad guy. That was just the way it had to be if my Adam was going to get through school.

Michael: It sounds like it took quite the toll on you.

Catrina: Yes it was a lot of work. And now that he is physically bigger than me, he thinks he's an adult, but he's not. Just because there's no man here doesn't mean he's taking over the male role. He can't order me around and tell me what to do.

Michael: It's interesting because Adam told me he didn't mind some rules but some he wanted changed.

Catrina: At age 16, then there will be this big loosening.

Michael: Was that how you were raised?

Catrina: Oh, me, I had no rules. I'd just hang around the alleys or down by the water, well not down by the water because that was where all the druggies were.

Michael: Are you worried about your son becoming a druggie?

Catrina: Oh I think he's too smart for that. He wants to be an athlete. And he knows, I have told him, that he can't get messed up with recreational drugs and still be an athlete.

Michael: I just don't want you as a family to do anything that doesn't feel right. But Catrina, your son just wants to be a normal kid. I mean, you weren't supervised. You turned out well.

Catrina: Well, not quite. I did all kinds of stuff and then a first marriage. And all the group therapy, and Al-Anon and all that. I'm tired now. I can't deal with the abuse.

Michael: What if we could find another compromise? Another solution.

Catrina: That's more lenient than I am now? I don't think so.

Michael: I wasn't thinking lenient. Quite the opposite. Your son says he wants some structure. He doesn't want to live with his dad. He just wants your rules with a little more flexibility. You're doing a great job. You've raised a wonderful young man. He doesn't have to become like your husband.

Catrina: No. And he won't.

Later, I invited Adam to join us in the session. He showed a remarkable amount of poise, never getting angry and gently asking his mother for more independence. She flatly refused. I'll admit it wasn't easy to contain my frustration. Clearly, Catrina's rules were unreasonable for a boy Adam's age. The fact that Adam did little to resist, and actually welcomed most of his mother's rules, was very different from my own experience as a child and the way I'd raised my own children. It took some time for me to reflect on my biased opinion of what would work for this family. I had to accept that Adam was okay with being seen as a bad child as long as he could somehow do the things he wanted to do. To him, this made sense. As a family outsider who thought I understood Adam's world because of how close I lived to it, Adam's choices seemed like awful compromises.

Keeping in mind that my client was Adam, not his mother, I began to help Adam increase his repertoire of coping strategies. Half joking at first, we began to talk about his life as if he was living in a prison. We explored all the strategies prisoners use to cope with their incarceration. As this idea took hold, I encouraged Adam to watch a number of movies that showed how people cope with detention. Though we never spoke to Catrina about Adam's sudden interest in movies like *Chicken Run, Brubaker, The Longest Yard, Shawshank Redemption* and *The Great Escape,* and television shows like *Prison Break,* Adam and I did find a great deal to talk about on the theme of non-violent resistance and what his life would be like when he turned 16 years old and was "let out on parole." I'd have preferred to include Catrina in these conversations but her reluctance to change unless it was turning a blind eye to Adam's behavior gave me a clue that it was better to not challenge Catrina directly. Adam was happy resisting what he came to refer to as "house arrest" and Catrina seemed pleased with the progress Adam was making clinically. Adam *appeared* to show more respect for her rules while all the while continuing to deceive her.

It was among the strangest case plans I'd ever negotiated, and not one I'm altogether proud of. Should I have colluded with Adam to secretly resist his mother's rules, or should I have tried harder to work with Catrina and help her to reconsider the way she was parenting her son? I found my work with Catrina very challenging because I couldn't believe that her behavior was justified. She had also threatened to end counseling for her son if I focused attention on her rather than the boy.

Eventually, Adam and I talked about his father's abusive behavior and the impact it had had on his mother. We found Adam other allies in his fight to break out of prison, including his father (who attended several sessions) and Adam's friends. Looking back, the intervention was successful, albeit in an atypical way. Both Adam and Catrina got what they wanted and the solutions made sense to each of them.

What Counselors Shouldn't Do

When clients appear stubborn and refuse to change, the problem is always the same. It's us, the counselor. The client's reluctance to change is an adaptive strategy to maintain personal coherence, a sense of order and connection in environments which are often toxic or where there are histories of neglect and trauma. The wise counselor acknowledges what psychodynamic therapists refer to as countertransference, the counselor's personal reactions that infiltrate clinical work. While an ecological practice does not focus on intrapsychic phenomena, counselors need to be aware that our personal baggage shapes our practice in often nasty ways.

There are a number of patterns to the interactions between counselors and clients that can undermine all phases of the work. While these behaviors may seem obvious and avoidable, my experience training counselors tells me these missteps are more common than we think. Unless we are taping sessions and receiving regular supervision on our work, it is easy to wind up in conversations with clients that reduce the effectiveness of our interventions. When employing an ecological approach to counseling it is best to avoid the following behaviors:

- *Telling the client what to do.* When counselors give advice, or try to convince a client that the solution the counselor favors is the best one, clients are likely to respond with resistance. They also seldom sustain the changes they make to please the counselor, if they make any changes at all. People come to see a counselor to engage in a process that helps them assert what is important to them and the solutions to problems that are most meaningful. They expect to be confronted on patterns of coping that are problematic, but seldom are the solutions found in the reservoir of the counselor's life experience.

- *Providing the client with too little information.* Just because solutions should not come from the counselor, that doesn't mean that counselors should not share information that can help a client make an informed decision. As case managers, we have knowledge of service delivery systems and the collected wisdom from our previous clients that may help those with whom we are working to explore new opportunities. As clinical therapists, we can ask questions that may help clients re-examine taken-for-granted assumptions about the world, their past, and how both shape their behavior. Clients want us to provide them with new ways of seeing the world, as long as we don't tell them what to do.

- *Unnecessarily avoiding confrontation and issues of safety.* While telling clients what to do can poison a therapeutic relationship, there are times when counselors need to confront behaviors that have the potential to harm the client and others. Ethically, we sometimes need to stop a client from acting recklessly, or at the very least, voice our concerns. Confrontation can occur without damaging the therapeutic relationship when the client is convinced the counselor is acting in the client's best interest.

- *Overly psychologizing client's problems and ignoring structural constraints.* It's easy to think about client's problems as the result of underlying psychological processes related to past trauma or disorder. While that may be the case, for people living in challenging contexts behavior is seldom explained by psychological processes alone. Intrapsychic phenomena are always complicated by structural barriers such as housing, neighborhood safety, the quality of educational institutions, or access to state funding. When we psychologize people's problems, we miss the important role that real world barriers play preventing people from experiencing well-being.

- *Failing to pay attention to the counselor's use of self.* Our own social location as counselors, who we are and what we bring to counseling, influences the five phases of intervention. When counselors fail to notice how they are impacting the therapeutic process, there is the risk that clients quickly disengage. What we wear to work, the small trinkets scattered around our office that tell clients about us and our values, symbols of our identity that speak to our social class like our accent and the car we drive, all become part of our interactions with clients. Who we are can inspire or create resentment, especially when service is mandated. While we may not be able to change who we are, or want to, we can be transparent. We can be sure to notice when what we are saying and doing reflects our values rather than the client's. For example, before we arrange to meet a client at an office across town, or encourage a sole parent to take her 6-year-old to gymnastics to burn off energy, do we consider that our client may not have a car, money, or feel comfortable walking into settings where people don't look like her nor struggle with the same life challenges?

Supervision and Self-supervision

As discussed in Chapter 1, intentional practice means that our work should reflect what we know is most likely to be helpful to our clients (Coulshed & Orme, 2006; Gambrill, 2008). I'm less concerned by what my trainees do than whether they can tell me afterwards what model their intervention adhered to. Intentionality makes our practice focused and ethical.

Video or audio recordings of our sessions are by far the very best way to observe the way we as counselors enhance or pollute the clinical process. I've often observed myself on a recording desperately trying to convince the client I'm right and that the correct way they need to change is the way I'm suggesting. Those are bad days. I can usually tell I'm failing miserably as a counselor when:

- I'm the one speaking more than the client.
- The solutions we are discussing were my suggestions.
- The client seems minimally engaged in planning for change.
- The client seems confused and uncertain what she should do when she leaves my office.
- The client is fearful of what others will say about the changes she is about to make and wary to make any change too fast.
- The client returns the following session and either has forgotten what she was supposed to do or remembers what we discussed but didn't make any effort to put the change she promised to make into practice.

Failed homework is often a very *helpful* sign that the counselor is pushing solutions that don't fit well with what the client wants. Far from a failure, when these things happen, clients and counselors have important information about what doesn't work and, potentially, what will. A wise counselor changes strategies and reflects on how much he is pushing the client to change and how much the client is motivated to do something different.

As counselors, we can't entirely fault ourselves for sometimes being over-zealous with our advice. After all, we may have helped dozens of people overcome similar problems and believe earnestly in the solutions that have worked. In Catrina's case, I was certain that her son would be safe if Catrina relaxed her curfew. I was also fairly certain that if she didn't, Adam would either escalate his behavior or become an angry older teen who distanced himself permanently from his mother. I knew Catrina didn't want to lose her son's love and yet she was unwilling to make concessions that would make it easier for him to remain connected. None of this, however, was of much use to Catrina. Only when I left her alone with her strong beliefs, and worked with Adam to resist the rules quietly, was I able to help the family remain intact. Adam colluded in the deception. He understood, by watching his mother and I talk during joint sessions, that she was afraid for his safety because of her own horrible past. While he was still upset with her, he came to understand that her behavior was motivated by both fear and love. Within two months, the family left counseling with less conflict and a plan for Adam to cope until his 16th birthday.

The Practicalities of Ethical Practice

Ethical practice is both doing what's right to help clients and avoiding doing anything wrong. In Adam's case, an ethical ecological practice meant helping him adapt to a situation that he couldn't change. It also meant adhering to an intentional model of practice that I knew would de-escalate conflict between Adam and his mother.

There are many ways to evaluate our practice to see if it is ethical. Exercise 7.1 provides a list of questions we can ask ourselves to assess whether our work reflects best practice principles and whether we are in compliance with the professional bodies to which we are accountable. I like to think of ethical practice in a very practical way, as reflected in each and every intervention we perform.

Chapter Summary

In this chapter, we've looked at how our personal experience as counselors can influence the clinical process. An effective practice is most likely that which is reflective as well as ecological in focus. As has been shown, the better we are at seeing how our biases influence our clients and the goals we set for counseling, the less likely we are to create resistance. Likewise, the more we use both cognitive and emotionally-focused interventions, the more likely we are to engage clients who are reluctant to participate in counseling. All these aspects of the work remind us that the counselor is a full participant in the clinical work, bringing her own thoughts, feelings, and past experiences to each session. The person of the therapist shapes the focus of the clinical work. Counselors can influence the goals clients set for themselves, or subtly change the focus of the work to satisfy the counselor's need to hold the client accountable. Even when we understand the techniques necessary to make this work effective, an ecological practice requires a deep sense of humility if counselors are to avoid the perils of being overly directive with people who live in complex and resource-poor social ecologies.

EXERCISE 7.1

Self-evaluation of Ethical Practices

To evaluate whether your practice is ethical, begin with questions that help put your intervention into context:

- What kind of service is being provided? _____
- Who initiated counseling? _____
- How many contacts are allowed by your agency or funder (if applicable)? _____
- How frequently can contact be made? _____

Next, consider aspects of your work. The better your answers are to the following questions (the more times you respond 'Yes'), the more likely it is that your interventions are being delivered ethically.

First, ask yourself "How well do I *engage* with clients?" Circle the answer that best describes your work.

- Are meeting times and interventions convenient and timely? *Answer: No, Sometimes, Yes*
- Is your client likely to feel comfortable where and when you meet with her/him/them (Will the client feel safe and that her/his/their confidentiality is respected)? *Answer: No, Sometimes, Yes*
- Is everyone invited to come to counseling who should be there (Or is the intervention inadvertently blaming an individual for a family, school, or community problem by including only them in the search for a solution)? *Answer: No, Sometimes, Yes*
- Are you clear with the client what your role is as a professional, and the boundaries to what you can and cannot do? *Answer: No, Sometimes, Yes*
- Are you clear what will happen if the client tells you she/he/they are at risk of being harmed, or harming someone else? *Answer: No, Sometimes, Yes*

When you conduct an *assessment*, is there sensitivity to the client's understanding of her/his/their problems and solutions?

- Have you asked questions about different parts of the client's social and physical ecology? *Answer: No, Sometimes, Yes*
- Has the client been given equal access to the results of the assessment so she/he/they can decide what are the most important factors that contribute to her/his/their problems (and possible solutions)? *Answer: No, Sometimes, Yes*
- If there is the need to assign a label to a client (for example, ADHD, Conduct Disordered), does the client understand what the label means and has the client been made aware of what is being recorded in her/his/their file? *Answer: No, Sometimes, Yes*

When developing a *contract*, how involved is the client?

- When deciding on a focus for the work, is everyone heard, even the most vulnerable (like children, or those with behavioral, physical, or psychological barriers to participation)? *Answer: No, Sometimes, Yes*

- Are your own boundaries respected (Are you asked to help in a way that is incongruent with your expertise, values, or resources)? *Answer: No, Sometimes, Yes*
- Does the client have the resources (financial, emotional, social) to fulfill the contract? (If not, is the contract routinely changed to be more achievable?) *Answer: No, Sometimes, Yes*

Next, consider the *work* phase:

- Are you accessible when needed (is counseling proceeding quickly enough to meet the client's needs)? *Answer: No, Sometimes, Yes*
- Is your work being done in a culturally sensitive way? *Answer: No, Sometimes, Yes*
- Is your work honouring people's own solutions? *Answer: No, Sometimes, Yes*
- Are you using methods you are confident can help people make the changes they want to make? *Answer: No, Sometimes, Yes*
- Are tasks you ask clients to try, like homework or in-session exercises, best practices that are likely to help stimulate the discovery of new solutions? *Answer: No, Sometimes, Yes*

As the work nears completion and you anticipate *transitions*, consider:

- Does the client have a say over whether she/he/they are ready to have less frequent contact with you? *Answer: No, Sometimes, Yes*
- Is there a network of supports for the client after counseling (has continuity of care been established)? *Answer: No, Sometimes, Yes*
- When necessary, have you advocated for services to meet the client's needs? *Answer: No, Sometimes, Yes*

Finally, ethical practice needs to be *evaluated*. Consider:

- Has the client had the opportunity to speak about her/his/their experience during counseling? (For example, did they ever feel blamed for problems? Supported when finding solutions?) *Answer: No, Sometimes, Yes*
- Have the sessions been helpful overall? *Answer: No, Sometimes, Yes*
- Is there a service that the client wanted (and thought more useful) but wasn't available? *Answer: No, Sometimes, Yes*
- Has counseling been provided in ways sensitive to the client's unique context or culture? *Answer: No, Sometimes, Yes*
- Has the client been asked for suggestions to improve service? *Answer: No, Sometimes, Yes*

CHAPTER 8

GETTING OUR ORGANIZATIONS TO ADOPT A SOCIAL ECOLOGICAL APPROACH TO CLINICAL PRACTICE, CASE MANAGEMENT, AND ADVOCACY

A recent study of clinical social workers working in private practice settings showed that even though most understood that their role should include case management and linking clients to social support networks, many hesitated to do more than provide individually-focused treatment (Groves & Kerson, 2011). This, despite clear guidelines from professional associations like the National Association of Social Workers, which identifies case management as a core competency. I suspect the same narrow definition of the counselor's role could be found among many other mental health professionals.

Sadly, there is a wide and troubling gap between what we know is important to our clients' psychosocial well-being and how we actually practice. The social workers who participated in the study I just mentioned said they'd like to expand their scope of practice but most perceived an ecological practice as too time consuming, potentially disempowering for their clients (they said clients should be able to navigate and negotiate for resources on their own), or they worried that they'd be seen by their colleagues as lower-status clinicians if they performed interventions that were perceived as less skilled.

I don't blame the clinicians for being reluctant to change. The most common feedback I receive on the principles and practices I've presented in the preceding chapters is that while they make sense, there is little support at the counselor's workplace for their implementation. Case management, advocacy, and helping clients grow their network of social supports are seen as unfunded and unnecessary activities discouraged by agency directors. "Good ideas," my colleagues tell me, "but how do I get my supervisors and funders to support an ecological model of practice?" My response is simple: an ecological practice (1) complements well other aspects of clinical work, (2) improves the effectiveness of interventions, and (3) makes it more likely the changes people make are sustainable. When done well, people become more resilient when the next crisis occurs, which means systems have the potential to save money and provide more services to even more people.

In my experience, agencies and funders mean well but under the pressure to meet service outcomes look at problems as the responsibility of individuals to solve because individual change is easier to measure than changes to the client's social ecology; what gets measured gets funded, regardless of whether the outcomes that are tracked are sustainable. Narrow prescriptions for success (the client will attend counseling six times; stop her substance abuse; reside with her parents) and fixed ideas about which outcomes are best (the client will get a job and put her children in subsidized childcare) choke the ability of clinicians to help people navigate and negotiate for the solutions they want for their problems. Organizations can be very difficult to work for if counselors perform nonconventional interventions like negotiating for better recognition of a client's atypical coping strategy, providing contextually relevant interventions, or refusing to close files while clients make the transition back to their community supports but still need a little more help to stabilize their lives.

Furthermore, organizations can struggle to support interventions that address social determinants of well-being despite mission statements that parrot the language of "community engagement," "strengths-based practice," "participatory case planning," "interagency collaboration," "social capital," and "social investment." A review of their actual on the ground practices can paint a very different picture (Ungar et al., 2012). Though social service providers are reticent to admit it, there is very little collaboration between agencies and very little support given to help a child's social ecology prepare itself to pick up when counseling ends (Greene & Ablon, 2006).

It shouldn't be this complicated given what we know about social ecologies and the long-term consequences of exposure to adverse childhood experiences (ACE), potentially traumatizing events (PTE), and the social determinants of health. As Larkin, Shields and Anda (2012) explain, understanding the early consequences of ecological factors like child abuse, exposure to community violence, poverty, and the mental illness of a parent should encourage investment by policy makers in the improvement of overall community health, family well-being, and the capacity building among social support networks. For young people who are still living in challenging contexts that expose them to traumatic events, we are learning that the best treatment is one that focuses on both individual and social processes that trigger negative emotional reactions. But individual trauma work is likely only useful after a client with signs of PTSD is embedded in a caring and supportive weave of relationships in a safe neighborhood. This has been the lesson learned from work with demobilized child soldiers, children exposed to war, and children recovering from maltreatment (Betancourt et al., 2010; Bonanno & Mancini, 2012; Klasen et al., 2010). A path to mental well-being is not exclusively one of self-reflection, forgiveness, mindfulness, or other change in cognition. Context matters more than psychology when the environment continues to brutalize an individual who has a history of trauma.

It is not surprising, then, that the research on ACE has shown very clearly that adult health depends on childhood experience (Anda et al., 2006) with a direct relationship between the number of adversities a child is exposed to and the likelihood of adult disorder. Table 8.1 summarizes the factors that predict long-term problems and the comorbid outcomes that have been found to be associated with ecological adversity. Odd, however, that while the ACE studies show that environments change children at the level of their neurobiology and behavior, we still think we can fix these problems by fixing children themselves. That's very strange given that the list of factors that are associated with later problems in life are *all* ecological. In other words, they are aspects of the child's environment that children need adults to change.

Perhaps the best argument for an ecological practice, then, is the differential impact it will have on the long-term development of vulnerable children. In this case, an ounce of prevention with those most at-risk really is worth a pound of cure later in their lives. If the argument, however, that shaping social ecologies improves the quality of life for clients isn't enough to change service delivery systems, then maybe the fact that there are big financial savings for agencies, communities, and governments when they invest in case management and community capacity building will promote investment in new models of practice (Hall et al., 2012).

Table 8.1 Adverse Childhood Experiences and associated adult outcomes (Anda et al., 2006)

Adverse Childhood Experiences	*Comorbid Outcomes*
<ul><li>Emotional abuse</li><li>Physical abuse</li><li>Contact sexual abuse</li><li>Exposure to alcohol or other substance abuse</li><li>Mental illness of caregiver</li><li>Violent treatment of mother figure</li><li>Criminal behavior in home</li><li>Parental separation/divorce</li></ul>	<ul><li>Mental health disturbances (panic, depression, etc.)</li><li>Somatic disturbances (sleep problems, obesity)</li><li>Substance abuse</li><li>Impaired memory of childhood</li><li>Sexuality (early intercourse, promiscuity, dissatisfaction)</li><li>Perceived stress, anger control problem, risk of partner violence</li></ul>

The Need for a Paradigm Shift

I don't mean to sound cynical, but too often even big bureaucracies that want to work more eco-logically struggle to do their work differently or spend their money in ways that will improve their clients' access to less formal supports (it is one thing to share a mental health worker with the community a day a week, but quite another to give that full-time position and its funding to a community agency). Even if staff are told to work more closely with communities they may be discouraged from leaving their offices to attend case conferences (it can be difficult to bill for indirect contact hours). Too often there is a reluctance to allow into the treatment room, residential facility, or community program the client's natural supports (issues of confidentiality or safety are frequently raised as barriers to facilitating smooth transitions), and the list goes on.

Appreciative Inquiry

While there is much to be discouraged by, the truth is that everywhere I travel I meet inspiring mental health professionals, educators, police officers, and caregivers who are making the shift to an ecological practice. The following exercise is an opportunity to mine your own experience for examples of success. The process of Appreciative Inquiry (Hammond & Royal, 2001) helps us identify what we are doing right and the conditions that were necessary for us to succeed as ecologically-oriented counselors in the specific contexts in which we work. Simply put, we become our own experts.

Exercise 8.1

An Appreciative Inquiry to Identify Best Practices

Step 1: Describe an experience at work (or as a volunteer) where you have been able to help a child, youth, or family get some, or all, of her/his/their needs met in a way that fit with her/his/their culture and context.

Step 2: Who, and/or what, was required to make this experience possible for you and the child, youth, or family? What did your employer, your colleagues, other service providers, the community, educational institutions, government departments, the client's extended family, and significant others do that made it possible for an ecologically-oriented intervention to work so well?

Step 3: Thinking about the future, what will you need to keep doing (or do even more of) to have more of these successes? What resources will be required? How will you recreate the success you've already had?

Step 4: How can you share your stories of success with your colleagues? Will sharing these stories help or hinder your efforts to work more ecologically?

I can understand the reluctance of systems to change. Unfortunately, there are few examples of evidence-based practices that show what most social workers, community-based psychologists, child and youth care workers, and public health nurses do is effective. Practice-based evidence, however, like that generated by Exercise 8.1, reminds us that making our counseling more eco-logical (which means becoming our client's ally, spending some of our clinical time performing the role of case manager, advocating for resources, and changing social delivery systems to better meet people's needs) can be very effective at increasing client well-being (Imber-Black, 1988; Madsen, 2009; Ungar et al., 2012).

Al Condeluci (2013), the Director of a large multiservice agency for people with disabilities in Pittsburgh, has suggested that there is a need for a paradigm shift in how we provide services to those who are vulnerable in our communities. If, for example, we look at why people with disabilities continue to struggle to be a part of their communities, or as Condulici says, to have "a house, a job, a ride and a friend," then it's clear that the highly medicalized model of care for people with disabilities has overstepped the bounds of its influence. There is nothing wrong with individual treatment for conditions that require intervention to alleviate acute or chronic symptoms: depression, anxiety, addiction. The problem is that the individual treatment paradigm is ineffective at providing people with all the other things they need to experience well-being. Individually focused interventions are simply not a good match to people's ecological needs.

Likewise, the map we are using to chart young people's problems and their solutions is wrong. We've started with a map that is for individual change processes even though children who face significant risks need their environments changed before individual changes will be sustainable. It's as if we are holding a geological survey map that shows mineral deposits beneath the surface of our city when what we need is a street map to know where we are and how to get where we need to go.

Two examples help illustrate this point. A child who experiences anxiety going to school may have good reason to fear playground bullies, or be so overprotected at home that he has never developed the psychological and social skills necessary to be independent. In either of these contexts, individualized treatment focused on building self-esteem or developing new coping strategies to avoid violence can only do so much. Likewise, interventions to address childhood obesity follow a similar pattern, albeit in very different ways. While obesity is known to affect a child's school engagement and academic performance because of its link to social stigma and mental health problems (Crosnoe & Muller, 2004; Florence, Asbridge & Veugelers, 2008; Taras & Potts-Datema, 2005), obesity prevention programs that are child-focused at school have little or no impact on changing children's body weight (Caballero et al., 2003). Programs that expand their focus beyond the child's behavior while at school and engage parents report much better results, although even these results are often mixed as over-eating is a more complex problem than any single intervention can address (Blom-Hoffman et al., 2008). Clearly, though, individualized treatment (even if delivered in a classroom or group setting) which focuses on cognitions, motivation, or lifestyle choices is unlikely to be effective unless a child's home, school, and community is adapted to make change possible (Alvaro et al., 2011).

As these examples show, providing treatment to individuals who live in challenging contexts is more effective when agencies view treatment as part of a continuum of services and supports that promotes community involvement and responsibility for children's complex needs. But how do we get agencies to see their responsibility to change systems rather than the individuals in systems? Helping them understand that clients are part of communities, and communities have the potential to contribute resources to a client's life is a first step. Simply defined, a community is a group of people who come together occasionally for some common cause or celebration. Those contacts, with their regularity and their ability to smooth over differences by focusing on what people have in common, creates the social capital that vulnerable people need to succeed.

Selling an Ecological Approach to Your Colleagues, Agency, and Community

Here are two strategies that I've found effective helping organizations adopt a more ecological approach to intervention.

Strategy 1: Test the Waters

While working as a Senior Clinical Case Consultant at a secure custody facility for young offenders, my clinical practice typically focused on cognitive behavioral interventions with the youth. The problem was that it was extremely difficult for young people to make the transition back to their communities and perform in the same way they performed while in custody. Frequent recidivism, breaches of probation, substance abuse, and school dropout were the result, even though the youth did very well while in a structured and safe environment.

Understanding the problem of recidivism to be partially the responsibility of a system that failed to provide the resources young people needed to make smooth transitions, I advocated for the primary caseworker for a particularly high-risk offender who was named Sobaz to continue working with the boy half a day a week after he was discharged. We knew Sobaz was returning to a family that would pressure him to leave school and a school where his peers would draw him back into a culture of drugs and delinquency. In custody his primary worker had formed an excellent bond with the boy and the two had developed a case plan that included education and drug treatment. Sobaz had become a leader among his peers on his living unit and had shown that with the right amount of mentoring, he could change. It made sense to continue to provide Sobaz the support he needed (and a reminder of who he had become) by inviting his unit worker to meet with him once a week after we transitioned Sobaz back into the community. The problem, however, was that the unit worker's job description did not include post-discharge contact with residents.

I began by talking about the young man's problems and the likelihood of recidivism during our discharge case conferences, manipulating the conversation in ways that focused our attention on the problems the boy would face that were beyond his control. The following is an example of the type of conversations I had with staff at the facility where I worked.

Michael (Senior Clinical Case Consultant): We know from review of Sobaz's case file that he tends to offend again quickly after release. I'm wondering if the gains we've made with him will be put at risk unless we change the environment into which we are placing him?

Unit Manager: We know that, but there's nothing we can do. He has to go home.

Unit Worker: Sobaz and I have talked about this. He knows the triggers. He knows what makes him get into trouble.

Michael: You've done amazing work with him. It's just that when I think of ways to help Sobaz find the supports he needs, and convince everyone he's changed, I'm just not sure he can do that on his own.

Teacher: I'm also worried that he may not go to school, even though he's doing great now. Let's face it, if he does offend again and he's back with us soon, at least we can help him get his education, right?

Unit Manager: Not our problem. I don't want to sound harsh, and I like the kid, but really. Not much we can do beyond our doors.

Michael: I know we can't change our work policies instantly, but in this case, where we all agree this kid is likely to reoffend, could we do an *experiment*? I was thinking that maybe we have Paul [the Unit Worker] be released half a day a week to work with Sobaz in the community. Remind him of everything he changed and help him connect to some new friends, maybe a recreation center. Whatever works.

Unit Manager: I get the idea, but there is no money for that, we'd have to backfill Paul on the unit and besides, that's not in his job description. Isn't that the job of the probation officer?

Michael: Paul, you know Sobaz best. Do you think he is going to join well with his probation officer? He strikes me as a kid who takes a long time to trust someone. Amazing that you got as far as you did with him.

Unit Worker: [*Speaking cautiously so as not to undermine the authority of his Unit Manager*] Sobaz isn't likely to trust his probation officer. I don't mind staying in touch. Maybe I could call him once a week?

Michael: I was thinking about that too. Great suggestion. But not sure it will be intense enough, at least at first. Really should be face-to-face contact. So here's a suggestion. What if we just use this opportunity to *test the waters*. Do an experiment. See if, say, eight weeks of weekly contact keeps Sobaz out of trouble. We document what happens and present our findings to senior management. Sell them on this as an idea. If it looks like it will work, we can then document what happened and fight for a policy change and some money. If it doesn't help, then we'll at least know we tried. The actual cost to backfill Paul will be quite small if we keep it to just an eight-week trial period. If it works, we may have a long-term solution for the kids that are most likely to repeat offend.

Unit Manager: I don't know. Seems like a lot of hassle.

Unit Worker: I'd be okay with doing it. We all like Sobaz. Might work.

Michael: [*Speaking to the Unit Manager directly*] If I could advocate on behalf of Sobaz, even have him come with me and try to convince the Director of our plan, would you be okay with that? If we could do this in a way that didn't cut into your budget?

Unit Worker: I could help too.

Unit Manager: I don't have a problem with you trying, especially if this is just a one time thing. If it is going to be something we do more, then I think we need to take it up with the Director and budget for it.

Michael: Exactly, but maybe if it works once, then senior management might be more interested in hearing from us when we ask for sustaining funds. Also, if it does work, or even works a little, Paul and Sobaz might be able to tell us what about this approach helps and what doesn't. I even wonder whether Sobaz might be intrigued to be part of something new. We would also have to let his family know. They might not like it.

Unit Worker: They're mostly okay with me, but that's in here. I sometimes think they're the biggest problem. Like they're going to expect Sobaz to become a delinquent again. Most of his family have been behind bars so I'm not sure they'll like seeing their kid spending more time with me or anyone else from the justice system. Know what I mean?

Michael: But worth a try?

Unit Worker: Oh, definitely. Without trying something, no way this kid is going to last out there and not get into a lot of trouble. Anything is better than nothing.

When I advocated for the money to have Paul, the Unit Worker, follow Sobaz into the community, the Director was skeptical but agreed it was a small price to pay to see if we should be thinking about these transitions in new ways. The high recidivism rate among young offenders had become a sore point politically and fingers were being pointed at the secure custody facility for failing to change the behavior of its residents. It was as if people expected us to fix the kids, not only while they were in custody but to ensure those changes were sustainable when the youth returned to their families, schools, and communities.

By keeping the intervention small, the costs low, and the potential for payoff large, I was able to get Paul released to work with Sobaz in the community for two months, then another two months of visits every 14 days. Sobaz did eventually break the law again, but it was over a year later and his crime was a very minor charge for shoplifting.

There were several reasons I was able to get the administrative structure of the institution to change. First, I was able to represent Sobaz's voice, explaining his world as he experienced it. In this sense, I negotiated with my colleagues for a definition of Sobaz's problems as related to the toxic context in which he lived and helped them to focus less on the young man's individual deficits. It would have been even better to have had Sobaz in the meeting to argue his view of his problems, but that was not common practice at those strategic team meetings.

Second, I didn't try to work alone. I formed an alliance with the Unit Worker and the Director. The Unit Manager never much liked the idea but was at least willing to go along with it as long as I didn't create more work for her.

I believe if I had tried to implement a system-wide change in policy as my first goal it would not have succeeded. After all, I had no proof that what I was proposing would effectively bring down recidivism rates and, as a consequence, save the system money in the long-term. Nothing brings momentum to an idea like success, even if it is just with one child.

Learning from this example, we can see that system stakeholders can be convinced to think ecologically when:

- It is in their best interest to do so (when it is likely they will have more success than they enjoy currently).
- Alliances are built that support this kind of thinking (it is difficult to succeed on one's own).
- The problems that are addressed have been troubling system managers and are in need of some new thinking (an ecological practice is best suited to the children with the most persistent problems and the fewest resources).
- Children and families need help to navigate and negotiate effectively (when resources are perceived as being in short supply, systems are more likely to want to work with other formal and informal supports).

Strategy 2: Think Context

A hospital-based clinical service for anxiety disorders offered a number of different treatments including individual psychotherapy and play therapy, a cognitive behavioral therapy group based on a manualized approach to treatment, and family counseling. In some instances, case conferences included educators and other professional consultants if a child's problems appeared to be more complex.

The strong emphasis on evidence-based practice with this population had led to very good results for many children, though workers had noticed that particular populations of children made it to their assessments but failed to sustain treatment, if they engaged at all. The children who tended to not receive adequate service were young people who self-identified as lesbian, gay, bisexual, or transgendered, Native American youth, rural youth, and youth from lower-income households. Anecdotally, service providers had heard that these youth experienced counseling as odd or insensitive to their needs, or that their parents lacked adequate transportation or could not take time off work to bring their children to the hospital for treatment. A review of files also showed that many of the referring agencies were not fully informed of the results of the assessments nor included in case planning process, even when the children and their families consented to the disclosure of their clinical records back to service providers in the community. Without the support of these community-based service providers to link clients with the hospital services, it was unlikely the rate of engagement in treatment was going to change.

With these problems in mind, and as a member of a hospital clinical team at the time, I asked for a meeting with the attending psychiatrist and other members of the anxiety disorders team, including a psychologist who offered cognitive behavioral therapy and a mental health nurse who ran the treatment group. Prior to that meeting I did a quick scan of the literature to find support for my argument that these clients should be more visible in our service. It wasn't difficult to locate studies of anxiety disorders among youth that showed that the populations which were mostly absent from our service had rates of anxiety equal to, and possibly higher, than the general population of all young people (D'Augelli & Hersherger, 1993; Owens, 1998; Sheldon-Keller et al., 1996).

Put succinctly, while our treatment groups for anxiety disorders were full, we weren't reaching the young people who came from more disadvantaged contexts. Furthermore, it had been shown that the young people we weren't seeing were using help lines and online chat forums to reach out for help with their anxiety rather than the hospital clinic that specialized in the disorder.

The following is an example of my conversation with the hospital team inviting them to find an ecological solution to the problem of engagement after assessment.

Michael: Our work is great, but there does seem to be populations of children who aren't appearing on our caseloads.

Psychiatrist: The service is free with referral. Though the recent report from the Help Line does suggest we are not reaching some young people.

Psychologist: That's worrisome.

Michael: I'm wondering if what we are offering is the right service for all children?

Nurse: But our evaluations are excellent. I'm in the schools all the time talking about the clinic and meet at least once a year with each school board to ensure they have what they need to make referrals.

Michael: Yes, it's like we're doing everything right with the people who engage, but I'm wondering if there are barriers to service that we don't control? That are out there in the community? If LGBT youth and Native youth aren't here I'm curious why.

Psychiatrist: And poor kids too.

Michael: If we wanted to we might want to think about advocating for our clinic to provide service directly in the schools? Would that help the kids whose parents can't take time off work? Maybe we also need to send out a very direct message to the kids we're not seeing. Find out where they are going for information and let those other services know what we do.

Psychologist: Are you sure you want to do that? I get it, but our caseloads are really high, and we already have a seven-month waitlist. Do we want to try to reach more children? Doesn't that set up expectations?

Nurse: I could maybe add one more group, even make it just for kids who identify as LGBT, but I'd need a student to intern with me.

Michael: That's a good idea, and would help with the waitlist a little. But there is likely more we need to do.

Psychologist: It's just finding the time to do all the work one-on-one and talk to parents and the school. If you want to take that on, I have no problem.

Michael: I'm not sure that I would be effective talking to the families and schools of children who are not my primary patients. But maybe I could try something. Work a little more often with the people in a child's life and report back how it goes. See what happens to my caseload.

Psychologist: Works for me.

Psychiatrist: Me too.

Notice that in the example above, I identify a particular population of children for whom traditional counseling is not effective. The first thing I do is to distinguish which children would benefit most from a more ecological approach. While all clients might find it helpful, the approach is best suited to those who are marginalized in their communities. Next, we brainstorm both problems extending programming to this population (for example, long waitlists, heavy caseloads, parents who can't bring their children to therapy) and possible solutions. The solution is to make changes that we each feel comfortable making but still respond to the contextual factors that affect children where they live. The nurse volunteers to add another group with a population-specific focus. The team as a whole will eventually do a little more advertising of the program, and I will begin to work with educators and parents more often in my practice to see if I can engage vulnerable populations better. Combined, our efforts introduce more complexity to our work as we expand the scope of our practice.

Ecologically-sensitive Casework

As these strategies show, we need to be able to convince those whose support we need for good casework that working to change a child's social ecology is clinical practice at its best. Ecologically sensitive clinical work that complements individually-focused interventions requires that the complexity of a client's coping strategies and the social context which shapes the client's choices be taken into account. The 20 skills discussed in Chapters 4 and 5 are not only useful when working with clients. They can also be adapted for use with our colleagues and employers to explore how we can make services more ecological. This means, for example, that:

- Functional outcomes (the behaviors we want to see happen) are negotiated with individuals, families, institutions, and communities, all of whom have a say over what is defined as a reasonable outcome that can be expected from counseling. Even when clients are convincing and able to explain what they need and why, that doesn't necessarily mean that service providers will listen when clients tell them what to do. As counselors, we need to help clients raise their voices and be heard.
- Maladaptive coping strategies should be explained as possible solutions. These atypical strategies may be functional in resource-poor contexts. If changed too quickly, new coping strategies can leave clients vulnerable in dangerous environments unless those environments are also changed.
- Change is viewed as a process that has a different amount of influence on different people who face different amounts of risk. As we saw in Chapter 6, an intervention dosage is difficult to predict without a thorough assessment of the individual's risk exposure.

If we use the 20 skills to change the systems in which we work, we can make service more ecologically oriented. In the descriptions that follow each of the skills, the focus is on what systems can do to change. Notice that the questions I've posed are for service providers (and informal supports) to answer. Questions for clients themselves are provided in Chapters 4 and 5. Of course, it is expected that clients, too, will participate as fully as possible in the design of their services though there may be good reasons for service providers to meet first to consider what they can do to change their models of practice and their agency's policies and procedures before trying to help clients.

Navigation Skills: Questions for System Change

1. Make resources available.

The counselor and her/his colleagues (in collaboration with the client) work together to identify which resources are available that could help the client succeed in different ways. The focus is on facilitating opportunities for the client to experience new resources as realistically available.

Questions for our colleagues and system managers:

- If the client is to change, what resources will she/he/they need?
- Are these realistically available? How can we (the service providers) help to make these resources available?
- Which resources has the client asked for? If we haven't made these available, why is that? Would the client be more or less likely to change if what she/he/they are asking for was made available?

2. Make resources accessible.

The counselor and her/his colleagues make the resources the client needs more accessible.

Questions for our colleagues and system managers:

- Of the resources that are available to the client, are there some that are difficult for the client to use? Are some inaccessible?
- Of the resources that are available, what steps could we take as clinicians to help the client access them?
- What policies and procedures could we change to make it easier for clients to access resources?
- In the past, when the client tried to access a resource, what happened? Who or what was responsible for making access possible, and who or what made access more difficult?
- In the absence of help from us, what has the client done to access the resources she/he/they need?

3. Explore barriers to change.

The counselor and her/his colleagues discuss the agency barriers to change that the client experiences, and which resources are most likely needed to address which barriers.

Questions for our colleagues and system managers:

- What characteristics of the client's personality, or behavior, cause the most difficulty for the systems that work with the client?
- What have we done to change how we work with the client so these will be less of a problem for us and the client?
- Are the characteristics of the client that we find the most troubling experienced by the client as problems?
- If the client changed her/his/their behavior, would we change the way we respond to the client and the resources we make available and accessible?

4. Build bridges to new services and supports.

The counselor and her/his colleagues build bridges to other services and supports that they know about and which they think may be of use to the client.

Questions for our colleagues and system managers:

- What solutions to the client's problem can we help make happen?
- Are there resources beyond our own service that we know about that could help the client?
- How can we build bridges to these other services and supports? What will other service providers need from us to become a part of our client's life?

5. Ask what is meaningful.

The counselor and her/his colleagues review what they know about which resources the client finds most meaningful given the client's context and culture.

Questions for our colleagues and system managers:

- Of the services and supports we have to offer, which are most valued by the client?
- How could we make the services we have more meaningful to the client?
- How will we show the client that we are sincere in our wish to help her/him/them find the resources they want? Who should speak with the client directly?
- What have we learned about people like the client and how she/he/they prefer to solve problems in her/his/their particular context and culture?
- Are there unique strategies that people like our client use to cope with problems?

6. Keep solutions as complex as the problems they solve.

The counselor and her/his colleagues find ways to provide the client with many different services and supports. In collaboration with the client's family, school, community, and other service providers, help is offered to the client to cope with complex problems.

Questions for our colleagues and system managers:

- Besides the core service we provide, what other services and supports should we help the client access?
- Given the complexity of the problems the client experiences, how can we as service providers ensure that the resources we provide meet all of the client's needs?
- Keeping in mind the services and supports we have provided in the past, what else could we do to make it more likely the client will succeed?

7. Find allies.

The counselor and her/his colleagues engage other service providers and supports to help the client put solutions into practice.

Questions for our colleagues and system managers:

- What other service providers and informal supports could we involve in the client's life to make change more likely?

- Can we ask these other service providers and supports for help directly, or are there procedures we need to go through to coordinate them?
- Given the client's specific problem, who in the client's family, community, or among other service providers has the expertise to help? If they can't help directly, what advice can they give us?

8. Ask whether coping strategies are adaptive or maladaptive.

The counselor and her/his colleagues review what they know about the client's life. Given the client's context, service providers need to consider whether the client's ways of coping makes sense in challenging contexts. Are those coping strategies adaptive or maladaptive? Says who?

Questions for our colleagues and system managers:

- Are the solutions the client is using bringing more advantages than disadvantages?
- Of the solutions the client has tried, which do we see as most desirable? Which are least desirable? Would the client agree with these assessments? If not, why not?
- How difficult would it be for the client to find other solutions to her/his/their problems?
- How can we as service providers lessen the negative consequences of the client's chosen coping strategies when those strategies appear to us to be maladaptive?

9. Explore the agency's level of motivation to change.

The counselor and her/his colleagues assess their agency and community's willingness to provide the client with what she/he/they say is necessary to change behavior.

Questions for our colleagues and system managers:

- How motivated are our systems to change the way we provide service?
- What would make us more motivated?
- If we did want to change the way we provide service to the client, would it be best to start with front-line staff, managers, or do we need changes to policies and procedures first?

10. Advocate.

The counselor and her/his colleagues advocate with, or on behalf of, the client to make resources more available and accessible.

Questions for our colleagues and system managers:

- What can we do to ensure the client succeeds? What personal contacts or resources can we make available and accessible that are ethical to share?
- Have we asked others what they can do to help the client?
- What policies and procedures do we need to change so that the client is able to succeed?

Negotiation Skills: Questions for System Change

1. Explore thoughts and feelings.
The counselor and her/his colleagues consider the client's thoughts and feelings about her/his/their problem and what participating in counseling could mean.

Questions for our colleagues and system managers:

- What does the client think her/his/their problem is?
- From the client's perspective, which behaviors, thoughts, or feelings are a problem?
- Do we agree or disagree with how the client feels about her/his/their problem?
- If one of us had the same problem, how would we handle it?
- What has the client's experience been of other service providers in the past? How ready is the client to accept help from another service?

2. Look broadly at the context in which problems occur.
The counselor and her/his colleagues discuss the context in which the client's problem occurs, how the problem is defined by others, and the social, economic, and political conditions that sustain the problem.

Questions for our colleagues and system managers:

- Which contexts, and which services, make the problem bigger/smaller?
- When is the client's problem more/less influential?
- How have services in the past, and in the present, changed the influence of the problem on the client's life?
- Which relationships add to the client's problem, and which make it go away?
- Culturally, what do people who share the client's culture say about the client's problem?
- What social, economic, and political conditions make the problem more likely to occur? Which make it less likely?

3. Explore who has responsibility for making change happen.
The counselor and her/his colleagues share responsibility for the client's coping strategies.

Questions for our colleagues and system managers:

- What responsibility do we have for helping the client make changes?
- Which solutions are under the control of the client? Which are under our control? Which solutions need the client and service providers to share responsibility to make them happen?

4. Make the client's voice heard.

The counselor and her/his colleagues ensure the client is heard when she/he/they identify the people and resources necessary to make life better.

Questions for our colleagues and system managers:

- What has the client told us she/he/they need?
- What has the client told us are the best strategies to deal with her/his/their problem?
- How willing and able are we to listen to the client?
- How have we behaved in the past when the client told us what she/he/they needed? How will our past behavior influence the client's confidence in the usefulness of our services and supports?

5. Consider new names for old problems.

When appropriate, the counselor and her/his colleagues may generate new ways to describe the client's problem.

Questions for our colleagues and system managers:

- What other ways do we describe the client's problem?
- How would new names for the client's problem influence the services and supports we provide?
- Which of the seven factors (associated with resilience) can we change as system providers to make the client's life better?
- How would others in the client's life describe the client's problem? What words would they use? Would these labels for the problem be better or worse for the client? How would these labels change the work we do with the client?

6. Find a description of the problem that fits.

Once the client chooses one (or more) new descriptions of the problem that fit with how she/he/they see the world, the counselor and her/his colleagues change their interventions.

Questions for our colleagues and system managers:

- Of the different ways we've suggested the client see her/his/their problem, which are most acceptable to the client?
- If we choose one of the client's preferred descriptions of her/his/their problem, what will that mean for the way our service contracts with the client?

7. Find resources the client values.

The counselor and her/his colleagues help the client find the internal and external resources that the client says she/he/they need to put new solutions into practice.

Questions for our colleagues and system managers:

- Of the seven factors that relate to resilience, which do we value most as service providers? How does our bias affect how we provide help to the client?
- Which resources would the client most like to have available and accessible?

- Which solutions will our agencies and communities most criticize? Are we strong enough to argue back that the client's choices are reasonably good ones given the challenges she/he/they face?

8. Expand possibilities for change.

The counselor and her/his colleagues expand the client's possibilities for change.

Questions for our colleagues and system managers:

- If we helped the client put these new strategies into practice, what personal strengths/assets/resources would she/he/they have that she/he/they don't have now?
- To put these strategies into practice, what resources can we make available from the client's family/school/community/neighbors/government?
- Have we overwhelmed the client? Or are our interventions paced to meet the client's needs in ways that the client wants?

9. Performance

The counselor and her/his colleagues identify times when the client has been performing new ways of coping and help the client to make others notice these changes.

Questions for our colleagues and system managers:

- When exactly have we seen changes to the client's behavior, thoughts, or feelings?
- How can we reflect the changes the client has made in our case notes, during case conferences, and in other places where we reflect on our intervention?

10. Perception

The counselor and her/his colleagues help the client find ways to convince others that she/he/they have changed, or are doing better than expected.

Questions for our colleagues and system managers:

- How can we convince others that the client has changed? What do others need to see? What do they need to hear about the client? Given the constraints of confidentiality, how much can we share? Would the client give us permission to share more about them with other service providers?
- Who must we get to notice the client's new ways of coping if the changes the client has made are to be sustained?
- Who will be most reluctant to acknowledge that the client has changed?
- Who can we ask to help us convince others that the client has changed?

Making Service Systems Work for Clients

Thinking back to times I've used these 20 skills for system change, I am reminded of my work with a community-based residential program that provided treatment for children with severe conduct disorder. While working there, I often developed case plans that required the children to make a slow transition back to their families of origin. The problem was that once the visits grew to more than an occasional overnight stay, the government department funding residential care would refuse to pay a per diem for the child if she was back home for more than a single night at a time. At a crucial period in the child's transition back into a supportive relationship with her parents, a decision had to be made to either (1) decrease the frequency of visitation, (2) prematurely discharge the youth from the residential service and risk placement breakdown, or (3) reduce the residential facility's budget by the amount that would be taken away by the funder if the child went home temporarily. The last option was definitely unworkable. After all, staffing had to be maintained regardless of whether a youth was sleeping in the residence (the staff were there for the other youth who remained on the living unit and in the case of an emergency, to offer support to the child who had returned home). Likewise, decreasing the frequency of visits (option 1) seemed counter-productive to the child's eventual reunification with her family. In the end, checkmated, we were forced to prematurely discharge the child from care.

That was unfortunate as research shows that services do the most good when clients respond favorably to statements such as: "Overall, I am satisfied with the services I received," "I helped choose my services," "I could get the service when I needed it," "Staff were sensitive to my cultural and ethnic background" (Ungar et al., 2012).[1] It takes more than formal services (counseling included) to ensure a child's optimal development under stress. Services must be designed in such a way that they are tailored to meet children's needs.

With no choice but to discharge, we held a team meeting that included, as a preliminary step, just the treatment team and supervisors at the residential facility. While it was unusual to hold a meeting about a child without the parents present, the focus of that first meeting wasn't the family. It was our system and what *we* needed to change to make ourselves more responsive to the family's needs. It was about changing our attitudes and challenging our workplace procedures before trying to help the family cope with their child's transition home.

Many of the 20 skills were used during that meeting. For example, to help the family navigate to the services and supports they needed, we considered:

- When the child returns home, what resources does the family have available and accessible that could replace the interventions we've done successfully with the child? Just as importantly, how can we help the family make better use of these resources?
- What barriers are there to them accessing these resources? How can we help the parents navigate their way around those barriers?
- What allies do we have in other systems who could help the family? How can we build bridges to these other formal and informal supports before discharge occurs?
- From the family's point of view, and especially the child's, what supports do they have that they would perceive as most useful? Most meaningful? How can we help strengthen these?
- If the child and the family slide back into previous patterns of behavior (in this case, allowing the child to stay home from school, or blaming the school and social workers for not "fixing" the child) will we be able to convince others that these are adaptive strategies in a context

where the parents are overwhelmed and the child unable to exercise self-control? Will these other service providers listen to us? How can we be more convincing? And how can we work with our colleagues to find more adaptive, socially desirable solutions?

- How motivated are we to expand the scope of our practice from direct treatment of the child to treatment of the family and advocacy for what the child and her family needs?
- How much time will staff be permitted to perform these functions of the case manager and advocate? Are we properly trained? Will others listen to us as we try to make services more complex, sustainable?
- Finally, recognizing that there will be other children in the future who are discharged prematurely, what changes to our policies and procedures should we recommend? What can we do as staff to make these changes happen?

We also spent time thinking about how we could help the family negotiate for what they needed. We considered:

- What did we know about the family's contact with other service providers in the past and present? What was the likelihood the family would see referrals to other agencies as helpful? How did they feel about the service they'd received from us? Did they want us to continue working with them after discharge?
- Once their child was home, how much stress was she likely to cause the family? Was it realistic to expect the family to handle her if her behavior escalated?
- Whose responsibility was it to sustain the changes the child had made in care? For example, how invested was the child's school in sustaining these changes? Would the school fully cooperate in case management? Did they see the child's success as their responsibility too?
- Had we provided enough space for the parents and child to tell us what they wanted changed?
- Had we provided the family with any new ways of seeing their child? When she had entered our care, she was known as a very angry out of control girl whose family was blamed for her misbehavior. By the time she was ready for discharge, we'd changed the way people saw the child. They understood she had several diagnosable disorders including ADHD, a severe learning disorder, and aspects of conduct disorder that would require years for the child to learn to control. Which of these labels had the family accepted? Had we done a good enough job explaining the child's behavioral problems to the parents and the child's educators? Were these diagnoses helpful to the family, or stigmatizing?
- With these new definitions of the child's problems, had we expanded possibilities for successful adaptation?
- Had we done enough to share our successes in the residential facility with the child's school? Community? Family? Did others understand what we had done to help the child? Had we made our techniques transparent enough for others to use them as well? Could what we did with the child in care be adapted to home, school, and community settings? Had we been concrete enough and described the techniques that could be useful with the child after discharge?
- Had we done enough to make people like the child? Did her family, educators, and the others in her life know the stories of her success in residential care? Had they seen proof of the child's success? And had we done a good enough job of documenting those changes?

In this case of a child who we had to discharge earlier than we would have liked, we were able to delegate one member of our treatment team as a liaison with the family and an advocate for services within our agency. The demands on the worker's time were not heavy (about a half day a week for ten weeks), but enough to make us realize that we couldn't provide this level of care for every child needing a smoother transition home. Furthermore, we were fortunate that the child lived relatively close to the residential facility. If she had lived further away, we would have had to work harder to find a local case manager with whom we could have coordinated our interventions.

Once we had considered what we as staff members and as an agency could do to help the family, we were much better prepared to meet with the family and help them navigate and negotiate. Obviously, they would have preferred option three, a slower transition of their child back home. Even with that possibility gone, there were still things we could offer to make it more likely the child would succeed at home and in school. With the child and family's consent, we made a point of identifying new resources that could support the child after discharge. We made our treatment strategies accessible to the school and family. We sat in on meetings between the child and the child's educators to help them replicate the environment that had helped the child succeed in care. We met with staff at a local boys and girls club who had agreed to provide after-school programming for the child. And we linked the parents to a family resource center where they could continue to get support while parenting a very challenging child.

My sense was that because we had met as a staff team first, and thought about the barriers to service that our service structures had imposed on the family, we were much more sensitive to the frustration the family was experiencing providing their daughter with continuity of care and an effective treatment plan. We also developed a better sense of what we needed to do to change our agency's policies and procedures to make them more sensitive to the complex social ecologies in which our clients lived.

Of course, even the best use of the 20 skills for system change won't necessarily stop bad things from happening when systems are too stuck in their ways to change. A community that is resilient provides a network of integrated services and supports that is there to pick up the pieces when things go wrong as much as it is there to help children develop the skills and structure enough challenge for them to develop their capacity for a lifetime of healthy coping. In this sense we need to make the resources a community offers (including their services) robust, useful, and sustainable, and ensure that community members and service providers have the ability to adapt and make use of resources when needed. Few of us ever think of seeing a counselor pre-emptively, or finding out what our house insurance really covers. The more a population is adaptive, able to exploit the opportunities that are available, the better they'll be able to thrive.

To illustrate, when researchers looked at why communities exposed to natural and human-made disasters recover quickly, they identified a short list of capacities that communities need to thrive (Bell, 2011; Norris, Sherrieb & Pfefferbaum, 2011). These include caring and supportive relationships, collective identification with a common goal and a shared culture or, at the very least, respect for differences. High on the list are also equitable access to resources like employment opportunities, medical care, and housing. When a community also has spiritual leadership, a creative class (people who can inspire through words and songs) and mechanisms to distribute wealth among those most in need, a community's social capital is likely to be great enough to weather the worst of storms. One need only contrast the length of time it took New Orleans to recover with Japan's recovery after its earthquake-tsunami-nuclear disaster. The difference in people's resilience between the two countries was not just their individual capacity to recover, but the structures that supported that recovery at the levels of government, individual communities, and families themselves.

To imply that individuals recover from disasters overlooks the obvious: it is the resilience of people's social ecologies before the disaster that predicts a community's resilience (Abramson et al., 2010). So it was when we were forced to design a plan for a child's transition back home that required discharge from treatment earlier than we would have liked. With our hands tied, and limits put on further treatment, our focus had to be on adapting the child's social ecology once back home. We literally had to change services to match what the child needed, even if it meant compromising the financial well-being of our agency temporarily by delegating a staff member to play the role of case manager after a child's discharge.

Chapter Summary

Many clinicians already make a great deal of effort to broaden the scope of their clinical practice, decenter the client and focus on changing the client's social ecology. The problem is that their agencies often consider these efforts a luxury or distraction. We have largely ignored the evidence that paying attention to contextual and cultural factors *first* makes for much better outcomes when we employ individual and family focused treatments to deal with complex problems like delinquency and depression (DuMont, Widom & Czaja, 2007; Wekerle, Waechter & Chung, 2012; Ungar, 2011).

An ecological approach to clinical practice gives mental health professionals a way to take theory and apply it to practice. There are very few roadmaps for counselors who want to integrate into their clinical work what they know about the social determinants of health, human development in diverse social ecologies, human rights, the politics of race, gender, ability and sexual orientation, resilience, and a host of other theories that explain the threats to young people's positive psychosocial growth. No wonder the agencies that provide services are sometimes reluctant to change the focus of their work, especially when the results are thought to be uncertain and their staff poorly trained to address broadly the social determinants of health.

In cases where people live in challenging contexts or face significant personal challenges, a more contextualized intervention can produce longer-lasting effects than one which is limited to individual change processes. The trick, as this chapter has shown, is to find ways to help organizations experiment with an ecological practice and document their successes. In this regard, we can adapt the 20 skills that help our clients navigate and negotiate. We can use them with our colleagues and agencies to help identify ways that systems also need to change. Of course, an ecological practice does not necessarily replace individual or family interventions. It does, however, greatly expand what guidance counselors, social workers, family therapists, nurses, child and youth care workers, psychologists, or other helping professionals do as part of their interventions. It also highlights the need to adapt our service delivery systems to make them more responsive to people's needs in challenging contexts.

Note

1 These questions are part of the Pathways to Resilience Youth Measure (PRYM). To view the measure, and for permission to use, please contact The Resilience Research Centre (rrc@dal.ca). For information on the PRYM and all its subscales, please see: Ungar et al. (2012).

CHAPTER 9

THE COUNSELOR AS ADVOCATE

Good advocacy has to be part of good counseling. Unless we change the quality of resources (ensuring they are available and accessible) and make it possible for people to control the resources they need, we are not going to create the conditions necessary for clients to transfer back into their communities the changes they've made in our offices and institutions.

Advocacy

To help clients get the quality services they deserve, the counselor can:

- Teach clients how to advocate for themselves.
- Join with clients and advocate together.
- Advocate on behalf of clients with the counselor's employer and other service providers.
- As a member of the wider community, use the counselor's professional status as a way to position themself in social policy debates.

Each of these types of advocacy has its own advantages, though different clients and different counselors may choose one over the other depending on their individual strengths (Are you a good public speaker? Does the client have the confidence to self-advocate?). Regardless of which form of advocacy one promotes, the goal is to help clients navigate and negotiate effectively for services and social policies that matter to them (Chung & Bemak, 2012). For example, school boards can be forced to provide special services for children with emotional and behavioral problems rather than suspending a child for misbehaving. Child Protection Services can be embarrassed into providing in-home supports before removing a child permanently from a family that has been systematically marginalized (for example, an Aboriginal family where the parents had been victims of abuse at residential schools where they were forcibly placed during their childhoods). The greater the client's exposure to adversity, the more important the counselor's role becomes as an advocate for responsive services.

The real impact of services comes, though, when they are provided to those who are most vulnerable. This differential impact (which I discussed in Chapter 2) has been demonstrated through research done by people like Maria del Carmen Huerta (2011) who works with the Organization for Economic Co-operation and Development as a social policy analyst. Huerta measured the impact of the birth of a child on the economic well-being of families. Sole parent families were hit hardest and dropped more quickly into poverty than two parent families. Her point was that countries that spend public funds on child support programs (like subsidized childcare for working parents) have higher maternal employment rates and lower child poverty. Likewise, Huerta showed that when we look at scores on standardized tests for grade two students, it is the children of immigrant families who benefit the most from early interventions to provide families with services that maintain their economic viability. We also know from other research that when parents (especially new immigrants) are less stressed by the demands of work, long commutes, and leaving their children unmonitored, parents report better mental health and children are protected against many developmental risks like early school leaving, substance abuse and risky sexual activity (Yoshikawa & Kalil, 2010).

The trick is to provide the right intervention to the right people to have the largest impact. Unfortunately, many children do not get the right dosage of an intervention, at the right time, in the right place. Making this situation even worse is the challenge many professional counselors experience getting their agencies to let them expand their scope of practice to include advocacy.

To illustrate how children navigate through a landscape of complex service systems and how counselors can advocate with them and for them, I've annotated below a detailed case description that was done as part of the Pathways to Resilience Study, a mixed methods examination of young people who are concurrent users of multiple services (child welfare, mental health, juvenile corrections, and special educational programs) and community supports (boys and girls clubs, programs and shelters for homeless youth) (Ungar et al., 2012). These children are a particularly vulnerable group with exceptionally high levels of need.

Kyle, who was 16 years old when he was interviewed for the study, was one of more than 500 youths who participated in interviews to assess service use patterns, risk factors, and resilience. Forty-four of these youth also had their case files reviewed from as many services as our team could access (see Ungar et al., 2012). In Kyle's case, not only were we able to interview him, we were also able to review his mental health, child welfare, and juvenile corrections files to see what services he'd received over time and in which combinations.

What we learned was that: (1) more services are not necessarily better and (2) counselors need to do more than see children like Kyle for individual treatment if they are going to influence the child's psychosocial development. They also need to be case managers who help children and their families be heard.

Case Study: Kyle

Kyle's family first became involved with child protection services when he was three years old. A complaint was filed with the Department of Community Services (DCS) by a neighbor who reported inappropriate parenting, harsh discipline, and drug and alcohol consumption by the parents. The claim was investigated but eventually the case was closed and no further contact was made with the family.

Kyle has one older brother. His parents were divorced just after Kyle's birth. Kyle has had no contact with his biological father who was diagnosed with paranoid schizophrenia before Kyle's birth.

With all these risk factors, it's not surprising that at the age of four, Kyle underwent assessment at a preschool clinic where he was diagnosed with ADHD. He was subsequently placed on Ritalin and his mother was referred to a parenting program to learn about the disorder. It doesn't appear that she attended, nor is it clear from our review of the files whether anyone contacted her to see why. When Kyle was six years old, a referral was made to a mental health clinic. However, once again, his file was quickly closed due to his mother's lack of follow-through and attendance.

This pattern is fairly typical of families in the study who face similar challenges. From what the research team could see through file reviews there were numerous offers by counselors to help Kyle and his family but little structured support to ensure the family could access services, little follow-up by a case manager to see if treatment was attended or if a different treatment was required, and little coordination between service providers to ensure continuity of the service plan.

From the time Kyle was three until he turned ten, there were at least seven referrals to DCS, each citing similar worries like domestic violence, inappropriate supervision, and substance abuse by Kyle's caregivers. All of these claims were investigated but none were fully substantiated. When Kyle was ten, his mother agreed to voluntarily work with staff from a community organization for at-risk youth and families. The hope was to prevent further investigations. A trained in-home support worker visited the family approximately once a week until Kyle was 15 years old. Unfortunately, Kyle's more serious challenges were still not being addressed in a way that engaged Kyle.

When Kyle was 13 years old he reported to his guidance counselor an incident of violence by his step-father toward Kyle's brother. This allegation was investigated and the mother was referred to the same community organization that was already providing her with an in-home support worker. About a month after the first incident, Kyle again reported to his guidance counselor another episode of violence by the step-father toward Kyle's brother. A new investigation was opened and Kyle's brother went to stay with family friends for four weeks. The case was soon closed due to a lack of evidence and Kyle's brother returned home.

At around this same time, Kyle was diagnosed with a rare form of cancer that is typically fatal unless there is a bone marrow transplant from a matched donor. Kyle was placed on medication that required careful monitoring and the hospital social worker, in an effort to keep Kyle alive, called DCS and indicated concern regarding Kyle's mother's ability to manage her son's illness. Kyle was referred to the department of pediatric oncology at the children's hospital, as well as an oncology social worker who helped him adjust to his illness and encouraged him to keep his weekly appointments.

Two months later, Kyle's mother told the hospital social worker that Kyle's brother was being verbally abusive toward both herself and Kyle. She asked for help and was again directed to the same community organization that was providing a weekly support worker in her home. The fact that Kyle's mother went again to an outside source for support suggests that her relationship with the in-home support worker may not have been very good. As Kyle's mother's own mental health deteriorated, her role overseeing Kyle's treatment also diminished. Kyle soon stopped complying with his medication, blood work, and other appointments. Hospital staff also noted in their files concerns about the financial burden Kyle's medication was placing on his mother and the need to advocate for long-term financial help.

Reviewing the enormity of the case plan and everyone's needs, it seemed to us that Kyle and his mother had done what they could to navigate and negotiate for services that were more intense and targeted toward the violence. Rather than being provided services that the family defined as necessary, however, they appear to have been referred repeatedly to the same in-home support that was ineffective at addressing the escalating problems the family was experiencing. At this point, Kyle's mental health service providers at the hospital began to advocate for more services, though they too were unable to secure the help the family needed.

Kyle's social worker reported that Kyle's chaotic home environment and the history of family violence warranted the assignment of a long-term social worker from DCS, as well as the possibility of removing Kyle from his home. DCS reviewed the file but once again closed it at intake because there were no overt child protection concerns. Out of frustration, Kyle's mother contacted the Children's Ombudsman and another referral was made to DCS. The family's case was reviewed for a second time and then closed. The mother was again directed to the same community organization that had already provided her with service.

A month later, DCS was forced to re-open Kyle's file after reports from the oncology social worker of domestic violence between Kyle's mother and brother, as well as between his mother and her partner, and hard drug use in the home. The mother's partner was served with an undertaking to leave the home, and DCS temporarily placed Kyle's brother into voluntary care at the mother's request. Once the mother's partner left the home, Kyle's brother was permitted to return.

Though these interventions were helpful, it was too little and much too late. Kyle was by this time 14 years old and, despite his illness, began to engage in risk-taking behaviors like lighting his clothes on fire, crossing a busy street extra slowly, and threatening suicide. Kyle was asked to meet with a psychiatrist who was convinced that the violence in the home was harming Kyle emotionally. A referral to a psychologist was made and, though it seemed odd given the nature of the psychiatric assessment, a recommendation was made to Kyle's school that he be provided an individualized learning plan to help him meet his educational and behavioral needs.

While Kyle was cooperative with his mental health team, his behavior at home and in the community became increasingly violent. The police were called to Kyle's home numerous times over the next year. Kyle was eventually charged with uttering death threats and assault with a weapon after pointing a knife at his brother and mother. Kyle was placed on probation with a daily curfew but continued to live at home. Soon after Kyle's mother called the psychologist to which the family had been referred to inform him of Kyle's threats to kill her. The psychologist recommended DCS take the necessary action to protect Kyle and those around him. In case notes, the escalation in Kyle's oppositional and defiant behavior was believed to have been the result of Kyle not feeling safe in his own home. His mother's ex-partner was stalking her and had entered the home when Kyle was home alone.

These issues of personal safety were not addressed directly. Instead, Kyle received more psychological and psycho-educational testing. These assessments were completed at the request of the youth justice court. Based on the results, it was recommended that Kyle be placed in a structured environment with one-on-one support. Instead, Kyle was assigned a community youth worker through DCS with whom he maintained a close connection for the next eight months, participating in programed activities several hours each week.

At the request of youth justice services Kyle was also referred to the Complex Case Committee. For the next year, his caseworkers tried to find him an appropriate placement. He was ineligible for any form of foster care because of his history of risky behaviors and his medical problems. Placement in a residential treatment program was never considered because a letter from his oncology social worker to the institution was "misplaced." A second request was turned down because Kyle had already accessed a large number of other services and was still maintaining contact with his community youth worker.

It was difficult from either the file reviews or interviews done with Kyle to know whether Kyle wanted a more restrictive placement, or if he wanted his home to change so he could return and live there. His behavior would suggest the latter. His violence seemed to be a reaction to an environment that would not change, while service plans developed with his mental health, oncology, education, DCS, and probation workers kept trying to change Kyle's behavior. It is worth noting that Kyle did better when he was provided a support worker in his own home who could advocate for his needs. However, with few changes in the chaos around him, his problem behaviors kept escalating. During the eight months working with his community worker, Kyle attempted suicide at least once.

Eventually, at the request of Kyle's mother, Kyle was taken into care and placed in a group home for 48 hours, after which he returned home, promising to behave better. Kyle told his probation officer at the time that he felt his mother "sensationalizes things" too much and that she blamed him for problems of her own.

Not surprisingly, Kyle's problems continued. Over the next two years, Kyle repeatedly breached his probation order and his mother asked DCS to take her son back into care. Kyle also began to abuse prescription medications like Valium that he could buy on the street. The mental health team at the hospital refused to admit Kyle into any specialized treatment program until there was a viable plan put in place for after his release from the program. DCS agreed to help and looked for a group home that could take Kyle. At the age of 15, Kyle was finally admitted to a residential mental health treatment program.

Two months after entering the program, a parental capacity assessment was conducted with Kyle's mother. It noted that her capacity to parent was poor and recommended that, oddly enough given that the focus of the assessment was the mother, Kyle, "should be provided treatment in a lock-down facility since youth is a danger to self, others and home visits may only sabotage any progress." Kyle completed ten months in a residential mental health treatment program and continued to have regular probation appointments. Overall, Kyle did well, though another youth in the program alleged that Kyle sexually assaulted her. The treatment program requested Kyle return to his mother but she refused. The program eventually decided the matter could be dealt with internally and Kyle was allowed to remain in the program.

After discharge, Kyle once again lived with his mother but refused contact with the transition team that provided aftercare. He also completed his period of probation, though a few days later he was charged with theft and sentenced to another six months of probation. Kyle's mother refused to take Kyle home from court if restrictions were not placed on him. The court agreed and Kyle was sent home with strict curfews and requirements regarding his attendance at school.

Within weeks, Kyle had left his mother's home after a dispute with his brother. He went to live with his father who was an intravenous drug user. Kyle was taken back into temporary care by DCS and placed at an emergency secure group home. Eventually, he was placed in a long-term group home and encouraged to have occasional visits with his mother. He was also provided mental health counseling services, adolescent addiction services for his marijuana and prescription drug abuse, and life skills programming, and he was given access to youth employment services so that he could look for work once he turned 16 years old. A year later, Kyle had finished treatment and returned home, but that situation soon broke down again and Kyle went to live in an emergency shelter for youth. DCS refused him any further help and his case was closed shortly after Kyle's 17th birthday. At this point, he was left completely without access to formal services except those from the voluntary sector that provided him temporary shelter.

Complex Needs, Complex Navigations

Working with a child like Kyle, many clinicians (myself included) can get quickly out-maneuvered. It can feel like the only solution is to pass the case over to a specialized team that can provide intensive in-home support or group work delivered by a separate team of professionals with graduate degrees (for example, Multisystemic Therapy [Henggeler & Lee, 2003]). While those interventions have been proven effective, how many of us and how many of our agencies have the money or staff resources to mount such programs?

An ecological model of practice is meant to increase the effectiveness of counselors already working in residential settings, hospital outpatient clinics, community-based family therapy clinics, secure treatment facilities, child welfare offices, and the many other places children like Kyle appear. It is meant to add to our practice the skills of case management and advocacy in ways that actually make our work more efficient and effective.

I have no doubt that, individually, Kyle's treatment providers all did their best to help Kyle. Their efforts were effective at different moments in Kyle's life, usually when Kyle or his mother found the service meaningful. For example, when Kyle was younger he responded well to interventions that made his home safer. When he was older, he was willing to collaborate with service providers who acknowledged that his behavior stemmed from the challenges he faced at home, the burden of coping with cancer, and the stress of multiple placements. Too often, however, the services that were offered were not the services that Kyle or his mother said they needed. It's the paradox of service. Families need help but are provided a limited selection of services, many of which they perceive as meaningless options. Changing that situation requires the counselor to have the skills of the advocate, the mandate of the case manager, and the focused interventions of the clinician. Kyle's oncology social worker fulfilled these roles for a short time, followed by departmental workers from DCS, and then a community youth worker. The dual roles of case manager and advocate, however, were never fully integrated by any of these individuals into their primarily clinical roles.

Kyle's case is not unique. My research suggests that like many other children with complex needs, living in challenging contexts, Kyle and his family would have benefited from interventions that were better matched to all their needs. In particular:

- Services that were provided through systems of care that embraced the complexity of the family's problems.
- Coordination between service silos and between service providers and the family's natural supports.
- Continuity in the relationships between Kyle, his mother, and service providers so that fewer people intervened.
- A say over who these service providers were.
- Follow-up by agency staff when Kyle or his mother missed appointments.
- Effort to build the family's capacity to cope with their problems on their own.
- Easier and earlier access to resources (like an outreach worker when Kyle was younger) to avoid more intrusive and restrictive interventions later in life.

There are glimmers of brilliance in Kyle's case record where each of these exemplary practices is evident. For example, DCS tried hard to keep one community agency and one in-home support worker available to the family over several years. On many occasions, interdepartmental meetings that included mental health and addictions counselors were held to coordinate case planning. And

DCS resisted, as long as they could, providing too many intrusive services to the family that might undermine the family's capacity to solve problems themselves. The problem, however, was not with services being made available. The problem was that the services that were provided were not always valued by Kyle and his mother, nor were family members heard when they asked for help in ways that made sense to them.

How to Argue for a Broader Mandate as a Counselor

There is a great deal written about the need to work across silos, to be client-centered and client-driven, socially just, and focused on strengths. Models of therapy like Rhea Almeida's Transformative Family Therapy (Almeida, Vecchio & Parker, 2008), Charles Waldegrave's (2000) Just Therapy, Bill Madsen's (2009) Collaborative Helping model, Angie Hart's (2007) Resilient Therapy, and Michael White's (2007) Narrative Therapy share similarities with an ecological practice. All account for the client's social context and the multiple sources of oppression people experience (racism, homophobia, sexism, able-bodyism, etc.) though my experience is that, with the exception of Madsen's approach in the United States and Hart's work in the United Kingdom, these other approaches to counseling: (1) tend to need more resources from the therapist and the therapist's agency than many are willing to provide; (2) are difficult to integrate into everyday clinical practice, especially when clinicians find other techniques like CBT more straightforward and less time consuming; (3) can require a high level of motivation on the part of the client (and the counselor) to participate in group sessions or sessions where there are third-party observers in the room. No wonder they are still a relatively small portion of the practice landscape even though each makes a wonderful contribution to interventions with clients. Case file reviews like Kyle's suggest that very little of the progressive thinking which is part of these other models of therapy has yet to be reflected in actual casework. How do we change the status quo? How do we champion the needs of our clients when there appear to be limited resources? Or as Madsen once told me over a cup of coffee, "How do we begin to be professionals who help people get to where they want to go?" Indeed, how do we join with our clients in their efforts to navigate and negotiate successfully?

In my experience, *showing is always better than telling*. Small strategic efforts to work a little differently with one individual or family (rather than an entire caseload) tend to be less stressful for agencies to accommodate. A small victory using the principles and practices discussed in previous chapters can create curiosity about alternative ways of intervening. Advocating for accommodations to a single client is simply easier than trying to redirect an entire system quickly enough to help the client you're seeing now.

The challenge, though, is knowing which innovations in service delivery are most likely to produce the most sustainable client change. Good research and case studies can help guide us as we turn our hand to advocacy.

Four System Changes Worth Advocating For

There are at least four service design strategies that counselors can advocate for that will increase the likelihood that their services will have a positive impact on children and families exposed to high levels of adversity. Specifically, we know that services are more just and responsive when they are designed as follows: (1) Complex services are much better than simple services that focus on just one aspect of people's problems (when their problems are complex); (2) Coordinated services are very effective with children and families who need the resources of multiple service providers; (3) It is important to maintain continuity with at least one worker or case manager even as people get their needs met from a community of professional and non-professional supports; (4) It is essential that interventions build the capacity of clients to access their own supports if they are to cope better after counseling ends.

1: Complex Services

A case study like Kyle's teaches us that the complexity of services should match the complexity of people's lives. While a small intervention that creates change can snowball and lead to new patterns of interaction, those interactions will be constrained by the complexity of the risk factors that a child or parent experiences. It was relatively easy to provide Kyle with treatment to help him comply with his cancer treatment, and it was easy to provide him with anger management and other cognitive behavioral therapies that gave him tools to change his reactions to the emotional triggers that upset him. None of these interventions, however, endured as long as Kyle continued to reside in a household where there was violence. The more a community of practitioners worked together to create a complex weave of services and natural supports, the more they were able to stabilize Kyle's behavior. Services are sufficiently complex when their number and interactions are numerous enough to match the complexity of the multiple problems people experience in challenging social ecologies.

To illustrate, Kenneth Dodge and his colleagues (Dodge et al., 2009) addressed child abuse as a community problem. In their work, they've understood abuse to reflect patterns of family dynamics that are affected by wider societal values, such as patriarchy. This argument builds on Henry Kempe and his colleagues' 1962 article on the "battered child syndrome" (Kempe et al., 1962). Kempe et al. caused a dramatic change in how professionals viewed and reported child abuse, making it much more likely to be detected and treated. In other words, the problem of child abuse was not just a problem of a parent abusing a child; it was a problem of whether child abuse was identified by health care providers as a deviant pattern of behavior that required intervention. A change in context and coordination of services between doctors and social workers resulted in many more children being identified as abused. Rather than simply putting in place more treatment for the victims, Kempe urged an upstream approach and introduced the need to tackle the complexity of social values and interprofessional collaboration if a solution was to be found to what had before seemed like a strictly intrafamilial problem. Today we take this complexity for granted, but half a century ago Kempe's words were a radical departure for a field that saw abuse in purely psychological terms.

We are currently seeing the same shift occur for trauma (Panter-Brick & Eggerman, 2012) and childhood illnesses like obesity (Pinhas-Hamiel et al., 2005), with individual treatments being found inadequate unless paired with ecological interventions that change the social fabric of a child's world. In each case, ongoing research is helping us understand the intersection between the environment and the individual. For example, returning to the subject of child abuse, our modeling of the antecedents of abuse are showing increasing complexity. They now include the need for safe, nurturing environments in families, schools, and communities (Daro, 2009). Abuse itself can be prevented if a child is able to avoid exposure to the disorganization and low social cohesion that makes abuse both more likely to occur and less frequently reported. To illustrate, Dodge's Durham Family Initiative (DFI; Dodge et al., 2009) showed good results in one county of North Carolina where the initial rate of child maltreatment in 2000–2001 was substantially higher than the national average. The intervention was complex, with help for parents to develop more competent strategies for disciplining their children and skills in self-care and care of others. Social supports were also encouraged to buttress the frustrations parents experienced because of economic, marital, and social stressors. At the neighborhood level, good social relationships were encouraged to help monitor parents' behavior and provide role models for good parenting, as well as childcare and informal knowledge exchange about effective parenting practices. At the community level, professional resources like mental health services, childcare, and pediatric care were made accessible. A change in community culture helped to convey to parents what was and was not acceptable behavior with regard to raising children. Finally, at the level of policy, local and state governments were engaged in discussions about the needs of parents for financial resources, access to medical care, emergency relief, and other supports for families. The DFI is a system of care initiative that, like other similar interventions, focuses on the conditions beyond the child and the family that can influence the incidence of problems like child abuse (Ager, 2006). Counselors, when effective, play an important role creating a complex network of services that are capable of meeting all of a child's needs.

2: Coordinated services

When members of the Conduct Problems Prevention Research Group (2007; Nix et al., 2005) looked at preventing behavioral problems among young people growing up in high-risk neighborhoods, they managed to identify 891 children from almost 10,000 Kindergarten students who showed signs of disordered behavior when first assessed. Using a random assignment to intervention and control groups, a ten-year intervention began that included parent behavior management training, child social cognitive skills training, reading support, home visiting, mentoring, and changes to classroom curriculum. It was not surprising that they were able to show that programming with multiple elements (complexity) could have a significant impact on children's outcomes, but that the size of that impact varied by the individual child's original level of risk exposure when the child was in Kindergarten. Fast Track, as the program was called, "had a statistically significant and clinically meaningful positive effect on preventing childhood and adolescent externalizing psychiatric disorders and antisocial behavior, but only among the highest risk subgroup of kindergarteners" (Conduct Problems Prevention Research Group, 2007, p. 1259).

The differential impact of the intervention is particularly important to making the argument that counselors need to be freed up to do case management and advocacy *for the most vulnerable of their clients*. Children with less severe forms of conduct disorder benefited far less from such an intense approach to education and behavior management than children with a diagnosable problem. Furthermore, the program focused on both management of problem behaviors and providing children with experiences that would nurture their resilience, like mentorship and reading support. The intervention was also complex, focused on changing the child, the child's school experience, the way the child was parented, and the child's connections to other supports in her community. Taken all together, the magic of the intervention and the reason for its success can be attributed to the coordination of services. Work was done with both parents and educators. The coordinated case planning that occurred to manage the child's behavior at school and at home created a well-integrated system of care that relied on both formal service providers and the informal resources of parents to address children's needs.

Coordination of services is one of the most important goals for a more ecological approach to counseling, but as we saw in Chapter 8, the skills required to make systems coordinate are not simple to master. A case conference may appear to bring service providers and natural supports together in the same room, but that doesn't mean there will be coordination in service plans unless there are also: (1) structures that make it possible for counselors and other professionals to work together, like dedicated meeting time in their schedules and releases of information that make coordination of services respectful of clients' right to confidentiality; and (2) the resources necessary to facilitate coordination, meaning the financial commitment to share staff, money, and physical resources like meeting space, in order to help a child experience their services as coordinated.

3: Continuity of service

Case studies of children like Kyle illustrate the disjointed way services are provided to children and families. Counselors do one piece of work, then disappear. On rare occasions a professional (like Kyle's oncology social worker) takes on the roles of case manager and advocate. This role is vital but it is seldom properly resourced. After all, if systems have not signed memorandum of understanding to collaborate, what will compel professionals to coordinate services and pool resources? A well-coordinated network of services is one that, ideally, ensures continuity in the relationship between the client and one or two professionals over time. Of course, we can't prevent counselors from changing jobs, but we can anticipate staff turnover and emphasize continuity with a single office or team of care providers so that disruptions in service are minimized. According to Duncan, Hubble and Miller (1997), the better counselors create a stable holding environment for their clients, the more engaged clients will be in the treatment process.

This all seems so obvious, and yet case file reviews show that most children and families who are exposed to higher levels of risk experience a great deal of discontinuity. Many different professionals enter their lives, often for very brief periods, and there is little reciprocity in their negotiations of treatment goals or sustainability in their relationships.

A more ecological approach to counseling suggests a number of solutions, from counselors working collaboratively with others in their agencies to ensure that someone maintains a relationship with the client, to working with the client's natural supports during sessions so that continuity is achieved beyond the time spent in counseling. Neither solution has to cost a great deal of money if, for example, the agency, or a partner agency, is committed to providing a community worker or in-home support to a client. In Kyle's case, though he had a community worker, it is unclear whether the worker was integrated into other parts of Kyle's treatment. Reading his file, one never saw any evidence that his in-home support worker and the community organization that provided that service had much contact with Kyle's psychiatrist, social worker, or probation officer. In other words, whereas many professionals assessed and offered Kyle treatment, little of it proved to be effective or coordinated. Could these professionals have increased their potential impact if they had worked with the community worker to ensure that his contact with Kyle reinforced the goals of counseling that was taking place outside of Kyle's home?

There is research to support this idea of including a person's support network in interventions that address serious problems. For example, Perry and Thurston (2007) found that programs that provide sexual health information and counseling to young men are more effective when participants bring their friends to sessions. It's these friends who provide a continuous source of support and reinforce the behavioral changes learned during counseling. Best of all, these friends are likely to continue to be a part of the person's life long after the intervention ends.

4: Capacity building service

When Brett Drake and his colleagues (Drake, Jonson-Reid & Sapokaite, 2006) looked at what factors predict a child being reported to Child Protection Services a *second* time, they found that children with mental health or substance abuse treatment records, special education eligibility, a caregiver with characteristics that put the child at risk (less formal education, mental health problems, and substance use), and those children using concurrently a service that was not child welfare related had a higher likelihood of being reported to authorities. Drake et al. conclude that while the first report may be dealt with adequately, low-level needs persist. Understood as an ecological problem, my experience tells me that these children were unable to navigate to what they needed, nor were their caregivers able to access the supports they required. Like Kyle, these families returned to child protection services because of simmering problems that weren't fully treated the first time around.

On the one hand, the solution is better interagency ties and cooperation, but on the other, families need the capacity to handle the next crisis themselves. This doesn't have to result in the responsibilization of families (Ungar et al., 2012), meaning we don't have to download responsibility to fix problems onto families who are already stressed. It means, instead, that systems of care include natural and community supports to help families develop for themselves new coping strategies that complement the efforts of counselors and other formal service providers. It also means ensuring families transition from service providers back into their own networks of support if the gains made during counseling are going to be sustained.

Helping children and families build their own capacity to access the resources that predict a more resilient child helps protect young people from the many expected and unexpected risks they will encounter. It may also prevent system providers from becoming exhausted, endlessly fixing problems rather than helping our young clients and their families develop the capacity to fix problems themselves.

Capacity building does not, however, guarantee positive outcomes. Young people with complex needs are not living a game of snakes and ladders where every setback and opportunity can be anticipated. Instead, children with complex needs live lives that are open systems. Their odds of succeeding are constantly changing because of their physical development and modifications to their social ecologies. Roll the dice and suddenly an anxious child is in grade ten and among a new group of peers where she feels comfortable to socialize. Roll the dice again and her uncle touches her inappropriately resulting in a charge of sexual assault, a family that suspects the girl of lying, and a visit to the emergency department where social workers assess the seriousness of the girl's threats to kill herself. Suddenly, the gains made in one part of the child's life (school) become threatened by the chaos in another. Navigation and negotiation for children with serious challenges looks more like a chessboard where even the rules of the game occasionally change.

Practicalities of Advocating

If the evidence is clear that clients do better when they receive services that are complex enough to meet all their needs, coordinated between service providers and the client's natural supports, are continuous over time, and capacity building, then why is it still so difficult for counselors to advocate for changes to their services? The answer is not the lack of will among counselors to change systems, but their lack of professional and agency mandate to advocate, their lack of time to coordinate services, and their lack of skill to train clients to advocate for themselves. Without a mandate, time, and the skills to advocate, counselors are forced to look down at their feet and provide highly individualized, family, or group therapy even when the need for a more ecological approach is warranted. Meanwhile, counselors who do advocate (and there are many) are likely to be told that the time they spend changing services is not an "evidence-based" treatment for their client's problems even if the research shows that the counselor's agency is offering services in an ineffective manner.

Let's be honest. Unless we can attribute change to the counselor, funders are going to wonder whether their investment in service is cost effective. It's a narrow view of what makes clients change that sets counselors up to fail. It ignores all the evidence that helping people with complex needs depends on much more than a clinical intervention (Tol et al., 2011).

Take, for example, a 15-year-old African American boy with whom I worked whose parents moved him from a racially-mixed community to an affluent white suburban community. It was an interesting strategy for two middle-class professionals except that when their son went to school he was bullied because he was a visible minority. The boy, Tony, grew up learning to defend himself, eventually choosing an identity as a gangsta' rapper with chains and baggy trousers and idealizing gang warfare. His choice was not unreasonable, and has been identified as a way that some Black youth protect themselves when marginalized (American Psychological Association Task Force on Resilience and Strengths in Black Children and Adolescents, 2008). The problem was that Tony's behavior also landed him in trouble with the law as his violence escalated and he was suspended from school for carrying a weapon. At home, he and his parents were constantly fighting, though when Tony was before the courts, they offered to take him home on house arrest rather than have him incarcerated.

My work with Tony was a good example of an ecological approach to counseling. Rather than work with Tony on anger management, which was the reason for his referral, we instead explored the numerous strategies he used to deal with racism and verbal abuse at home, his experience of racism in his community, and his preference to stand up for himself rather than letting himself be put down. By the time we began working on cognitive techniques to help him control his angry outbursts, the work was easier because we'd made changes to Tony's environment that decreased his exposure to racism.

Counseling began by talking about Tony's family to find out what they knew about coping with racial prejudice. Tony's father, for example, had gotten the principal of his high school reassigned to another school because of inappropriate comments the principal had made about Black students. Tony's solution to his experience of racism was different but it echoed his father's strategy: there were ways of fighting back and winning. Tony's preferred strategy, however, was both atypical and controversial, especially in the eyes of his parents. Tony asked me to help him negotiate with his school board a transfer to a school where there were more Black students, which meant a return to the other side of the city which was where his parents had grown up. At first, it seemed like an odd request as it would put Tony in a neighborhood that had a higher rate of crime and would reverse the efforts Tony's parents had made to leave the inner city by moving to the suburbs. Tony, however, saw the change of schools differently: "That way, if I'm at that school in the city, and if anyone calls me a n_____ there will be 20 other guys there to beat the shit out of him." It wasn't a perfect solution, but it was Tony's preferred coping strategy and one I had to admit would likely work.

I helped Tony negotiate the transfer with his school board, coaching him on how to advocate for himself while also doing some lobbying behind the scenes to get Tony accepted into a new high school. Tony's parents also had to be convinced the move was a good idea. Eventually, the pieces fell into place and Tony enjoyed a remarkable amount of success the next school year. Though some of his troubling behaviors persisted, such as his drug use and conflict with his parents, he did better at modulating the intensity of these problems and managed to avoid school-related violence.

The solution was not just an individual plan, but a complex intervention that involved Tony's family, his school board, his probation officer, and his community. My role wasn't to just be Tony's anger management coach. I became an advocate who had to convince a school board that this delinquent kid from the suburbs would do much better in a school that already had its fair share of troubled youth.

In Tony's case, there was clearly a need to help him with anger management, his drug abuse, and his impulsivity. There was also a need to address the posttraumatic stress related to his earlier experiences of abuse at home and bullying at school. However, it was the more decentered, contextualized aspects of therapy that helped to create conditions for Tony to change his behavior. Arguably, the changes Tony made to his problem behaviors resulted from the changes those helping him made to Tony's social ecology. Thinking about the seven factors that predict resilience discussed in Chapter 1, it's easy to see that by helping Tony address the racism he experienced, and changing schools, we adapted his relationships and helped him feel a greater sense of belonging, a heightened sense of integration with others of his same ethnoracial group (and the safety that came with that integration), a sense of power from having been consulted on his case plan, an alternative identity as a student rather than a delinquent, and much more. Overall, we reduced Tony's exposure to the risk factors associated with his violence and made his environment responsive to his needs. Far more was achieved this way than could have been achieved if work had been limited to treating Tony's anger or experience of past trauma.

Why Community Work Works

Changing service ecologies adds to the efficacy of individual and family interventions. Organizations can adapt the way they provide services to individuals in ways that facilitate navigation and negotiation. If we review the seven factors associated with resilience (see Table 1.1) we can see that each has both an individual and a structural component that can be changed at the level of either an organization, community, or social policy (see Figures 9.1 and 9.2). Of course, there are limits to what a counselor has time to do. But acknowledging for clients that oftentimes the changes that need to be made are not within the power of clients to make can reassure them that their problems are not theirs to fix on their own. Frequently, clients are being coached to adapt to maladjusted, dysfunctional systems that thwart their efforts to succeed. If, for example, we ask a youth who self-identifies as lesbian, gay, bisexual, or transgendered to attend school when school is not a safe place to be, how does that make any sense? Change the child's school, family, peer group, and community, and maybe, just maybe, the child will change too.

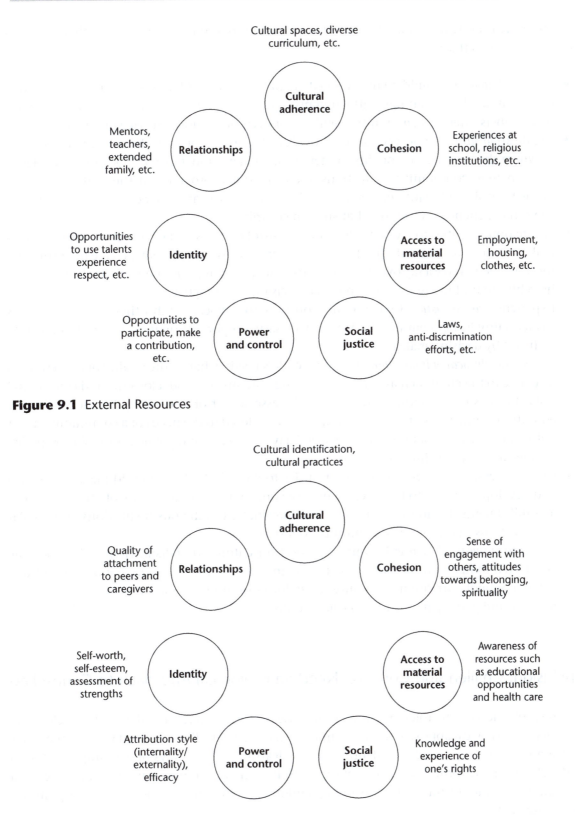

Figure 9.1 External Resources

Figure 9.2 Internal Resources

With this reasoning in mind, for each individual action that increases resilience, there will also be systemic changes that:

- Foster *relationships*: Build a child's social capital. Help a child access new people who will create sustainable, meaningful attachments. These people may be the child's extended family members, friends, community members, or even professional service providers.
- Create an *identity* that others respect: Provide a child with opportunities to experience pride in where she lives, her nationality, or her ethnic background. Open opportunities for her to participate in community institutions like recreational programs at the YMCA or a local music festival. Put her into places where others see her as a part of her community and where she can experience respect for what she can contribute.
- Create opportunities to feel *powerful* and in control of one's life: Give a child the chance to make decisions for himself. At school, in the community and at home, create opportunities for the child to have a say over the decisions that affect him. When he does make a decision, help him to find the resources to put that decision into practice.
- Experience *social justice*: Coach a child on how to advocate with others to ensure she is treated fairly in her community. When necessary, support affirmative action. Help a child be heard by decision makers.
- Access the *physical or built capital* to meet a child's needs: Change the quality of the resources available to the child such as adequate housing, safe streets, food, clothing, and educational opportunities (for example, a teacher's aide, assessment of a learning disorder, a flexible education plan). Advocate for better built capital tailored to the needs of a community's most vulnerable citizens. For example, subsidized day care spaces and public transit. Ensure policy makers are aware of children's needs.
- Create a *sense of belonging* and opportunities to contribute: Find a child places to engage and develop strategies to help a child make a contribution to the welfare of others that uses a child's talents. Connect a child, when appropriate, to religious institutions and secular organizations that promote community cohesion.
- Promote *cultural adherence*: Encourage respect for cultural pluralism. Help a child become connected to her cultural traditions and the institutions that promote her unique culture. Change school curriculum to ensure the cultures of minorities are reflected. Help a child identify and participate in cultural celebrations.

Conclusion: Challenging Contexts Need an Ecological Approach to Counseling

For some professionals, the roles of advocate and case manager will feel familiar and be welcomed. For others, an ecological approach to intervention and the 20 skills I've described in earlier chapters will demand a shift in professional identity and the learning of new ways of working with clients and the client's many formal and informal supports. It's a change in professional competency that is needed if we are to nurture resilience among children, youth, and families who face significant levels of adversity.

Clinical work that focuses on the needs of individuals and what they can do to change has been shown to be effective, up to a point. Interventions that account for the quality of young people's social ecologies and the need for these to also change are an important part of good counseling.

When individuals, families, and their communities face challenges, whether chronic (for example, poverty and exposure to street violence) or acute (a natural disaster, relocation to a new community, or the sudden death of someone close) interventions that shape a young person's social ecology are even more important to sustaining well-being.

If the case examples and research discussed throughout this book teach us anything it is that counseling is more effective when we think about relational, systemic, and meaning-making processes and how these are affected when people live in challenging contexts. If we've devalued work like this, it is an excusable oversight. After all, we haven't had many good models that we could show our supervisors and funders. We haven't been able to argue that what we do with a client's supports is just as important as what we do with the client directly.

Thankfully new approaches to clinical work are emerging.

REFERENCES

Abramson, D. M., Park, Y. S., Stehling-Ariza, T. & Redlener, I. (2010). Children as bellwethers of recovery: Dysfunctional systems and the effects of parents, households, and neighborhoods on serious emotional disturbance in children after Hurricane Katrina. *Disaster Medicine and Public Health Preparedness, 4*, 17–27. doi: 10.1001/dmp.2010.7.

Ager, A. (2006). What is family? The nature and functions of families in times of conflict. In N. Boothby, A. Strang & M. Wessells (Eds.), *A world turned upside down: Social ecological approaches to children in war zones* (pp. 39–62). Bloomfield, CT: Kumarian Press.

Allen, E., Bonell, C., Strange, V., Copas, A., Stephenson, J., Johnson, A. M. & Oakley, A. (2007). Does the UK government's teenage pregnancy strategy deal with the correct risk factors? Findings from a secondary analysis of data from a randomized trial of sex education and their implications for policy. *Journal of Epidemiology and Community Health, 61*(1), 20–27. doi: 10.1136/jech.2005.040865.

Almeida, R. V., Vecchio, K. D. & Parker, L. (2008). *Transformative family therapy: Just families in a just society.* New York, NY: Pearson.

Alvaro, C., Jackson, L. A., Kirk, S., McHugh, T. L., Hughes, J., Chircop, A. & Lyons, R. F. (2011). Moving Canadian governmental policies beyond a focus on individual lifestyle: Some insights from complexity and critical theories. *Health Promotions International, 26*(1), 91–99. doi: 10.1093/heapro/daq052.

American Psychological Association Task Force on Resilience and Strengths in Black Children and Adolescents (2008). *Resilience in African American children and adolescents: A vision for optimal development.* Washington, DC: Author. Retrieved from www.apa.org/pi/cyf/resilience/html (accessed January 12 2010).

Anda, R. F., Felitti, V. J., Bremner, J. D., Walker, J. D., Whitfield, C., Perry, B. D. & Giles, W. H. (2006). The enduring effects of abuse and related adverse experiences in childhood: A convergence of evidence from neurobiology and epidemiology. *European Archives of Psychiatry and Clinical Neuroscience, 256*(3), 174–186.

Arcelus, J. B., Bellerby, T. & Vostanis, P. (1999). A mental-health service for young people in the care of the local authority. *Clinical Child Psychology and Psychiatry, 4*(2), 233–245. doi: 10.1177/1359104599004002009.

Bandura, A. (1998). Exercise of agency in personal and social change. In E. Sanavio (Ed.), *Behaviour and cognitive therapy today: Essays in honor of Hans J. Eysenck* (pp. 1–29). Oxford, UK: Pergamon.

Barkham, M., Connell, J., Stiles, W. B, Miles, J. N. V., Margison, F., Evans, C. & Mellor-Clark, J. (2006). Dose-effect relations and responsive regulation of treatment duration: The good enough level. *Journal of Consulting and Clinical Psychology, 74*(1), 160–167. doi: 10.1037/0022–006X.74.1.160.

Bateson, M. C. (2008, June 17). Keynote address. American Family Therapy Academy Annual Meeting, Philadelphia.

Beah, I. (2007). *A long way gone: Memoirs of a boy soldier.* Vancouver, BC: Douglas & MacIntyre.

Beckett, C., Maughan, B., Rutter, M., Castle, J., Colvert, E. & Vedder, P. (2006). Immigrant youth: Acculturation, identity, and adaptation. *Applied Psychology: An International Review, 55*(3), 303–332.

Bell, C. C. (2011). Trauma, culture, and resiliency. In S. M. Southwick, B. T. Litz, D. Charney & M. J. Friedman

(Eds.), *Resilience and mental health: Challenges across the lifespan* (pp. 176–188). New York, NY: Cambridge University Press.

Bell, K. (2012). Towards a post-conventional philosophical base for social work. *British Journal of Social Work, 42*, 408–423. doi: 10.1093/bjsw/bcr073.

Belsky, J. (1980). Child maltreatment: An ecological integration. *American Psychologist, 35*(4), 320–335. doi: 10.1037/0003-066X.35.4.320.

Belsky, J. & Pluess, M. (2009a). Beyond diathesis-stress: Differential susceptibility to environmental influence. *Psychological Bulletin, 135*(6), 885–908. doi: 10.1037/a0017376.

Belsky, J. & Pluess, M. (2009b). The nature (and nurture?) of plasticity in early human development. *Perspectives in Psychological Science, 4*(4), 345–351. doi: 10.1111/j.1745-6924.2009.01136.x.

Belsky J., Bakermans-Kranenburg, M. J. & van Ijzendoorn, M. H. (2007). For better and for worse: Differential susceptibility to environmental influence. *Current Directions in Psychological Science, 16*(6), 300–304. doi: 10.1111/j.1467-8721.2007.00525.x.

Benight, C. C. & Cieslak, R. (2011). Cognitive factors and resilience: How self-efficacy contributes to coping with adversities. In S. M. Southwick, B. T. Litz, D. Charney & M. J. Friedman (Eds.), *Resilience and mental health: Challenges across the lifespan* (pp. 45–55). Cambridge: Cambridge University Press.

Benson, P. L. (2003). Developmental assets and asset-building community: Conceptual and empirical foundations. In R. M. Lerner & P. L. Benson (Eds.), *Developmental assets and asset-building communities: Implications for research, policy, and practice* (pp. 19–46). New York, NY: Kluwer.

Berry, J. W., Phinney, J. S., Sam, D. L. & Vedder, P. (2006). *Immigration youth in cultural transition: Acculturation, identity, and adaptation across national contexts.* Mahwah, NJ: Erlbaum.

Betancourt, T. S., Borisovea, I. I., Williams, T. P., Brennan, R. T., Whitfield, T. H., de la Soudiere, M., . . . & Gilman, S. E. (2010). Sierra Leone's former child soldiers: A follow-up study of psychosocial adjustment and community reintegration. *Child Development, 81*(4), 1076–1094.

Blom-Hoffman, J., Wilcox, K. A., Dunn, L., Leff, S. S. & Power, T. J. (2008). Family involvement in school-based health promotion: Bringing nutrition information home. *School Psychology Review, 37*(4), 567–577.

Blundo, R. (2001). Learning strengths-based practice: Challenging our personal and professional frames. *Families in Society: The Journal of Contemporary Human Services, 82*(3), 296–304.

Bonanno, G. A. (2013). How prevalent is resilience following sexual assault? Commentary on Steenkamp et al. (2012). *Journal of Traumatic Stress, 26*, 392–393. doi:10.1002/jts.21803.

Bonanno, G. A. & Mancini, A. D. (2012). Beyond resilience and PTSD: Mapping the heterogeneity of responses to potential trauma. *Psychological Trauma: Theory, Research, Practice, and Policy, 4*(1), 74–83. doi: 10.1037/a0017829.

Bonanno, G. A., Westphal, M. & Mancini, A. D. (2011). Resilience to loss and potential trauma. *Annual Review of Clinical Psychology, 7*, 511–535. doi: 10.1146/annurev-clinpsy-032210-104526.

Bottrell, D. (2009). Understanding "marginal" perspectives: Towards a social theory of resilience. *Qualitative Social Work, 8*(3), 321–339. doi: 10.1177/1473325009337840.

Bronfenbrenner, U. (1979). *Ecology of human development.* Cambridge, MA: Harvard University Press.

Bronfenbrenner, U. (2005). *Making human beings human: Bioecological perspectives on human development.* Thousand Oaks, CA: Sage.

Brown, D. K. (2004). *Social blueprints: Conceptual foundations of sociology.* New York, NY: Oxford University Press.

Brown, T. M. & Rodriguez, L. F. (2009). School and the co-construction of dropout. *International Journal of Qualitative Studies in Education, 22*(2), 221–242. doi: 10.1080/09518390802005570.

Browne, G. (2003). Integrated service delivery: More effective and less expensive. *Ideas that Matter, 2*(3), 3–8.

Burton, L. (2007). Childhood adultification in economically disadvantaged families: A conceptual model. *Family Process, 56*(4), 329–345. doi: 10.1111/j.1741-3729.2007.00463.x.

Caballero, B., Clay, T., Davis, S. M., Ethelbah, B., Rock, B. H., Lohman, T., . . . & Stevens, J. (2003). Pathways: A school-based, randomized controlled trial for the prevention of obesity in American Indian school-children. *The American Journal of Clinical Nutrition, 78*(5), 1030–1038.

Cacioppo, J. T., Reis, H. T. & Zautra, A. J. (2011). Social resilience: The value of social fitness with an application to the military. *American Psychologist, 66*(1), 43–51. doi: 10.1037/a0021419.

Cauce, A. M., Paradise, M., Embry, L., Morgan, C. J., Lohr, Y., Theofelis, J., . . . & Wagner, J. (1998). Homeless youth in Seattle: Youth characteristics, mental health needs and intensive case management. In M. H. Epstein, K. Kutash & A. Duchnowski (Eds.), *Outcomes for children and youth with emotional and behavioral disorders and their families: Programs and evaluation best practices* (pp. 611–632). Austin, TX: Pro-Ed.

Chettleburgh, M. G. (2007). *Youth thugs: Inside the dangerous world of Canadian street gangs.* Toronto, ON: Harper Collins.

Chung, R. C. & Bemak, F. P. (2012). *Social justice counselling: The next steps beyond multiculturalism.* Thousand Oaks, CA: Sage.

Cicchetti, D. (2010). A developmental psychopathology perspective on bipolar disorder. In D. J. Miklowitz & D. Cicchetti (Eds.), *Understanding bipolar disorder: A developmental psychopathology perspective* (pp. 1–32). New York, NY: Guilford.

Cohen, L. R., Hien, D. A. & Batchelder, S. (2008). The impact of cumulative maternal trauma and diagnosis on parenting behavior. *Child Maltreatment, 13*(1), 27–38. doi: 10.1177/1077559507310045.

Condeluci, A. (2013, September 17). Promoting resilience among people with acquired brain injuries. Keynote address, Annual conference, Brain Injury Canada. Kelowna, BC.

Conduct Problems Prevention Research Group (2007). Fast track randomized controlled trial to prevent externalizing psychiatric disorders: Findings from grades 3 to 9. *American Journal of the Academy of Child and Adolescent Psychiatry, 46*(10), 1250–1262.

Conger, R. & Armstrong, M. (2002). Bridging child welfare and juvenile justice: Preventing unnecessary detention of foster children. *Child Welfare, 81*(3), 471–494.

Copp, H. L., Bordnick, P. S, Traylor, A. C. & Thyer, B. A. (2007). Evaluating wraparound services for seriously emotionally disturbed youth: Pilot study outcomes in Georgia. *Adolescence, 42*(168), 723–732.

Coulshed, V. & Orme, J. (2006). *Social work practice.* London, UK: Palgrave Macmillan.

Crosnoe, R. & Muller, C. (2004). Body mass index, adolescent achievement, and school context: Examining the educational experiences of adolescents at risk of obesity. *Journal of Health and Social Behavior, 45*(4), 393–407. doi: 10.1177/002214650404500403.

Cruz-Santiago, M. & Ramirez-Garcia, J. I. (2011). "Hay que ponerse en los zapatos del joven": Adaptive parenting of adolescent children among Mexican-American parents residing in a dangerous neighborhood. *Family Process, 50*(1), 92–114. doi: 10.1111/j.1545-5300.2010.01348.x.

Cyrulnik, B. (2011). *Resilience: How your inner strength can set you free from the past.* New York, NY: Penguin.

D'Augelli, A. R. & Hersherger, S. L. (1993). Lesbian, gay and bisexual youth in community settings: Personal challenges and mental health problems. *American Journal of Community Psychology, 21*(4), 421–448.

Daro, D. (2009). The history of science and child abuse prevention: A reciprocal relationship. In K. A. Dodge & D. L. Coleman (Eds.), *Preventing child maltreatment: Community approaches* (pp. 9–28). New York, NY: Guilford.

Dei, G. J. S., Massuca, J., McIsaac, E. & Zine, J. (1997). *Reconstructing "dropout": A critical ethnography of the dynamics of black students' disengagement from school.* Toronto, ON: University of Toronto Press.

Dickerson, V. C. & Zimmerman, J. L. (1996). Myths, misconceptions, and a word or two about politics. *Journal of Systemic Therapies, 15*(1), 79–88.

Dishion, T. J. (2000). Cross-setting consistency in early adolescent psychopathology: Deviant friendships and problem behavior sequelae. *Journal of Personality, 68*(6), 1109–1126. doi: 10.1111/1467-6494.00128.

Dodge, K. A. & Coleman, D. L. (2009). Introduction: Community-based prevention of child maltreatment. In K. A. Dodge & D. L. Coleman (Eds.), *Preventing child maltreatment: Community approaches* (pp. 1–8). New York, NY: Guilford.

Dodge, K. A., Murphy, R., O'Donnell, K. & Christopoulos, C. (2009). Community-level prevention of child maltreatment: The Durham family initiative. In K. A. Dodge & D. L. Coleman (Eds.), *Preventing child maltreatment: Community approaches* (pp. 68–81). New York, NY: Guilford.

Dohrn, B. (2002). The school, the child, and the court. In M. K. Rosenheim, F. E. Zimring, D. S. Tanenhaus & B. Dohrn (Eds.), *A century of juvenile justice* (pp. 267–309). Chicago, IL: University of Chicago Press.

Dominelli, L. & McLeod, E. (1989). *Feminist social work*. London, UK: Macmillan.

Donnon, T. & Hammond, W. (2007). A psychometric assessment of the self-reported Youth Resiliency: Assessing Developmental Strengths Questionnaire. *Psychological Reports, 100*(3), 963–978.

Dotterer, A. M., McHale, S. M. & Crouter, A. C. (2009). Sociocultural factors and school engagement among African American youth: The roles of racial discrimination, racial socialization, and ethnic identity. *Applied Developmental Science, 13*(2), 61–73. doi: 10.1080/10888690902801442.

Drake, B., Jonson-Reid, M. & Sapokaite, L. (2006). Re-reporting of child maltreatment: Does participation in other public sector services moderate the likelihood of a second maltreatment report? *Child Abuse & Neglect, 30*(11), 1201–1226.

DuMont, K. A., Ehrhard-Dietzel, S. & Kirkland, K. (2012). Averting child maltreatment: Individual, economic, social, and community resources that promote resilient parenting. In M. Ungar (Ed.), *The social ecology of resilience: A handbook for theory and practice* (pp. 199–217). New York, NY: Springer.

DuMont, K. A., Widom, C. S. & Czaja, S. J. (2007). Predictors of resilience in abused and neglected children grown-up: The role of individual and neighborhood characteristics. *Child Abuse & Neglect, 31*(3), 255–274.

Dumont, M. & Provost, M. A. (1999). Resilience in adolescents: Protective role of social support, coping strategies, self–esteem and social activities on experience of stress and depression. *Journal of Youth and Adolescence, 28*(3), 343–363. doi: 10.1023/A:1021637011732.

Duncan, B. L., Hubble, M. A. & Miller, S. D. (1997). Stepping off the throne: It's easy to be too enamored with our own theories. *Family Therapy Networker, 21*(4).

Duncan, B. L., Miller, S. D. & Sparks, J. A. (2004). *The heroic client*. New York, NY: Jossey-Bass.

Ebersöhn, L. (2007). Voicing perceptions of risk and protective factors in coping in a HIV & AIDS landscape: Reflecting on capacity for adaptiveness. *Gifted Education International, 23*(2), 1–27. doi: 10.1177/026142940702300205.

Farmer, E. M. Z., Burns, B. J., Phillips, S. D., Angold, A. & Costello, E. J. (2003). Pathways into and through mental health services for children and adolescents. *Psychiatric Services, 54*(1), 60–66. doi: 10.1176/appi.ps.54.1.60.

Feder, A., Nestler, E. J., Westphal, M. & Charney, D. S. (2010). Psychobiological mechanisms of resilience to stress. In J. W. Reich, A. J. Zautra & J. S. Hall (Eds.), *Handbook of adult resilience* (pp. 35–54). New York, NY: Guilford.

Feldman, G. (2007). Cognitive and behavioural therapies for depression: Overview, new directions, and practical recommendations for dissemination. *Psychiatric Clinics of North America, 30*(1), 39–50.

Fergusson, D. M. & Horwood, L. J. (2003). Resilience to childhood adversity: Results of a 21-year study. In S. S. Luthar (Ed.), *Resilience and vulnerability: Adaptation in the context of childhood adversities* (pp. 130–155). Cambridge, UK: Cambridge University Press.

Flemons, D. G., Green, S. K. & Rambo, A. H. (1996). Evaluating therapists' practices in a postmodern world: A discussion and a scheme. *Family Process, 35*(1), 43–56. doi: 10.1111/j.1545-5300.1996.00043.x.

Florence, M. D., Asbridge, M. & Veugelers, P. J. (2008). Diet quality and academic performance. *Journal of School Health, 78*(4), 209–215. doi: 10.1111/j.1746-1561.2008.00288.x.

Folkman, S. (2011). *The Oxford handbook of stress, health, and coping*. New York, NY: Oxford University Press.

Friborg, O., Hjemdal, O., Rosenvinge, J. H., Martinussen, M., Aslaksen, P. M. & Flaten, M. A. (2006). Resilience as a moderator of pain and stress. *Journal of Psychosomatic Research, 61*(2), 213–219.

Gambrill, E. (2008). Evidence-informed practice. In K. M. Sowers, I. C. Colby & C. N. Dulmus (Eds.), *Comprehensive handbook of social work and social welfare: Social policy and policy practice* (pp. 3–28). New York, NY: John Wiley & Sons.

Gergen, K. J. (2001). Psychological science in a postmodern context. *American Psychologist, 56*(10), 803–813. doi: 10.1037/0003-066X.56.10.803.

Germain, C. B. & Gitterman, A. (1980). *The life model of social work practice*. New York, NY: Columbia University.

Gewirtz, A., Forgatch, M. & Wieling, E. (2008). Parenting practices as potential mechanisms for child adjustment following mass trauma. *Journal of Marital and Family Therapy, 34*(2), 177–192. doi: 10.1111/j.1752-0606.2008.00063.x.

Gillham, J. E., Reivich, K. J., Freres, D. R., Chaplin, T. M., Shatté, A. J., Samuels, B., . . . & Seligman, M. E. P. (2007). School-based prevention of depressive symptoms: A randomized controlled study of the effectiveness and specificity of the Penn resiliency program. *Journal of Consulting and Clinical Psychology, 75*(1), 9–19.

Godsall, R. E., Jurkovic, G. J., Emshoff, J. & Stanwyck, D. (2004). Why some kids do well in bad situations: Relation of parental alcohol misuse and parentification to children's self-concept. *Substance Use & Misuse, 39*(5), 789–809.

Greene, R. W. & Ablon, J. S. (2006). *Treating explosive kids: The collaborative problem-solving approach.* New York, NY: Guilford.

Groves, L. C. & Kerson, T. S. (2011). The influence of professional identity and the private practice environment: Attitudes of clinical social workers toward addressing the social support needs of clients. *Smith College Studies in Social Work, 81*(2/3), 218–233. doi: 10.1080/00377317.2011.589314.

Haapasalo, J. (2000). Young offenders' experiences of child protection services. *Journal of Youth and Adolescence, 29*(3), 355–371.

Hall, J., Porter, L., Longhi, D., Becker-Green, J. & Dreyfus, S. (2012). Reducing adverse childhood experiences (ACE) by building community capacity: A summary of Washington family policy council research findings. *Journal of Prevention & Intervention in the Community, 40*(4), 325–334. doi: 10.1080/10852352.2012.707463.

Hammond, S. A. & Royal, C. (2001). *Lessons from the field: Applying appreciative inquiry, revised edition.* Boulder, CO: Thin Book Publishing.

Hansen, M., Litzelman, A., Marsh, D. T. & Milspaw, A. (2004). Approaches to serious emotional disturbance: Involving multiple systems. *Professional Psychology: Research and Practice, 35*(5), 457–465. doi: 10.1037/0735-7028.35.5.457.

Hansson, E. K., Tuck, A., Lurie, S. & McKenzie, K. (2012). Rates of mental illness and suicidality in immigrant, refugee, ethnocultural, and racialized groups in Canada: A review of the literature. *Canadian Journal of Psychiatry, 57*(2), 111–121.

Hart, A., Blincow, D. & Thomas, H. (2007). *Resilient therapy: Working with children and families.* London, UK: Routledge.

Hart, A., Hall, V. & Henwood, F. (2003). Helping health and social care professionals to develop an "inequalities imagination": A model for use in education and practice. *Journal of Advances in Nursing, 41*(5), 480–489.

Harvey, M. R. (2007). Towards an ecological understanding of resilience in trauma survivors: Implications for theory, research, and practice. *Journal of Aggression, Maltreatment & Trauma, 14*(1/2), 9–32. doi: 10.1300/J146v14n01_02.

Heinonen, T. & Spearman, L. (2006). *Social work practice: Problem solving and beyond.* Toronto, ON: Thomson.

Hellriegel, K. L. & Yates, J. R. (1999). Collaboration between correctional and public school systems serving juvenile offenders: A case study. *Education and Treatment of Children, 22*(1), 55–83.

Henggeler, S. W. & Lee, T. (2003). Multisystemic treatment of serious clinical problems. In A. E. Kazdin & J. R. Weisz (Eds.), *Evidence-based psychotherapies for children and adolescents* (pp. 301–324). New York, NY: Guilford.

Henggeler, S. W. & Sheidow, A. J. (2012). Empirically supported family-based treatments for conduct disorder and delinquency in adolescents. *Journal of Marital & Family Therapy, 38*(1), 30–58. doi: 10.1111/j.1752-0606.2011.00244.x.

Henggeler, S. W., Schoenwald, S. K., Borduin, C. M., Rowland, M. D. & Cunningham, P. B. (2009). *Multisystemic therapy for antisocial behavior in children and adolescents.* New York, NY: Guilford Press.

Hobfoll, S. (2011). Conservation of resources theory: Its implication for stress, health, and resilience. In S. Folkman (Ed.), *The Oxford handbook of stress, health, and coping* (pp. 127–147). New York, NY: Oxford University Press.

Huerta, M. (2011, December). Keynote: Children and family policies across the OECD. Presentation at the annual meeting of Eurochild, Cardiff, UK.

Imber-Black, E. (1988). *Families and larger systems: A family therapist's guide through the labyrinth*. New York, NY: Guilford.

Ivey, A. E. & Ivey, M. B. (2007). *Intentional interviewing and counseling*. Belmont, CA: Thomson-Brooks/Cole.

Jaffee, S. R., Caspi, A., Moffitt, T. E., Polo–Tomas, M. & Taylor, A. (2007). Individual, family, and neighborhood factors distinguish resilient from non–resilient maltreated children: A cumulative stressors model. *Child Abuse & Neglect, 31*(3), 231–253.

Jané-Llopis, E. & Anderson, P. (2005). Mental Health Promotion and Mental Disorder Prevention. A policy for Europe. Nijmegen: Radboud University Nijmegen.

Kataoka, S. H., Zhang, M. S. & Wells, K. B. (2002). Unmet need for mental health care among U.S. children: Variation by ethnicity and insurance status. *American Journal of Psychiatry, 159*(9), 1548–1555. doi:10.1176/appi.ajp.159.9.1548.

Kemp, S. P., Whittaker, J. K. & Tracy, E. M. (1997). *Person-environment practice: The social ecology of interpersonal helping*. New York, NY: Aldine.

Kempe, C., Silverman, H. F., Steele, B., Droegemueller, W. & Silver, H. (1962). The battered child syndrome. *Journal of the American Medical Association, 181*(1), 17–24.

Kirby, M. J. & Keon, W. J. (2006). *Out of the shadows at last: Transforming mental health, mental illness and addiction services in Canada*. The Standing Senate Committee on Social Affairs, Science and Technology, Ottawa, ON. Retrieved from www.parl.gc.ca/content/sen/committee/391/soci/rep/rep02may06-e.htm (accessed May 14 2011).

Klasen, F., Oettingen, G., Daniels, J., Post, M., Hoyer, C. & Adam, H. (2010). Posttraumatic resilience in former Ugandan child soldiers. *Child Development, 81*(4), 1096–1113. doi: 10.1111/j.1467-8624.2010.01456.x.

Kroll, L., Rothwell, J., Bradley, D., Shah, P., Bailey, S. & Harrington, R. C. (2002). Mental health needs of boys in secure care for serious or persistent offending: A prospective, longitudinal study. *The Lancet, 359*(9322), 1975–1979.

Lal, S. (2012). *Resilience in youth recently diagnosed with psychosis: A qualitative inquiry*. (Doctoral dissertation). Retrieved from WorldCat database. (OCLC No. 820560742).

Landau, J., Mittal, M. & Wieling, E. (2008). Linking human systems: Strengthening individuals, families, and communities in the wake of mass trauma. *Journal of Marital and Family Therapy, 34*(2), 193–209. doi: 10.1111/j.1752-0606.2008.00064.x.

Larkin, H., Shields, J. J. & Anda, R. F. (2012). The health and social consequences of adverse childhood experiences (ACE) across the lifespan: An introduction to prevention and intervention in the community. *Journal of Prevention & Intervention in the Community, 40*(4), 263–270. doi: 10.1080/10852352.2012.707439.

Laub, J. H. & Sampson, R. J. (2003). *Shared beginnings, divergent lives: Delinquent boys to age 70*. Cambridge: Harvard University Press.

Lebow, J. (2006). *Research for the psychotherapist*. New York, NY: Routledge.

Lerner, R. M. (2006). Resilience as an attribute of the developmental system: Comments on the papers of Professors Masten & Wachs. In B. M. Lester, A. S. Masten & B. McEwen (Eds.), *Resilience in children* (pp. 40–51). Boston, MA: Blackwell.

Leschied, A. W., Nowicki, E. Rodger, S. & Chiodo, D. (2004). Better to build a child than fix an adult: Report to the Canadian National Crime Prevention Council on the Predictors of risk for youth who proceed to the adult justice system and the programs that work to reduce that likelihood. Toronto, ON: Centre for Addiction and Mental Health.

Lewin, K. (1951). *Field theory in social science; selected theoretical papers*. D. Cartwright (ed.). New York: Harper & Row.

Liberman, A. (2007). Adolescents, neighborhoods, and violence: Recent findings from the project on human development in Chicago neighborhoods. Washington, DC: U.S. Department of Justice, Office of Justice Programs, National Institute of Justice.

Litrownik, A. J., Taussig, H. N., Landsverk, J. A. & Garland A. F. (1999). Youth entering an emergency shelter care facility: Prior involvement in juvenile justice and mental health systems. *Journal of Social Service Research, 25*(3), 5–19. doi: 10.1300/J079v25n03_02.

Loeber, R., Burke, J. D. & Pardini, D. A. (2009). Development and etiology of disruptive and delinquent behavior. *Annual Review of Clinical Psychology, 5,* 291–310. doi: 10.1146/annurev.clinpsy.032408.153631.

Loeber, R., Farrington, D. P., Stouthamer-Loeber, M. & Van Kammen, W. B. (1998). Multiple risk factors for multi-problem boys: Co-occurrence of delinquency, substance use, attention deficit, conduct problems, physical aggression, covert behavior, depressed mood, and shy/withdrawn behavior. In R. Jessor (Ed.), *New perspectives in adolescent risk behaviour.* New York, NY: Cambridge University Press.

Lourie, I. S., Stroul, B. A. & Friedman, R. M. (1998). Community-based systems of care: From advocacy to outcomes. In M. H. Epstein, K. Kutash & A. Duchnowski (Eds.), *Outcomes for children and youth with emotional and behavioral disorders and their families: Programs and evaluation best practices* (pp. 3–19). Austin, TX: Pro-Ed.

Luthar, S. S. (2006). Resilience in development: A synthesis of research across five decades. In D. Cicchetti & D. J. Cohen (Eds.), *Developmental psychopathology: Risk, disorder and adaptation* (pp. 739–795). New York, NY: Wiley.

Luthar, S. S. & Brown, P. J. (2007). Maximizing resilience through diverse levels of inquiry: Prevailing paradigms, possibilities, and priorities for the future. *Development and Psychopathology, 19*(3), 931–955. doi: 10.1017/S0954579407000454.

Madigan, S. (2006). Watching the other watch: A social location of problems. In C. Brown & T. Augusta-Scott (Eds.), *Narrative therapy: Making meaning, making lives* (pp. 133–150). Thousand Oaks, CA: Sage.

Madigan, S. & Law, I. (1998). *Praxis: Situating discourse, feminism and politics in narrative therapies.* Adelaide, Australia: Dulwich Centre.

Madsen, W. C. (1999). *Collaborative therapy with multi-stressed families: From old problems to new futures.* New York, NY: Guilford.

Madsen, W. C. (2009). Collaborative helping: A practice framework for family-centered services. *Family Process, 48*(1), 103–116. doi: 10.1111/j.1545-5300.2009.01270.x.

Madsen, W. C. & Gillespie, K. (2014). *Collaborative helping: A strengths framework for home-based services.* New York, NY: Guilford Press.

Malmgren, K. W. & Meisel, S. M. (2002). Characteristics and service trajectories of youth with serious emotional disturbance in multiple service systems. *Journal of Child & Family Studies, 11*(2), 217–229. doi: 10.1023/A:1015181710291.

Manassis, K. (2012). *Problem solving in child and adolescent psychotherapy: A skills-based collaborative approach.* New York, NY: Guilford.

Masten, A. S. (2001). Ordinary magic: Resilience processes in development. *American Psychologist, 56*(3), 227–238. doi: 10.1037/0003-066X.56.3.227.

Masten, A. S. (2006). Promoting resilience in development: A general framework for systems of care. In R. J. Flynn, P. M. Dudding & J. G. Barber (Eds.), *Promoting resilience in child welfare* (pp. 3–17). Ottawa, ON: University of Ottawa Press.

Masten, A. S. & Obradović, J. (2006). Competence and resilience in development. In B. M. Lester, A. S. Masten & B. McEwen (Eds.), *Resilience in children* (pp. 13–27). Boston, MA: Blackwell.

Masten, A. S., Monn, A. R. & Supkoff, L. M. (2011). Resilience in children and adolescents. In S. M. Southwick, B. T. Litz, D. Charney & M. J. Friedman (Eds.), *Resilience and mental health: Challenges across the lifespan.* Cambridge, UK: Cambridge University Press.

McAdams, D. P. (2005). A psychologist without a country, or living two lives in the same story. In G. Yancy & S. Hadley (Eds.), *Narrative identities: Psychologists engaged in self-construction* (pp. 114–130). London, UK: Jessica Kingsley.

McKay, M. M., Stoewe, J., McCadam, K. & Gonzales, J. (1998). Increasing access to child mental health services for urban children and their caregivers. *Health and Social Work, 23*(1), 9–15.

Mikami, A.Y. & Hinshaw, S. P. (2006). Resilient adolescent adjustment among girls: Buffers of childhood peer rejection and attention-deficit/hyperactivity disorder. *Journal of Abnormal Child Psychology, 34,* 825–839. doi: 10.1007/s10802-006-9062-7.

Miller, A. L., Rathus, J. H. & Linehan, M. M. (2007). *Dialectical behavior therapy with suicidal adolescents.* New York, NY: Guilford.

Miller, M. W. & Harrington, K. M. (2011). Pathways to resilience: Personality factors in resilience to traumatic stress. In S. M. Southwick, B. T. Litz & D. Charney (Eds.), *Resilience and mental health: Challenges across the lifespan* (pp. 56–75). Cambridge, UK: Cambridge University Press.

Moffitt, T. E., Caspi, A., Rutter, M. & Silva, P. A. (2001). *Sex differences in antisocial behaviour.* Cambridge, UK: Cambridge University Press.

Murphy, R. A. (2002). Mental health, juvenile justice, and law enforcement responses to youth psychopathology. In D. T. Marsh & M. A. Fristad (Eds.), *Handbook of serious emotional disturbance in children and adolescents* (pp. 351–374). New York, NY: John Wiley & Sons.

Naess, A. (1989). *Ecology, community and lifestyle: Outline of an ecosophy.* Cambridge, UK: Cambridge University.

Naess, A. & Jickling, B. (2000). Deep ecology and education: A conversation with Arne Naess. *Canadian Journal of Environmental Education, 5*(1), 48–62.

Ng-Mak, D. S., Salzinger, S., Feldman, R. S. & Stueve, C. A. (2010). Pathologic adaptation to community violence among inner-city youth. *American Journal of Orthopsychiatry, 74*(2), 196–2008. doi: 10.1037/0002-9432.74.2.196.

Nix, R. L., Pinderhughes, E. E., Bierman, K. L. & Maples, J. J. (2005). Decoupling the relation between risk factors for conduct problems and the receipt of intervention services: Participation across multiple components of a prevention program. *American Journal of Community Psychology, 36*(3/4), 307–325. doi: 10.1007/s10464-005-8628-9.

Norris, F. H., Sherrieb, K. & Pfefferbaum, B. (2011). Community resilience: Concepts, assessment, and implications for intervention. In S. M. Southwick, B. T. Litz & D. Charney (Eds.), *Resilience and mental health: Challenges across the lifespan* (pp. 162–175). Cambridge, UK: Cambridge University Press.

Orlinsky, D. E., Rønnestad, M. H. & Willutzki, U. (2004). Fifty years of process-outcome research: Continuity and change. In M. J. Lambert (Ed.), *Bergin and Garfield's handbook of psychotherapy and behavior change* (pp. 307–390). New York, NY: Wiley.

Owens, R. E. (1998). *Queer kids: The challenges and promise for lesbian, gay and bisexual youth.* Binghamton, NY: The Haworth Press.

Pancer, S. M., Nelson, G., Hasford, J. & Loomis, C. (2012). The better beginnings, better futures project: Long-term parent, family, and community outcomes of a universal, comprehensive, community-based prevention approach for primary school children and their families. *Journal of Community & Applied Social Psychology, 23*(3), 187–205. doi:10.1002/casp.2110.

Panter-Brick, C. & Eggerman, M. (2012). Understanding culture, resilience, and mental health: The production of hope. In M. Ungar (Ed.), *The social ecology of resilience: A handbook of theory and practice* (pp. 369–386). New York, NY: Springer.

Parton, N. (2002). Postmodern and constructionist approaches to social work. In R. Adams, L. Dominelli & M. Payne (Eds.), *Social work: Themes, issues and critical debates* (pp. 237–246). London, UK: Palgrave.

Perry, C. & Thurston, M. (2007). Meeting the sexual health care needs of young people: A model that works? *Child: Care, Health and Development, 34*(1), 98–103. doi: 10.1111/j.1365-2214.2007.00741.x.

Peterson, C., Park, N., Pole, N., D'Adrea, W. & Seligman, M. E. P. (2008). Strengths of character and post-traumatic growth. *Journal of Traumatic Stress, 21*(2), 214–217. doi: 10.1002/jts.20332.

Pettit, G. S., Laird, R. D., Dodge, K. A., Bates, J. E. & Criss, M. M. (2001). Antecedents and behavior-problem outcomes of parental monitoring and psychological control in early adolescence. *Child Development, 72*(2), 583–598. doi: 10.1111/1467-8624.00298.

Pinhas-Hamiel, O., Singer, S., Pilpel, N., Fradkin, A., Modan, D. & Reichman, B. (2005). Health related quality of life among children and adolescents: Associations with obesity. *International Journal of Obesity, 30*, 267–272. doi:10.1038/sj.ijo.0803107.

Pinnock, D. (1997). *Gangs, rituals and rites of passage*. Cape Town, South Africa: African Sun Press.

Prilleltensky, I. (2012). Wellness as fairness. *American Journal of Community Psychology, 49*(1/2), 1–21. doi: 10.1007/s10464-011-9448-8.

Rogoff, B. (2003). *The cultural nature of human development*. Oxford: Oxford University Press.

Root, E. & Madsen, W. C. (2013). Imagine: Bringing vision into child protective services. *Journal of Systemic Therapies, 32*(3), 74–88. doi: 10.1521/jsyt.2013.32.3.74.

Saathoff, A. J. & Stoffel, E. A., (1999). Community based domestic violence services. *Domestic Violence and Children, 9*(3), 97–110.

Sagatun-Edwards, I. & Saylor, C. (2000). A coordinated approach to improving outcomes for substance-abusing families in juvenile dependency court. *Juvenile and Family Court Journal, 5*(4), 1–16. doi: 10.1111/j.1755-6988.2000.tb00028.x.

Sanders, J., Mumford, R., Liebenberg, L. & Ungar, M. (2014). Consistent service quality: The connection between service quality, risk, resilience and outcomes for vulnerable youth clients of multiple services. *Child Abuse & Neglect, 38*(4), 687–697.

Scheper-Hughes, N. (2008). A talent for life: Reflections on human vulnerability and resilience. *Ethnos, 73*(1), 25–56. doi: 10.1080/00141840801927525.

Schwartz, S. J. (2008). Self and identity in early adolescence. *Journal of Early Adolescence, 28*(1), 5–15. doi: 10.1177/0272431607308662.

Seccombe, K. (2002). "Beating the odds" versus "changing the odds": Poverty, resilience, and family policy. *Journal of Marriage and Family, 64*(2), 384–394. doi: 10.1111/j.1741-3737.2002.00384.x.

Selekman, M. D. (2006). *Working with self-harming adolescents: A collaborative, strengths-based therapy approach*. New York, NY: Norton.

Sheldon-Keller, A. E. R., Koch, J. R., Watts, A. C. & Leaf, P. J. (1996). The provision of services for rural youth with serious emotional and behavioral problems: Virginia's comprehensive services act. *Community Mental Health Journal, 32*(5), 481–495.

Shernoff, D. J. & Schmidt, J. A. (2008). Further evidence of an engagement-achievement paradox among U.S. high school students. *Journal of Youth and Adolescence, 37*, 564–580. doi: 10.1007/s10964-007-9241-z.

Shin, R., Daly, B. & Vera, E. (2007). The relationships of peer norms, ethnic identity, and peer support to school engagement in urban youth. *Professional School Counseling, 10*(4), 379–388.

Simich, L., Maiter, S., Moorlag, E. & Ochocka, J. (2009). Taking culture seriously: Ethnolinguistic community perspectives on mental health. *Psychiatric Rehabilitation Journal, 32*(3), 208–214. doi: 10.2975/32.3.2009. 208.214.

Smith, M., Gallagher, M., Wosu, H., Stewart, J., Cree, V. E., Hunter, S. . . . & Wilkinson, H. (2011). Engaging with involuntary service users in social work: Findings from a knowledge exchange project. *British Journal of Social Work, 42*(8), 1460–1477. doi: 10.1093/bjsw/bcr162.

Sroufe, L. A., Egeland, B., Carlson, E. A. & Collins, W. A. (2005). *The development of the person: The Minnesota study of risk and adaptation from birth to adulthood*. New York, NY: Guilford.

Stiffman, A. R, Chen, Y., Else, D., Doré, P. & Cheng, L. (1997). Adolescents' and providers' perspectives on the need for and use of mental health services. *Journal of Adolescent Health, 21*(5), 335–342.

Stiffman, A. R., Hadley-Ives, E., Doré, P., Polgar, M., Horvath, V. E., Striley, C. & Elze, D. (2000). Youths' access to mental health services: The role of providers' training, resource connectivity, and assessment of need. *Mental Health Services Research, 2*(3), 141–154.

Sue, D. W. & Sue, D. (2003). *Counseling the culturally diverse: Theory and practice*. New York, NY: John Wiley & Sons.

Swanson, D. P., Spencer, M. B., Dell'Angelo, T., Harpalani, V. & Spencer, T. R. (2002). Identity processes and the positive development of African Americans: An exploratory framework. In R. M. Lerner, C. S. Taylor & A. Von Eye (Eds.), *Pathways to positive development among diverse youth* (pp. 73–100). New York, NY: Jossey-Bass.

Swenson, C. C., Randall, J., Henggeler, S. W. & Ward, D. (2000). The outcomes and costs of an interagency partnership to serve maltreated children in state custody. *Children's Services: Social Policy, Research, and Practice, 3*(4), 191–209. doi: 10.1207/S15326918CS0304_1.

Swenson, R. R. & Prelow, H. M. (2005). Ethnic identity, self-esteem, and perceived efficacy as mediators of the relation of supportive parenting to psychosocial outcomes among urban adolescents. *Journal of Adolescence, 28*, 465–477.

Taras, H. & Potts-Datema, W. (2005). Chronic health conditions and student performance at school. *Journal of School Health, 75*(7), 255–266.

Taylor, J. M., Gilligan, C. & Sullivan, A. M. (1995). *Between voice and silence: Women and girls, race and relationship*. Cambridge, MA: Harvard University Press.

Tol, W. A., Barbui, C., Galappatti, A., Silove, D., Betancourt, T. S., Souza, R. . . . & van Ommeren, M. (2011). Mental health and psychosocial support in humanitarian settings: Linking practice and research. *Lancet, 378*(9802), 1581–1591. doi: 10.1016/S0140-6736(11)61094-5.

Tomm, K. (1988). Interventive interviewing: Part III. Intending to ask lineal, circular, strategic, or reflexive questions? *Family Process, 27*(1), 1–15.

Totten, M. (2000). *Guys, gangs & girlfriend abuse*. Peterborough, ON: Broadview.

Tsemberis, S. J., Moran, L., Shinn, M., Asmussen, S. M. & Shern, D. L. (2003). Consumer preference programs for individuals who are homeless and have psychiatric disabilities: A drop-in centre and a supported housing program. *American Journal of Community Psychology, 32*(3/4), 305–317.

Tummala-Narra, P. (2007). Trauma and resilience: A case of individual psychotherapy in a multicultural context. *Journal of Aggression, Maltreatment, & Trauma, 14*(1/2), 205–225. doi: 10.1300/J146v14n01_11.

U.S. Department of Health and Human Services. (1999). Children and Mental Health. In *Mental Health: A Report of the Surgeon General* (pp. 117–220). Rockville, MD: U.S.

Ungar, M. (2004). *Nurturing hidden resilience in troubled youth*. Toronto, ON: University of Toronto Press.

Ungar, M. (2005). Pathways to resilience among children in child welfare, corrections, mental health and educational settings: Navigation and negotiation. *Child and Youth Care Forum, 34*(6), 423–444. doi: 10.1007/s10566-005-7755-7.

Ungar, M. (2007). The beginnings of resilience: A view across cultures. *Education Canada, 47*(3), 28–32.

Ungar, M. (2008). Resilience across cultures. *British Journal of Social Work, 38*(2), 218–235. doi: 10.1093/bjsw/bcl343.

Ungar, M. (2011). *Counselling in challenging contexts: Working with individuals and families across clinical and community settings*. Belmont, CA: Brooks/Cole.

Ungar, M. (2012). Social ecologies and their contribution to resilience. In M. Ungar (Ed.), *The social ecology of resilience: A handbook of theory and practice* (pp. 13–32). New York, NY: Springer.

Ungar, M. (2013). Resilience, trauma, context and culture. *Trauma, Violence & Abuse, 14*(3), 253–264. Doi: 10.1177/1524838013487805.

Ungar, M. & Liebenberg, L. (2011). Assessing resilience across cultures using mixed methods: Construction of the Child and Youth Resilience Measure. *Journal of Multiple Methods in Research, 5*(2), 126–149. doi: 10.1177/1558689811400607.

Ungar, M. & Liebenberg, L. (2013). Ethnocultural factors, resilience, and school engagement. *School Psychology International, 34*(5), 514–526. DOI: 10.1177/0143034312472761.

Ungar, M., Liebenberg, L. & Ikeda, J. (2012). Young people with complex needs: Designing coordinated interventions to promote resilience across child welfare, juvenile corrections, mental health and education services. *British Journal of Social Work*. doi: 10.1093/bjsw/bcs147.

Ungar, M., Liebenberg, L., Armstrong, M., Dudding, P. & van de Vijver, F. J. R. (2012). Patterns of service use, individual and contextual risk factors, and resilience among adolescents using multiple psychosocial services. *Child Abuse & Neglect, 37*(2/3), 150–159. doi: org/10.1016/j.chiabu.2012.05.007.

Ungar, M., Liebenberg, L., Landry, N. & Ikeda, J. (2012). Caregivers, young people with complex needs, and multiple service providers: A study of triangulated relationships and their impact on resilience. *Family Process, 51*(2), 193–206. doi: 10.1111/j.1545-5300.2012.01395.x.

Ungar, M., Brown, M., Liebenberg, L., Othman, R., Kwong, W. M., Armstrong, M. & Gilgun, J. (2007). Unique pathways to resilience across cultures. *Adolescence, 42*(166), 287–310.

Wackernagel, M. & Rees, W. E. (1996). *Our ecological footprint: Reducing human impact on the earth.* Gabriola Island, BC: New Society.

Waldegrave, C. (2000) "Just therapy" with families and communities. In G. Burford & J. Hudson (Eds.), *Family group conferencing: New directions in community-centered child and family practice* (pp. 153–163). New York, NY: Aldine de Gruyter.

Walsh, F. (2011). *Normal family processes: Growing diversity and complexity.* New York, NY: Guilford Press.

Webb, M. B. & Harden, B. J. (2003). Beyond child protection: Promoting mental health for children and families in the child welfare system. *Journal of Emotional & Behavioral Disorders, 11*(1), 45–54. doi: 10.1177/106342660301100107.

Weedon, C. (1997). *Feminist practice and poststructuralist theory.* Cambridge, MA: Blackwell.

Weine, S. M., Levin, E., Hakizimana, L. & Kahnweih, G. (2012). How prior social ecologies shape family resilience amongst refugees in U.S. resettlement. In M. Ungar (Ed.), *The social ecology of resilience: A handbook of theory and practice* (pp. 309–324). New York, NY: Springer.

Wekerle, C., Waechter, R. & Chung, R. (2012). Contexts of vulnerability and resilience: Childhood maltreatment, cognitive functioning and close relationships. In M. Ungar (Ed.), *The social ecology of resilience: A handbook of theory and practice* (pp. 187–198). New York, NY: Springer.

Werner, E. E. & Smith, R. S. (1992). *Overcoming the odds: High risk children from birth to adulthood.* Ithaca, NY: Cornel University Press.

Werner, E. E. & Smith, R. S. (2001). *Journeys from childhood to midlife: Risk, resiliency, and recovery.* Ithaca, NY: Cornell University Press.

White, M. (2007). *Maps of narrative practice.* New York, NY: Norton.

Wilson, K. & Melton, G. B. (2002). Exemplary neighborhood-based child protection programs. In G. B. Melton, R. A. Thompson & M. A. Small (Eds.), *Toward a child-centered, neighborhood-based child protection system* (pp. 197–213). Westport, CT: Praeger.

Wood, P. A., Yeh, M., Pan, D., Lambros, K. M., McCabe, K. M. & Hough, R. L. (2005). Exploring the relationship between race/ethnicity, age of first school–based services utilization, and age of first specialty mental health care for at-risk youth. *Mental Health Services Research, 7*(3), 185–196. doi: 10.1007/s11020-005-5787-0.

Yoshikawa, H. & Kalil, A. (2010). The effects of parental undocumented status on the developmental contexts of young children in immigrant families. *Child Development Perspectives, 5*(4), 291–297. doi: 10.1111/j.1750-8606.2011.00204.x.

INDEX

T - #0102 - 170519 - C0 - 276/216/12 - PB - 9781138800731